THE NET AFTER DARK

DARK

LAMONT WOOD

John Wiley & Sons, Inc.
New York • Chichester • Brisbane • Toronto • Singapore

Publisher: Katherine Schowalter
Editor: Tim Ryan
Managing Editor: Mark Hayden
Editorial Production & Design: North Market Street Graphics

Designations used by companies to distinguish their products are often claimed as trademarks. In all instances where John Wiley & Sons, Inc. is aware of a claim, the product names appear in Initial Capital or all CAPITAL letters. Readers, however, should contact the appropriate companies for more complete information regarding trademarks and registration.

This text is printed on acid-free paper.

This publication is designed to provide accurate and authoritative information in regard to the subject matter covered. It is sold with the understanding that the publisher is not engaged in rendering legal, accounting, or other professional service. If legal advice or other expert assistance is required, the services of a competent professional person should be sought.

Library of Congress Cataloging-in-Publication Data:

Wood, Lamont, 1953–
     The net after dark : the underground guide to the coolest, newest,
and the most bizarre hangouts on the Internet, CompuServe, AOL,
Delphi, and more / Lamont Wood.
          p. cm.
     Includes index.
     ISBN 0-471-10347-0 (paper ; acid-free paper)
     1. Computer networks.   I. Title.
TK5105.5.W64   1995
005.7'13—dc20   94-34512
                                                                CIP

Printed in the United States of America
10 9 8 7 6 5 4 3 2 1

CONTENTS

INTRODUCTION

Most online books endlessly belabor the technical merits of YMODEM over XMODEM, or show you how to get Dow-Jones stock prices fed live right into your living room. You say business isn't your thing? Well, then, there are books that show you how to turn your PC into a digital, interactive PBS channel and find the size of the oldest living anaconda, or how many panda bears are mating in China. It's all so convenient now. So nice. So modern. So . . .

Boring!

Let the corporate drones digitize their encyclopedias and magazines, slap them on a CD, and hawk them online. Big deal. Maybe they'll be a big hit with the polyester crowd, but they've got no style, no attitude. And they don't realize that people like us were cruising the Net when they were selling CB radios. We create our own online cultures and guard the gates. We know about the latest developments in technology and culture because we're the ones making it happen.

This is the underground—we're not talking about pro-grammed entertainment or prepackaged news and financial feeds. We're talking about real people, the techno-shamans of the computer age, cutting-edge software, and live action. This book will show you the secret paths to the Net's dark-est corners. You'll see where the hip hang out, and you'll get all the lingo and smart tips you need to show some style.

SYMBOLISM

We use several symbols throughout this book to help you decide if you want to visit a part of the Net before you set out:

 Addresses with this icon next to them are mailing lists.

 These addresses are for live conferences, chat lines, and other interactive destinations.

This gauge indicates an address's signal-to-noise ratio. A 5 on the gauge means you'll find a lot of focused information, software, and ideas here. A 1 indicates lots of posturing, chaos, and noise.

Conference devoted entirely or predominantly to the posting of factual material, such as announcements, data files, transcripts, and press releases. Think of a professional journal that prints occasional letters from readers.

Conference with a lot of heavy, technical discussion. What give-and-take there is, is all hard-core, factual, and to the point. Think of the peer-review process for grant funding, or one of those professional retreats where they have to maintain a distinguished reputation lest the taxman ask why the thing was held in Barbados.

Conference with a lot of give-and-take, most of it on-topic, carried on in a good-natured fashion, the participants eager to establish the facts when the facts are an issue. Personalities are an issue only as they directly impact the subject material. Think of an impromptu bull session before the beginning of a college class.

Conference dominated by gossip, complaints, and unfounded personal opinions. Factual questions may be posed, but are rarely answered. References to the stated topic keep surfacing, although the topic getting the most attention at any given moment is likely to be random. Flames flare, but eventually subside due to the indifference of most of the users. Think of a random bull session in a locker room.

Conference given over to flames, feuds, cat fights, gossip, innuendo, whining, ranting, paranoid ravings, wild assertions, or bizarre posturing. Think of a riot in a South American prison.

Mail list with the professional quality of newspaper or magazine, only online.

Mail list that amounts to an online publication with evident involvement from the subscribers. Think of church newsletter.

Mail list reflecting the traffic of a passably on-topic conference. Think of a batch of letters from people in the same organization.

Mail list reflecting the unedited traffic of a gossipy conference. Think of a batch of random letters from friends and acquaintances, with an occasional annual report thrown in.

 The dog must have gotten it.

BOOK FAQ

From: Wiley

Subject: Frequently asked questions (FAQ) about this book.

Message-ID: <Book FAQ chapter of "The Net after Dark">

Summary: Common questions and answers about the book you are holding, *The Net after Dark*, and the subject material it covers, concerning the online world and artifacts of human activity that you can find there.

Archive name: "The Net after Dark."

This is the most recent version of this FAQ.

List of questions in the Book FAQ:

Q0: How come the list begins at zero instead of one?

Q1: What do you mean, FAQ?

Q2: What does this book cover?

Q3: How is this book organized?

Q4: Why go online?

Q5: Okay—what kind of stuff can you find online?

Q6: What is that Internet thing everyone's talking about?

Q7: How is all this related to the Information Superhighway?

Q8: What do I need to get online?

Q9: Is it true you can find tons of dirty pictures online, free for the taking?

Q0: How come the list begins at zero instead of one?

A0: This is a computer book. Computers always start counting at zero.

Q1: What do you mean, FAQ?

A1: FAQ means "frequently asked questions." FAQ files are the means by which the Internet—and especially Usenet newsgroups—documents itself. In the PC world, similar overview files usually have names like read.me, readme.txt, or readme.1st. FAQ files are usually laid out like this one, with a list of questions, followed by the Q&A itself, so you can look over the questions and then jump forward to whatever answers you are interested in.

Q2: What does this book cover?

A2: The net as a human place, and the exciting things people do there. Cyberspace is more than a collection of machines and software—it is also a place where people live part of their lives. Therefore, the book also covers the "culture" of various sources and hangouts, lest you commit some gaffe that will cause the locals to turn against you. Remember, the online world is the creation of the participants, and its various haunts have personalities that are the product of their mutual efforts. They do not take kindly to people who think they can log in and take over.

Plus we'll look at the incredible wealth of information and software you can tap into, paying particular attention to neat stuff for PC users. Some of it is free, some of it is shareware.

Q3: How is this book organized?

A3: There are four sections (besides this Book FAQ):

Chapter 1: The Layout of the Net—An overview of the online world and the nature of the things you can find there.

Chapters 2–12: Attractions—The cool stuff you can find online.

Chapters 13–15: Routes—How to use one online service to access info on another online service. Learn stuff like how to cross from Delphi over to the Internet without an Internet account.

Appendix—Technical information about getting online, and a glossary.

Q4: Why go online?

A4:   The resources stored on your computer, in your desk drawer, under your bed, are finite. The resources of the online world are, functionally, infinite. (It's growing faster than you can explore it.)

And what's out there includes the hottest, newest material on the hottest, newest subjects. The future direction of technology and culture is being mapped there. If you are not online, you are blind to it all. If you begin to feel irrelevant, it may be because you are.

Q5: Okay—what kind of stuff can you find online?

A5:   Vast treasure troves of software, engaging conversation with programmers, government watchers, conspiracy peddlers, humorists, and the techno-elite. Good, hard information on topics ranging from artificial life to back rubs. Things that will make you think, make your mouth drop, or just leave you rolling on the floor with laughter.

An easier question to answer might be: What can you not find online?

Q6: What is that Internet thing everyone's talking about?

A6:   As explained in Chapter 15, the Internet is an interconnection of academic, government, and corporate computers set up so that a user sitting at one can send mail to, login to services on, or fetch files from any of the others. (Restrictions apply, of course.) The result is a globe-spanning computer system offering awesome potential to individual users.

Q7: How is all this related to the Information Superhighway?

A7:   The Internet is a major lane on the Superhighway, although the term is used for the entirety of the online world that impacts the common citizen, including cable TV systems, BBS echo networks (explained in Chapter 14), database services, and the phone system itself.

Q8: What do I need to get online?

A8:   A computer, communications software, a modem, and a phone line, plus some knowledge as to how they work (see the Appendix in this book). Usually you will need some kind of account with an online service, or access to a local BBS that offers an Internet connection.

Q9: Is it true you can find tons of dirty pictures online, free for the taking?

A9:   Ultimately, there is only data. It is you, the perceiver, who invests it with meaning. Think about it. And see Chapter 11.

LAYOUT OF THE NET

The Net—a glowing, teeming labyrinth of computer networks. Every day, the noxious blare of corporate trumpets announces another new virtual store. Want to buy a car from Ford? Check out JCPenney's new White Sale? Yes, you can do that. Lucky you. But meanwhile, far beneath the neon lights of the virtual stores, lies the real Net. In its dark, crooked alleyways, dedicated cybernauts gather in groups large and small, furtive and boisterous, to swap software, stories, and their latest techie breakthroughs. This is where things *really* happen on the Net.

You can join the underground groups, no matter what your point of origin—the Internet, AOL, CIS, Delphi, or a local BBS. You'll discover that you can do and find almost anything on the Net.

In this chapter, I'm going to give you a quick overview of what you need to explore on the Net, and describe all the different file

formats, compression programs, forums, newsgroups, and chat systems you'll run into. If you're a seasoned veteran of the Net, then you can safely skip this chapter and start navigating the alleyways described in the rest of the book. If you need to know how to cross from one service to another (how to get Internet e-mail from AOL, for example), then check out Chapter 13.

The space shuttle Endeavor gets a lift in this graphics file of a photo found on the Internet.

WHAT'S OUT THERE

The Net is not a museum that houses some dead collection of technology, but a living place. It's throbbing with the creations and interactions of the people who spend their time there and make it worth your while to participate. Those creations and interactions fall into six main categories:

☞ Files and file downloading
☞ Electronic mail
☞ Conferences (also called forums)
☞ Programs
☞ Chatting
☞ Behaviors

FILES

You've probably heard of the incredible variety of files out there on the Net—cryptography algorithms, virtual worlds,

Ready to rock!

MUD games, scripts from *The Simpsons,* naughty pictures, sound clips from Monty Python, videos of Mr. Bill, and other fun stuff. To use most of these files, you have to download them first. Only in a few cases will you be able to run files remotely or view graphics files remotely. One exception is text files, which you can often read remotely, but if they are of any length (and you're paying by the hour for your connect time) you'll probably want to download them first. If you intend to edit them, you'll obviously want to download them. The section in this chapter called "Downloading" will give you some tips for getting those files you want fast.

Of course, downloading is only half the problem—there are about as many file formats and compression schemes as there are Elvis impersonators. The section called "File Compression" later in this chapter will help you deal with all the different compression formats and utilities.

Text Files

Most text files on the Net are usually straight ASCII files with the .txt extension. Any word processor can be used to read them, or you can use the DOS EDIT command by going to the DOS prompt and typing **edit** *filename*. You can also just display it on your screen by entering the DOS command **type** *filename* | **more**.

Documentation for Windows applications is often in the .wri format used by Windows Write.

E-mail correspondents who use the same word processors often like to send word processing files. That normally requires the use of a file transfer protocol, explained presently.

Graphics Files

Graphics files are files that, when loaded into a viewer or paint program, will be rendered as pictures on the screen or as a printout. Notice that you have to first acquire or download the files, and then load them into a viewer or paint program—pictures do not normally pop on your screen when you're online. (Well, there are services with graphical front-end programs that download icons as you go along, and there is specialized viewing software for use over the Internet. But with all but the fastest connections it takes at least a couple of minutes to transmit any picture worth looking at.) Some communications software lets you see the picture as you are downloading it—it's not that fun to watch, but at least if the graphic turns out to be junk, you can abort the download before you waste any more time on it.

Graphics files typically have file extensions like .gif. tif, .pcx, .jpg, .bmp, and .eps. If your viewer or paint program lists the extension of a file you have acquired, it should be able to display it (unless, of course, some errant person gave it the wrong extension—and that happens). In almost all cases, you will need a file transfer protocol (described presently) to download a graphics file.

Software and Data Files

Software for Unix, MS-DOS, Windows, Macintosh, and Amiga machines are commonly found online, often in different subdirectories of online repositories. You will need file transfer protocols (described presently) to download them.

Data represent the files those programs need to operate. Sometimes the data are in readable text files or in a formatted text scheme called "comma-delimited ASCII." Usually, though, they are not readable, and you will need a file transfer protocol (described presently) to download them. Meanwhile, programs and their data files are often compressed

Check This Out:

(continued from page 6)

resulting file as easily (it's now chopped into one-line paragraphs) and especially because you can't use file compression, and so the transmissions will take about twice as long. But a little time sacrificed up front can save you a lot of headaches later.

You can uncover many pictures like this on the Net.

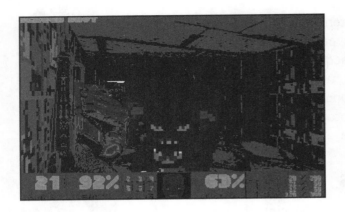

together into a single "archive" file, so let's examine the subject of file compression.

File Compression

To cut transmission times and line congestion, files residing remotely are usually compressed (processed by an algorithm that encodes the data in a more compact form).

DOOM, the hottest game around, is available on the Net.

Compression ratios vary depending on the type of file you're working with—I've seen the results vary from a savings of zero (for graphics files that already employ a compression scheme) to 80 percent, with the average for text files being around 50 percent.

Once the file arrives at your end, you will have to decompress it before you can use it. There are several main methods used for compression, and therefore for decompression. You can usually spot the method that was used by the file extension of the compressed file (see Chapter 15 for information concerning special file formats you find on the Internet).

.zip—"Zipping" is the most common method used to compress PC files. Files with this extension were compressed with PKZIP from PKWare and need PKUNZIP to decompress them. (Unix and other platforms use a compatible version, just called ZIP and UNZIP, from InfoZIP.) It will compress single files or groups of files. The usual command for decompress file.zip is **pkunzip** *filename.zip*. (The latest version from PKWare is 2.04g—it can handle files compressed with version 1, but version 1 won't know what to do with files compressed by version 2.04g.)

.arj—This file extension requires a file called arj.exe. It's probably the second most popular compressor after zip, and prized for its multidisk capabilities. On the other hand, there does not seem to be a Unix version. To extract file.arj, you'd type **arj e *filename.arj***. Single files or lists of files can be included in an archive.

.zoo—This extension requires the use of zoo.exe. It can archive files, individually or in groups, with path names and comments. To extract file.zoo, you'd type **zoo e *filename.zoo***.

.lzh—Files with this extension were compressed, individually or in groups, with lha.exe, and you need it for decompressing. To extract file.lzh, you'd type **lha e *filename.lzh***.

.arc—Files with this extension are rarely seen anymore, but were compressed with pkpak, individually or in groups, and you need pkunpak.exe to decompress them. You'd type **pkunpak *filename.arc*** to decompress file.arc.

.Z—Files with this extension are usually found on Unix systems and were shrunk with a standard Unix facility called "compress." Unix allows longer file names than DOS, and instead of changing the file extension, the software just adds .Z to the end of the name. If you have downloaded such a file to a PC machine without first decompressing it, you need a program called comp430d.exe. To decompress file.Z, you'd type **comp430d -d *filename.Z***.

.gz—Files with this extension are usually found on Unix systems and were compressed with a Unix facility called gzip. To extract such files on a PC, you will need a program called gzip.exe. For file.gz, you'd type **gzip -d *filename.gz***.

.?q?—Files in which the middle letter in the file extension was changed to a q were "squeezed" with a file called sqpc.com (or something similar) and for desqueezing need nusq110.exe. For file.txt, which was changed to file.tqt, you'd type **nusq110 *filename.tqt***.

.lbr—Files with this extension were "libraried" into a single file with lu.exe (or luu.exe). They are not compressed by lu.exe, although it is common to do so with one's favorite compression facility before librarying them. To break the library apart, and also unsqueeze any .?q? files, you need lue220.exe. For a file named file.lbr, you'd type **lue220 *file-name.lbr***.

.tar—Tape archive, the Unix version of .lbr. It's often combined with .Z compression.

.uue—Uuencoded files, in which binary files are translated to an ASCII format so they can be sent as e-mail on the Internet or posted in Usenet newsgroups.

Check This Out:

The SimTel Software Repository and the Garbo site (see Chapter 8) or their mirrors contain probably all the extraction software you'll need:

.zip—pkz204g.exe in the SimTel /pub/msdos/zip/ directory.

.arj—.arj241a.exe in the SimTel /pub/msdos/archiver/ directory.

.zoo—zoo210.exe in the SimTel /pub/msdos/zoo/ directory.

.lzh—lha213.exe in the SimTel /pub/msdos/archiver/ directory.

.arc—pk361.exe in the SimTel /pub/msdos/archiver/ directory.

.Z—comp430d.zip in the SimTel /pub/msdos/compress/ directory.

.gz—gzip124.zip in the SimTel /pub/msdos/compress/ directory.

.?q?—nusq110.com in the SimTel /pub/msdos/starter/ directory.

.lbr—lue220.com in the SimTel /pub/msdos/starter/ directory.

.tar—either tar4dos.zoo, tar314us.zip, or tstar311.zip in the Garbo /pc/unix/ directory.

.uue—uuexe525.zip in the Garbo /pc/decode/ directory.

Files with the .exe extension are "self-extracting" files that expand into the program files and documentation when run. For the Macintosh, .cpt and .sit are compressed files, while .hqx is the ASCII encoding of binary files.

DOWNLOADING

You can read a text file online and save it as a file on your hard drive at the same time—all you have to do is read it on the screen while having your modem software save the incoming text to disk. This will not work with other kinds of files, such as programs and graphics. There are several reasons for this:

☞ Some of the bytes will have the same values as ASCII screen control characters, causing the display to go berserk.

☞ Sooner or later (probably sooner) one of the bytes will have the value of the ASCII end-of-text character, halting the display long before the end of the file.

☞ A single garbled byte that would not matter in a screen display could prove catastrophic in a program file, and problematic in a graphics file.

The answer is to use a downloading protocol, of which you will probably find several built into any given modem software package. Such protocols do several basic things:

☞ Transmit the data in blocks, without displaying it on the screen.

☞ Check each block for possible errors, usually through a check-sum comparison.

☞ Demand retransmission of defective blocks.

☞ Usually display a progress indicator on the screen. (Otherwise, nothing would be happening on the

Check This Out:

For file compression and decompression, you can get by with PKUN-ZIP most of the time. If you are getting files from a Unix machine (which usually means you're on the Internet), check into how to decompress .Z files—which your Unix host can usually do for you. On the other hand, if you spend enough time fishing online, you will eventually need every flavor of unzipper mentioned here.

Saving Face:

There is an exception to the downloading requirement: the Usenet newsgroups on the Internet. Program and graphics files often appear there as conference postings, using an encoding method—uuencoding, or similar schemes—that turn files into alphabet soup. But there are no control codes in the soup, so they can be sent by e-mail, or posted in a conference. See Chapter 15 for details.

screen, leaving you to bite your nails until the process is completed.)

The online procedure is that, at some point in browsing, you will be given a menu that includes a download option. You select it, and then you are asked for the file name(s) you want (if they are not already selected through some other fashion), and then presented with a list of protocols. You select the one you want to use. Then either the remote system automatically invokes your protocol and the file transfer begins or you have to toggle to your modem control software and tell it to be prepared to receive file X using the selected protocol.

The commonest protocols include the following:

☞ XMODEM—oldest protocol in circulation; slow, but nearly always available
☞ YMODEM—improved version of XMODEM, with several variants
☞ KERMIT—slow but reliable protocol inherited from the minicomputer world
☞ ZMODEM—favorite of the cognoscenti
☞ CompuServe B—used on CompuServe; not quite as fast as ZMODEM

"Which one do I use?" is a common lament. First, check your modem software to see which ones it supports. Then note which protocols are offered by the remote system. If there is not much overlap, you have your answer (usually XMODEM). If there are plenty at both ends, you should probably try ZMODEM. If there are line problems, try Kermit.

ELECTRONIC MAIL

Which is worse—to logon and find no mail waiting, or to find 127 urgent messages? The question comes up more and more these days, as e-mail is the primary method of communications between Net denizens. Not only does e-mail arrive (or at least become available to the addressee) within seconds, but it carries more impact then paper mail, since its arrival implies that the sender is a member of the same group of digital literati as the recipient.

Electronic mail (e-mail) consists of files sent to your address on a particular online service. When you logon, the service will normally inform you that you have mail, and you can then invoke the service's mail facilities to read or download it, or perhaps send a reply. Some services have facilities through which you can tell if the recipient of your message has read it yet.

Most e-mail material is simple ASCII text files, which you can capture as you read, or simply capture for later reading. Many systems allow you to "append" binary files, which the system will have you download as described earlier.

The sender need only know your online address to send you mail. (To get your mail, you need both your address and password to logon successfully.) Mail sent between systems or on the Internet normally uses the Internet addressing scheme of name@system.domain.country. Domain and country are usually abbreviations (such as edu for an educational domain, and de for Germany), while the country suffix is usually left off for U.S. addresses.

Addressing mail sent within a commercial service (i.e., the sender and receiver both have accounts there) is usually simpler, and you can often use the recipient's given name. If the same name belongs to more than one subscriber, you'll be asked to choose which one you want from a list.

We won't examine e-mail further in this book, since it is not for public consumption. But be aware that cases where it did get consumed publicly have funded some upscale legal careers.

Saving Face: The @ is pronounced "at."

CONFERENCES

They have many names: conferences, roundtables, special interest groups (SIGs), forums, newsgroups, bulletin boards. They all amount to the same things—places online where you can post messages, which, when read back, form a written conversation.

The messages are either original postings or replies or comments on a posting, comments on comments, etc. An original and all the comments on it, and comments on those comments, is called a "thread." Conferencing software usually has some feature that lets you follow selected threads—or ignore selected threads. The system will usually keep track of which messages you have read, so that when you login the next time you will see only new ones listed (or, rather, the list starts with the latest one you haven't read).

Conferences are often moderated, meaning that one of the participants oversees the direction that the talk is going and tries to keep it on the stated topic and smooth over any feuding. The moderator may be an employee of the commercial service carrying the conference, or the moderator may simply be one of the more vocal participants. The moderator may have the power to remove offensive or off-topic messages, or he or she may have to rely purely on moral persuasion.

Conferences are what make the Net a human place. Everything else you see online was put there by some third party, but conferences are grassroots phenomenon—they cannot be manufactured.

PROGRAMS

By programs I mean software that is running on a remote machine, which you use from your desktop machine, your machine acting as the terminal of the remote machine. Also, the program is the main reason for logging in—everything else we will talk about in this chapter also involves running software on a remote machine, but in those cases—such as downloading or conferencing—the software is incidental. Programs offered for their own sakes online include:

☞ Games
☞ Database inquiries
☞ Catalog sales

It is possible to run graphic programs—such as arcade games—remotely, despite the comparatively slow speed of modems, but to do so requires "front-ends" by which your local machine is programmed to respond to graphic commands from the remote machine. If such a front-end is required, it is usually available for downloading from that machine.

CHATTING

If conferencing amounts to non-real-time conversations, chatting is real-time conversations. The users sit at their keyboards and type messages that the other users can see. The situation is similar to two people at different ends of a teletype connection, except that there can be far more than two users involved.

Sometimes the system will automatically add prefixes to all messages indicating who is typing it, and will separate the input from different users who would otherwise overtype each other. In other cases it is convenient to have modem software that can go into "chat mode" and separate incoming from outgoing text.

Many conferences will sponsor periodic chat sessions—often starring some celebrity in the field—in which the participants will go online at the same time and converse in real time.

```
Quit spraying spittle and train yourself to shut up.

Look me in the eye when I grab you by the neck.

If they pinned a tin star on your tie and made you deputy blowhard
the tack would fall out the first time you bent over to drool
on your shoes.  You couldn't even be a substitute blowhard; you
couldn't fill in for five minutes while the regular blowhard
was in the bathroom.

The only dignity you find is in pesthood.

You have the clotted smugness of a mosquito fed to bursting
off a corpse in a ditch.

You've been the wad of chewing gum stuck to the underside of
this newsgroup for as long as I know,

You are more boring than sand. You are more boring than bricks.
If you stood still in San Francisco the building inspectors
would garb you in unreinforced-masonry citations.

God forbid you discover your own insipidity in one great moment
of truth.

I have never heard anyone speak your name without a
sort of slight frown, as of a beetle discovered in cheese.

No matter how deep you burrow our mud will never be yours.
Stop trying. You pollute this place. Go forth and find your own.
```

Snippets of flamage found on the Internet. Alas, few flamers ever achieve any particular eloquence.

BEHAVIORS

Ever wonder what it would be like to be run out of town, like a character in an old horse-opera Western? Well, it happens online, and it can happen to you.

There is something about the pure-text online world that turns some people into verbal savages, adopting modes of expression they would never think of using face-to-face. Perhaps it is the absence of facial and tonal clues, for these carry a lot of information when conversing face-to-face, and their absence may cause some people to overreact. Perhaps it is the anonymity that cyberspace offers—the "mask of the modem." Whatever the cause, you never need to go far to see the result online, and it's called "flaming."

But there are other things that you can do online that are less obvious than infantile flaming, but nearly as irritating to other users. Some just involve a failure to follow common sense, but others are more subtle. Consider the following conference posting (lines beginning with >> indicate text copied from a message being commented on):

```
-- Last response --16 Mar 1994 00:34:02 GMT              alt.achoo
Thread 21 of 31
Article 9823 Twit                                    No responses
mush@uk.edu                       Mike H. at University of Katmandu


In his last posting, nit.wit writes:

>> I have not been able to unzip the compressed files I have
>> found on-line here at abandon.hope.edu. I have tried zoo, .Z,
>> gzu, pkunzip, arc, uudecoding, and some others I can't spell.
>> Can anybody here help me?


RTFM, bozo!

Mike Handbiter
University of Katmandu
mush@uk.edu

          ||||||
          (o o)
|------oOOOo-( )-oOOOo-------------------------------------------|
|---------------------"Still Hanging On!"-----------------------|
|--------------------------------------------------------------|
|------------------------------|-------------------------------|
|---"Never Committed!"---------|  100 Palace Square            |
|------------------------------|  Katmandu, Nepal             |
|"Well, they tried, but it     |  mush@uk.edu                 |
|wasn't legal or anything, and |------------------------------|
|they knew it, so there."      |------------------------------|
|--------------------------------------------------------------|
```

The person who posted this conference contribution broke several subtle and not-so-subtle rules. Let's review them:

☞ His signature (the preformatted text that many people add to the bottom of their messages, often called a "sig") was excessively long. Four lines is enough to

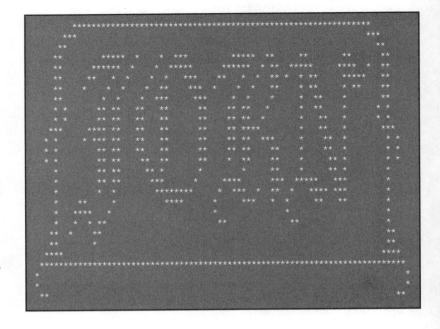

impress the world with your wit. After you've posted a dozen messages in one conference, one line is too much. Some of the leading lights of the Internet do without any sigs.

☞ He quoted excessively from the message he was responding to.

☞ He used (or at least implied) vulgarities.

☞ He made a personal attack on another user.

☞ He offered no real information to someone who specifically asked for some.

Yes, what we have here is an example—a tiny, isolated one—of flaming. In isolation, it can be silly, almost entertaining. In an ongoing conference, it's cancer that can feed on itself.

Consider: User Alpha posts a laboriously written and researched, closely felt message. User Beta scans over it and dashes off an objection to something he misread. Alpha, wounded by what he sees as a gratuitous attack, lashes back. They fall into a round of squabbling over what they "really meant." Other users try to settle things and end up squabbling, too, while still others begin flaming all the squabblers and then fall to fighting among themselves. Everybody else goes away in disgust, and after the flames die away the conference collapses into the backwaters of cyberspace, marked only by the stiff silence you detect in a room where an argument has just happened.

To prevent things from going to pieces, it is up to the moderators or the other users to try to get the flamers back on course, or at least take their feud elsewhere. It may require a little cajoling e-mail. At the other extreme, it may require booting the flamers and erasing the flame thread. It can require every diplomatic skill you ever knew you had, and if you don't watch yourself you, too, can become one of the flamers. To disagree without being disagreeable sounds easy from an armchair, but can be tricky when sitting in front of a keyboard, feeling you should do something, while trying to decide what that might be.

Meanwhile, there are people who post inflammatory nonsense just to get responses. They may even believe some of their paranoid ravings, assuming they have any inner lives. Anyway, responding to them in any way is a mistake. Posting a reply means you are agreeing to play their game. Thoughtful e-mail pointing out the error of their ways will be shrugged off as a timid, halfway effort to play. Ignore them and they will eventually go away. In the meantime you might want to get a mail reader with a "kill file," which will filter out their postings.

A variant of flaming is "baiting." It's usually seen on the Internet, where malefactors are harder to pursue. Following a pathetically predictable pattern, someone overcome with his own cleverness will pop into a newsgroup or conference and assert that all the other participants are nerds, geeks, dweebs, and/or weenies unable to even imagine the level of sexual prowess that he himself embodies. It's amazing that such people are able to master the user of a computer.

Replying, of course, is a waste of time, since the baiter will almost certainly never be seen or heard from in that conference again.

Other Behaviors to Avoid

Besides overt flaming and the other etiquette gaffes pinpointed here, there are a number of other pitfalls you should seek to avoid if you want to enjoy life online. Some are behaviors you should guard against in yourself, and some are dangers posed by other users.

Obvious Ignorance

Read the conference for a while before you start posting. On Usenet, search out the FAQ file. That way you won't be dredging up topics that were beaten to death a year earlier. And read threads to the end before commenting, lest you post a question that someone else has already answered.

Too-Cute Language

Conferences are read by people all over the globe, and their interpretation of colloquialisms may not match yours. If English is their second language, your subtle wit and word play may escape them entirely.

And anytime you see that you have written purple, glowing prose of which you feel deep pride, highlight it, and then press the DEL key.

Shouting

MESSAGES IN UPPERCASE COME ACROSS AS SHOUTING. Messages in upper- and lowercase do not. But if the whole message is uppercase, they will understand that you're stuck in the 1970s (maybe even the 1870s) and understand.

Illegibility

In material meant to be read online, lines should be no more than eighty characters long, and there are those who insist that seventy-two should be the limit. Do not include control-code strings in the text. Do not use left margins. Begin paragraphs with indents or blank lines, but not both. Use spaces rather than tabs.

When in doubt, send or post some test material and then go back and read it.

Lurking

Those who read conferences but never post are referred to as "lurkers." They are tolerated, but only that, since they add no value to the conference.

Blathering

Stay on the topic. Or at least show some awareness that you've wandered off, and be appropriately sheepish. Some services keep a tight rein on their conferences, since they want to maintain a reputation for serious, professional discussion well worth the online fee. Others are more philosophical. Every conference seems to seek its own comfort level within the rules.

Chain Letters

So you've thought up this great scheme. You'll post a message online, asking people to send a few dollars to a list of names (yours is on top of the list), add their names to the list, and send the list to another group. You'll threaten them with a hex if they don't comply. Since countless people read online stuff, and since there's a member of your target audience born every minute, money will come pouring in. Right?

Wrong. First, few people are that stupid, since they can see that only those who originated the scheme are likely to get anything. Second, you're not the first to think up the scheme. Your state legislature, parliament, sovereign, or glorious leader, for instance, probably thought a great deal about it decades before you were born, calling it a Ponzi scheme, pyramid scheme, wire fraud, chain letter, or, most importantly, a felony.

The sad thing is that a devout data surfer is likely to come across such sociopathic nonsense every couple of days, often in postings titled MAKEMONEY or MAKE.MONEY.FAST. The originator probably did get a cascade of responses—from irate users, who quickly pressured his site administrator into closing the offender's account.

Dubious Causes

A British schoolboy got about thirty-three million get-well cards after a story circulated online about a dying child wanting postcards. He has since had a successful operation and his mother has been begging people to knock it off. Outcries against government initiatives to tax modems arise from time to time, despite an absence of such government initiatives. (There are deep-seated fears of such a tax in certain corners of Europe, where the phone system is, or until recently was, owned by the government. In the United States, the Bell System had to abandon its anti-interconnect posturing—which extended even to noise-supression rubber cups for mouthpieces—after a court decision in the late 1960s, and all efforts by local phone companies to charge extra for modem connections died out about a decade ago.)

Crass Commercialization

There have been organizations that have used the Net as if it were another medium for junk mail, blithely posting announcements in any and all likely conferences. What they got in return were floods of hate mail—thirty thousand in one reported Internet case, bringing their host to its knees and getting their account revoked on three different services. Net denizens welcome participation—that is what makes the Net worth their time—but they resent exploitation.

The nodes belong to the organizations that own them. Cyberspace—the sum total of the human activity you see on the Net—is created on those machines by the users. Abuse cyberspace and the users will feel you are abusing them. Keep that in mind and you'll suffer less.

Hacking

We'll assume you are concerned about the subject, rather than interested in perpetrating something yourself. Yes, youths who know a few ASCII codes and Unix commands too many do sometimes get in trouble after wreaking havoc in cyberspace. As an average user who wants to protect yourself, the main thing is to avoid having your password fall into the wrong hands. Do not give it out over the phone or online, no matter how plausible the reason the other person is giving. Remember, when hackers get together, they are far less likely to talk about technical details than things like how to trick telephone operators into giving out unlisted numbers. (Consensus: Tell the operator you found this guy's wallet, see . . .) It seems the Net is far more susceptible to what they call "social engineering" than to bit twiddling.

In other words, hacking isn't technical wizardry, its con artistry, and you should protect yourself online the same way you would protect yourself on the street, by being careful about who you trust.

While you're at it, make sure your password is genuine gibberish rather than a word that has sentimental meaning to you—a word a hacker could surmise after examining the contents of your wallet or purse (as some have boasted). Other hackers say they can get into nearly any system if given the opportunity to try a list of about two hundred of the most commonly used passwords—mostly common nicknames and epithets, and individual letters of the alphabet.

And in case you were wondering but were too embarrassed to ask, no, just owning a modem does not leave your PC naked to hackers. You have to leave it configured and turned on, with the modem software in phone-answering mode. If you are doing this, it is because you are a "sysop" (system operator) of a BBS (bulletin board system). Software intended for operating a BBS usually includes ways to restrict callers' access to the innards of the system.

Check This Out:

The existence of hackers is not a valid reason to avoid putting a system online. If it were, you'd have to get rid of voice mail, since voice mail systems also get taken over by hackers. Or even phone lines, since there are people who make abusive calls. You can't live in houses, since there are burglars who break into them. Nor can you drive cars, because of carjackings. Do you see where we're headed here? Alternately you might try ordinary precautions and common sense, and keep your eyes open.

Viruses

Yes, there are viruses (viri?) out there—programs that attach themselves to legitimate software and thus propagate from computer to computer. More than two thousand have been counted, grouped into about three hundred genres. Some print political or demented messages on the screen, some wipe out your hard disk, some do no damage at all, and some just waste computer power and disk space by their mere presence. Some online software collections scan all files for viruses, some do not. The best (almost foolproof) way to protect yourself is to use only shrink-wrapped off-the-shelf software. Barring that, there are anti-virus scanners you can get from any software store. You should also keep a system diskette that you can boot from if you suspect a virus on your hard disk.

Besotted Sexism

Most systems will let you choose your own online name, which is the one that appears automatically on your e-mail and conference postings, and during your chat sessions. Sadly, women are best advised not to use their own names if obviously feminine. Women report that bizarre sexual aggressiveness from the male participants is so common and so uncomfortable that many women are driven offline by it. As with flaming, the mask of the modem encourages the perpetrator to do things he normally would not do. Or, components of behavior normally cloaked by other components get starkly exposed in this text-only world.

As for what name to choose, "Bloodaxe" is always a good choice, or something else with a Dark Ages, heroic—yet unisex—ring. It hints that in the game of male one-upmanship, you have nothing left to prove. And when they find you're not really playing the game, the joke's on them.

ARTIFICIAL INTELLIGENCE

Artificial intelligence (AI) is a field in which you take nothing for granted. If you've ever mused about the meaning of meaning, about how is it that you understand when asked "How is it that you understand?" or how you recognize the face of someone you haven't seen for ten years, then you'll be able to fit right in. If such questions make you dizzier than a bottle of cheap gin, then you might want to skip this chapter.

Commercial AI, darling of a lot of futuristic investors in the mid-1980s, peaked about 1988 and today has withdrawn into niches, the hype giving way to workaday expert system shells. Otherwise, AI has largely retreated back into academia. What you'll find on the Net offers limited scope to the personal computer user—leading-edge AI these days is done on big-iron Unix machines. This chapter can point you in directions that should prove fruitful, but unless you have an academic computing department under you, there may be only so far you can go.

Saving Face:

Before you start hanging out with the experts, load the following terms directly into your cerebral cortex:

A-life—Artificial life. Or, rather, computer simulations of living systems—or, at any rate, of complex systems that interact with each other and the environment on the basis of preset rules. Dr. Frankensteins need not apply.

Admissibility—Testing a solution to problems to make sure the solution can find the goal.

Case-Based Reasoning—Decisions based on analysis of similar past cases.

Cellular Automata—Computer simulations of (or models inspired by) the behavior rules of one-celled animals.

Cyc—A project at MCC (Microelectronics Computer Technology Corporation) in Austin, Texas, to build common sense into a computer using an enCYClopedic database, perhaps eventually permitting the machine to simulate a PSYCHe.

Expert Systems—A shirt-sleeves branch of AI, expert systems try to capture and replicate the knowledge and decision-making processes of a human expert in a particular niche.

Fuzzy Logic—Formulae that process ranges or intervals of data to arrive at concrete results.

Life—A game that illustrates the basic theory behind artificial life.

Lisp—A programming languages popular with AI practitioners. (There are versions of Lisp for the PC.)

Neural Nets—Systems that can be trained rather than programmed.

NLP—Natural language processing, the trick of getting a computer to understand (or, rather, respond to) a human language.

Prolog—A programming language popular in AI. (There are versions available for the PC, particularly Micro Prolog.)

Strong AI—The idea that computers can be made to think like people do, assuming people actually do so.

Validation—Confirmation that the results of an AI system have some connection to the real world.

Verification—Confirmation that an AI system works.

Weak AI—The idea that a computer can be made to simulate or model human reasoning patterns rather than actually think.

NET RESOURCES

AI forums are either all noise or all music, depending on your viewpoint. Remember, AI concerns the understanding of knowledge, which involves the definition of knowledge, which gets you into deep waters—philosophically speaking—pretty fast. If inquiries into the meaning of meaning intrigue you, this is your field.

comp.ai

This Usenet newsgroup is the heaviest and/or airiest of them all, with bearded critiques of articles in the *Journal of Artificial Intelligence Research,* and questions about "optimal loco-motion simulation."

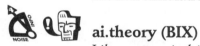

ai.theory (BIX)

Like comp.ai, this BIX conference is steeped in speculative philosophical inquiry, with participants debating, among other things, the ethics of "roboticide," while others hunt down specialized software and learned but obscure papers. Plus you see people passing around problems in predicate calculus: "Tony, Mike, and John belong to the Alpine Club. Every member of the Alpine club who is not a skier is a mountain climber. Mountain climbers do not like rain, and anyone who does not like snow is not a skier. Mike dislikes whatever Tony likes and likes whatever

Saving Face:

While life may not be a game, remember, Life is. The rules: You have a rectangular grid, and each cell is either empty or filled. New "generations" are produced as follows: Fill an empty cell if three of its neighbors are full; otherwise leave it empty. A full cell dies of loneliness if it has one or no neighbors, lives on if it has two or three neighbors, dies of crowding if it has four or more neighbors. Diagonals count. Certain initial patterns will die out immediately, some will spread fitfully and fade away, some will get caught in recurring patterns, and some will spread energetically.

The screen of Transmigration Analysis 1.0, downloaded from CompuServe's AI Expert forum as the file clife.zip. It attempts to show whether successful transmigration of your personal identity (mind and/or soul, presumably to another continuum after death) is possible without physical connection and/or intermediate storage. AI is often found hand in hand with speculative philosophy.

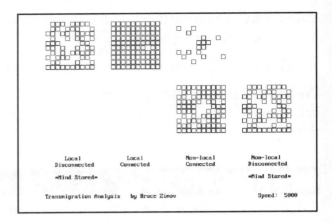

Tony dislikes. Tony likes rain and snow. Is there a member of the Alpine club who is a mountain climber but not a skier?" Yes, this stuff is a hobby for some people.

AI Expert Forum (CIS)

The CompuServe AI Expert forum, this is also abuzz with talk about philosophy, "evolutionary computation," Zen and the art of creating life, and whether language is learned, inborn, or both. There is a healthy software library, including Tierra and Qnet (mentioned later) and a lot of tutorials.

alife

The a-life mail list is for those involved in a-life research (which cuts across computer science, the natural sciences, math, medicine, and probably every other major field) plus interested members of the public. Send your request to **alife-request@cognet.ucla.edu**.

neuron

The neuron mail list deals with all aspects of neural networks, both computer and biological. Send your request to **neuron-request@cattell.psych.upenn.edu**.

Things To Play With

As mentioned, the problem with the flavors of AI you can find on the Net is that most of the software is written in Lisp or Prologue, or otherwise embedded in environments inaccessible to the user on the street. Even those written for the PC often turned out to be—when downloaded—files of C source code. You'd need a C compiler and the knowledge to use it to get started. Bearing that in mind, there is still some interesting AI stuff out there.

Tierra

Tierra is an a-life cellular automata simulation for studying the evolution of digital organisms. Instead of DNA, you have a simulated computer and operating system, with executable machine code that cannot only evolve but suffer mutations through random bit-flippings. It's available on MS-DOS as well as Unix, but only C source code is available—you have to be able to compile it.

CompuServe Access Information: Enter the AI Expert forum and select the Libraries option, and then the Browse command, using the All option, and then Tierra as the keyword. Documentation is in separate files.

Internet Access Information: Anonymous ftp to **tierra.slhs.udel.edu** or **life.slhs.udel.edu**. Look for directories named almond, beagle, doc, and tierra.

Saving Face:

If you're not careful, you'll miss the AI Expert forum on CompuServe and end up in the Automobile Information Center, which is all about new, used and collectible cars, car alarms, and car-buying services. Actually, car buying might be a good place to apply AI. Considering the audio-animatronic nature of some car salesmen, perhaps it already has been applied there.

Qnet

If you yearn to delve into neural networks in the privacy of your own home, then Qnet may be the answer. It's a shareware program ($149) in either Windows or DOS formats, requiring a 486, or fast 386 with a coprocessor.

The documentation seems quite friendly, showing you how to tell if your data is random noise or not, and demonstrating OCR and stock market analysis. The OCR application seemed like a more realistic example of what neural networks can do. As for the stock market application, if future stock prices could truly be predicted from patterns in past fluctuations, presumably the big boys with their mainframes would have figured out the trick and cornered all the marbles by now. (Such technical analysis always seemed to me akin to predicting future ripples in a pond based on past ripples, without any knowledge of who's throwing rocks in the water, or why.)

CompuServe Access Information: Enter the AI Expert forum and select the Libraries option, and then the Browse command, using the All option, and then Qnet as the keyword to locate the file qunet10.zip.

Eliza

Hang around in AI long enough and you'll hear about Eliza, the therapy program that got a lot of people excited about the subject of AI in the 1970s. Like a Rogerian therapist, it will look for patterns in what the patient says, and try to draw him or her out on that basis. Presumably, a trained therapist would do a better job than a machine, but there were those who liked the privacy and nonjudgemental interaction the computer offered. Anyway, since it appeared, Eliza has migrated to Prolog and Lisp, but the MS-DOS versions around appear to be compilations of the same simplistic version that was written for the PC in the 1970s.

Internet Access Information: Anonymous ftp to either **ftp.cc.utexas.edu** through the /pub/AI_ATTIC/Programs/

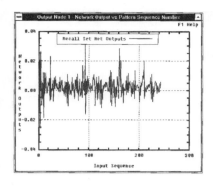

Graph of 216 weeks of S&P 500 stock market weekly average movements (starting in January 1988), fed in to train a Qnet network. Qnet was then asked to predict the next twenty-seven weeks' directions and amounts of movement. The result: If you waited for a prediction of at least a half-percent move, you would be trading in 30 percent of the weeks and would be right 75 percent of the time. Your mileage may vary.

Classic subdirectory, or to **uscd.edu** to the pub/pc-ai subdirectory.

Other AI Haunts

comp.ai.edu
Calls for papers, notes on conferences, searches for compilers, and rants about various academic advisers are the focus here.

comp.ai.fuzzy
"A fuzzy subset F of a set S can be defined as a set of ordered pairs, each with the first element from S, and the second element from the interval [0,1], with exactly one ordered pair present for each element of S." Got that? People spend their time here asking about how to apply fuzzy logic to control systems or how to perform fuzzy data acquisition.

```
HI! I'M ELIZA. WHAT'S YOUR PROBLEM?

> I have to use computers all day.
SAY, DO YOU HAVE ANY PSYCHOLOGICAL PROBLEMS?

> The thought that a PC can be made to sound like a shrink intrigues me.
WHAT DOES THAT SUGGEST TO YOU?

> That I am easily intrigued.
I SEE.

> Is there nothing else?
I'M NOT SURE I UNDERSTAND YOU FULLY.

> I mean, you stopped talking after I said I was easily intrigued.
COME COME ELUCIDATE YOUR THOUGHTS.

> Gosh, such a big word: elucidate.
CAN YOU ELABORATE ON THAT?

> I am not sure if I can spell it.
SAY, DO YOU HAVE ANY PSYCHOLOGICAL PROBLEMS?

>
```

Text of a short session with an old PC version of Eliza, found through the AI_ATTIC subdirectory at ftp.cc.utexas.edu. Not much therapeutic intervention was achieved before it looped back to the opening question.

The periodically posted FAQ lists other sources of information, including ftp sites.

comp.ai.genetic
Don't come here if you're looking for information about genetics—the talk here is about the use of genetic algorithms for things like allocating retail space and simulating the annealing of metals. Plus there is talk of evo-

```
Diana Develops a Meaningful Relationship

A story of little literary merit written for your edification by
Scirocco, the steamy and torrid software system from Hectare Ltd.

Nothing had gone right for Diana since that unhappy evening at
the tennis club. Try as she might, she could not shake off her
gloom. That day would transform her life, though as yet she did
not know it. As so often before, fate took her all unawares.
Their eyes met, just for a moment. Then a steady gaze that
seemed to bore into her very soul and lock her eyes to his. The
space between them seemed to shrink, the people between them
merged into a blur. Yes, you guessed it, her contact lens had
fallen out.

Although she strove against it she seemed to melt in his
presence, like a Mars bar in a mixed sauna. His enigmatic smile,
his brooding eyes seemed to beckon her without her knowing why.
"Not to beat about the bush," he sighed, "couldn't we, you know,
find somewhere private?"

They soon discovered they shared a passion for horses. Each
weekend they would sit down and work out which colts to geld just
for a giggle, and then sit, close and silent on the sand, as the
sun set. She felt a flush come over her. At first she knew she
was blushing, and then the feeling spread down to take over the
core of her being.

"You're the sort of girl to make Barnacle Bill the Sailor reform"
he breathed, going down on one knee and pulling two tickets for a
matinee performance of Starlight Express from his anorak.
Suddenly she felt she could not help herself, no longer could she
control her feelings.

Gritting her teeth, her heart pounding, she slapped his face
hard, again and again. That would show him how not to treat
someone who had just undergone the trauma of a sex-change
operation.

This software doesn't just make Barbara Cartland look as slow as
an XT with cassette tapes instead of disks. It can run
simulations, interpret data, drive speech synthesizers in real
time and generally fool you into thinking it's really
intelligent. Because it is really intelligent (or at least very
clever).

For more information, contact Hectare Ltd, Brewmaster House, The
Maltings, St Albans, AL1 3HT, England. Telephone: (0727) 41455
fax: (0727) 47846.
```

One of many possible outcomes from the story.exe program found through the AI_ATTIC subdirectory at ftp.cc.utexas.edu. Generally, the heroine—beset by romantic and other stimuli—swoons over the hero, but then manages to scurry off in the end, with or without him. The first and the last two paragraphs are always the same. The accompanying documentation warns that the humor is very British and very politically incorrect—and never gets X-rated no matter how many times you run it.

ARTIFICIAL INTELLIGENCE

lutionary computation, book announcements, and conference announcements.

comp.ai.jair.announce

JAIR is the *Journal of AI Research*, and if we are to trust the title, this newsgroup is used for *JAIR* announcements.

comp.ai.jair.papers

Obviously, this is the place to look for papers of the *JAIR.*

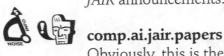

comp.ai.nat-lang

Nat-lang refers to natural languages—computer software that you can talk to in English or something. Here you see endless searches for online dictionaries, plus announcements of conferences and symposia, and discussions of ongoing projects. Heavy stuff, all in all.

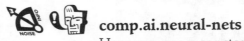

comp.ai.neural-nets

Here you see a constant search for financial modeling software, literature citations, advice on particular widgets, specific software utilities—these people need to build a neural net to handle their network searching.

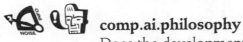

comp.ai.philosophy

Does the development of AI offer humanity the promise of immortality? How does one test for consciousness? How does one define consciousness? Where does Buddhist cognition fit in? Is it safe to trust facts? Exactly how does one go about creating a new universe? If questions like these are keeping you up at night, better camp out here.

comp.ai.shells

"Modelization using Petri Nets" is about as commonplace as it gets here, among conference announcements and calls for papers that are even more arcane. The periodically posted FAQ file lists places where you can download free expert system shells, generally written in Prolog, Lisp, or C, which you'll have to compile yourself.

comp.ai.vision
This is actually the periodic posting of a mail list on the subject of machine vision.

ail-l
This mail lists covers **AI** and the law, including automated legal research. Send your request to **listserv@austin.onu.edu**.

ai-medicine
This popular mail list concerns the use of computer-based medical decision support. Send your request to **ai-medicine-request@med.stanford.edu**. Ftp archives are available at **lhc.nlm.nih.gov** in the /pub/ai-medicine/ directory. (There is also mail list concerning medical decision-making, called SMDL-L, from **listserv@dartcms1. dartmouth.edu**; and MedInf-L concerning medical data processing, at **listserv@dearn.bitnet**.)

ai-stats
This mail list deals with the use of AI in statistics. Send your request to **ai-stats-request@watstat.uwaterloo.ca**.

IE digest
This mail list serves academics looking into the use of AI (including neural networks, genetic algorithms, and expert systems) to model economic and financial systems. Calls

for papers and other academic announcements are included; paper announcements and queries are welcome. Send your request to **IE-list-request@cs.ucl.ac.uk**. An archive of the mail list and related material is accessible via anonymous ftp at **cs.ucl.ac.uk** in the /ie/ directory.

AG-EXP-L

This mail list covers the use of expert systems in agriculture. Send your request to **list-serv%ndsuvm1.bitnet@cunyvm.cuny.ed**.

ECTL

ECTL is the Electronic Communal Temporal Lobe, a mail list for speech interface enthusiasts. Send your request to **ectl-request@ snowhite.cis.uoguelph.ca**, and include your name, institution, department, daytime phone, and an e-mail address. The list has an anonymous ftp archive site at **snowhite.cis.uoguelph.ca** in the /pub/ectl/ directory, with lists of speech-related products, back issues of ECTL, and technical report abstracts.

Artmoral

This mail list is devoted to the discussion of theories of artificial morality, as defined in the book *Artificial Morality: Virtuous Robots for Virtual Games* by Peter Danielson. Experimenters use the Prolog computer language. Send your request to **artmoral-list-request@ unixg.ubc.ca**.

Other Access Information: There are also AI conferences on the major general discussion BBS echo networks, including FidoNet, NorthAmeriNet, ILink, and GlobalLink.

MULTIMEDIA

Slip the word *multimedia* into conversation with a couple of corporate stiffs and they'll bounce off the walls like bug-eyed Chihuahuas on amphetamines. Multimedia: It's the biggest marketing tool since the discovery of sex, it's the future of education, it's the future of entertainment, it slices, it dices—it even does julienned fries!

Right. You've probably noticed that anything hyped as everything for everybody usually turns out to be nothing, period. But in the case of multimedia, once you filter out all the noise, forget all the marketing hype, and just look at what's being done, you can find some really innovative stuff.

For software to qualify as multimedia, it must have some combination of:

- ☞ Text
- ☞ Still graphics
- ☞ Animation
- ☞ Video
- ☞ Sound

Animation here means moving text, artwork or graphical "sprites" across the screen, and *video* means digitized versions of TV or film material. *Sound* can mean either digitized recordings from any source or MIDI music. Some animations and videos also have sound. There are two problems with handling multimedia material on the Net:

☞ There are more file formats than days of the year.
☞ Sound and graphics files are rather large.

The only way to approach the file format morass is to become familiar with the ones that pertain to your machine and software, and ignore all rest. Even within the boundaries of one software package, though, formats multiply like rabbits as the tech-wizards compulsively take yesterday's favorite and "improve" it. Fortunately, there are always other tinkerers posting conversion utilities—just look around for files with the number "2" in them, names like jpeg2gif and 3ds2plg.

Saving Face:

For the PC, the following file formats are very popular:

.AVI—Windows full-motion video file (Audio Visual Interleave), which can be sound or silent, and running one to thirty frames per second, although fifteen to twenty is average.

.BMP—Windows bitmap (equivalent to .DIB).

.DCX—Intel fax format, used also for graphics.

.DIB—Windows Device Independent Bitmap (equivalent to .BMP).

.EPS—Encapsulated PostScript, not always viewable on-screen.

.FLC—Like FLI, but offering higher resolution.

.FLI—Autodesk animation files, silent, about ten frames per second.

.GIF—CompuServe's Graphics Interchange Format (widely used elsewhere) in either the GIF87a or the slightly fancier GIF89a versions.

.JPG—JPEG File Interchange Format, JPEG being the Joint Photographics Experts Group; offers enormous compression at the cost of image quality.

.MID—Data for MIDI (Musical Instrument Digital Interface) devices, which synthesize music rather than play back recordings of it.

.PCT—Apple and Macintosh graphics format, often supported by PC packages in the spirit of togetherness.

.PCX—Graphics files in the Zsoft Paintbrush format, also supported by Windows Paintbrush.

.TGA—TARGA Truevision format, supporting twenty-four-bit color.

.TIF—Tagged Image File Format, widely used in desktop publishing.

.WAV—Windows Waveform, the digitized recorded sound format used by Windows; requires a soundboard and speakers.

.WPG—WordPerfect Graphics.

VFW—Not a file format, but the abbreviation for Video for Windows, which uses the .AVI format.

As for the bloated file sizes, well, that's just the way it is, friend. (For example, you can logon to AOL and download high-quality audio samplings from Firesign Theater albums—a total of fifteen seconds of sound tucked in a zipped file 323K bytes long.) Unless you enjoy Net access via high-speed dedicated lines or have a bottomless bank account, cyberspace may not be the most practical place to forage for multimedia material. Buying a CD ROM of files might be a better choice. Consider: If it takes you one minute to load a platter into a CD ROM drive, that's equivalent to downloading almost eleven million bytes per second. Kinda makes that new 28.8K bps V.34 modem look downright glacial, doesn't it?

All this may explain why decent multimedia material in cyberspace is tough to come by. Sure, there are plenty of illustration-quality graphics (and other, more *decorative* ones posted purely for their own sake—see Chapter 11), and there are plenty of recorded sounds, but only a few scattered snippets of animations and videos.

COMMERCIAL SERVICES

Commercial services do carry a lot of multimedia material. (Of course, you have to pay to download it.) The following nodes have some great caches.

 Multimedia Forum (CIS)

The CompuServe Multimedia Forum had a lengthy selection of software utilities and file players, and leans heavily toward the serious user interested in authoring his or her own presentations. The discussion conferences focus on questions about finding the right software for a specific project or about getting balky components to work together.

 Cyberforum (GEnie)

The GEnie Cyberforum has a multimedia magazine called *LiveWire*, which you can download and run, with versions for the Macintosh, the Amiga, and the PC with VGA graphics. Even zipped, the PC version was almost 500K bytes long. It turns out to be, mostly, a full-screen advertisement from which you can read articles about events on GEnie. The use of dancing icons and jarring background music apparently qualifies it as

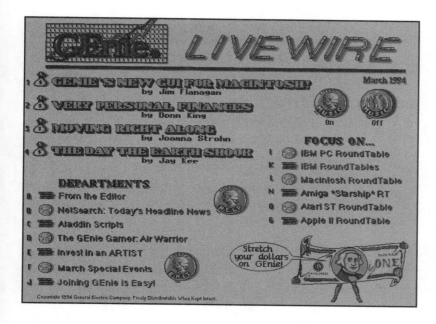

Welcoming screen of the LiveWire multi-media magazine from the GEnie Cyberforum. Basically, it's a text presentation program for articles concerning GEnie, with some background music and dancing icons.

multimedia. But, as mentioned in the Virtual Reality chapter, the Weekly Cyberspace Report is worth reading. The tone in the discussion conferences is serious, if not always technical. The files library offer quite a few pictures in the .GIF format, and some animations in the .FLI format.

Multimedia (AOL)

AOL has a large collection of multimedia material. The Software Library section under the Multimedia option under the Computers and Software Department also contains sound files, animations, and utilities. Pictures can be found under the Graphics and Animation option. Much of the conference traffic is from people struggling to install multimedia hardware or software—the field contains no shortage of "gotchas." The Multimedia option on AOL also includes a conference for the Multimedia Marketing Council, which is

Saving Face:

These multimedia forums are for professional users—you should only ask specific technical questions that lend themselves to concise answers. If you don't have a lot of background knowledge on multimedia, then lurk for a while to learn what you need before posting messages.

Check This Out:

The FAQ for comp.publish.cdrom.multimedia is an excellent primer on CD ROM technology, CD ROM publishing, and the CD ROM market.

active in setting multimedia technical standards for the PC.

IMA (BIX)

BIX includes a conference for the IMA, the Interactive Media Association, whose online membership list should be a valuable resource to anyone interested in approaching the industry.

Multimedia (BIX)

BIX's multimedia conference is dominated by talk of problems and (sometimes) solutions.

Music (BIX)

The BIX music conference concerns the performance and composition of music, although there is some discussion of MIDI.

INTERNET SOURCES

If you're downloading a lot of files from Internet nodes, it's courtesy to do it during off hours. Don't go grabbing forty megs of animation files at ten-thirty in the morning or some network administrator may decide to take them offline.

comp.graphics

The Internet harbors somewhat more sophisticated users than the commercial systems, but the thrust is still the same: system questions. It's just that on the Internet the questions are more technical and concern fancier (often Unix) systems, with users spread from Sweden to South Africa to Hong Kong. There's also an ongoing quest for software tricks and pointers.

alt.binaries.multimedia

Most of the postings appear to be software utilities rather than multimedia presentations, but there are a few of the latter also. Most items are first zipped and then uuencoded, and are bigger than the ones you see in the rest of the alt.binaries hierarchy—and they aren't small.

NetJam

The NetJam mail list is for collaborative musical composition—the subscribers pass around their MIDI files. If you want to join in, send your request to **netjam-request@xcf.berkeley.edu**.

GodlyGraphics

This mail list is for the discussion of Christian uses of computer graphics, with emphasis on Amiga hardware. Send your request to **GodlyGraphics-request@acs.harding.edu**.

OTHER SOURCES AND HANGOUTS

Some of the following Internet Usenet newsgroups are conferences in which people post material they have recorded (for whatever reason) or dug out of their archives in response to the request of another participant. And so you see people swapping files from opposite sides of the globe. To participate, however, requires a working knowledge of the uuencoding procedures used in Usenet, explained in Chapter 15.

alt.binaries.sounds.misc

Here you'll see people posting sound bites, mostly in the .WAV format used by Windows, amid accompanying requests for snippets of this or that actor, Sousa marches, or movie quotes. Most of the material is fated to replace the boings, bongs, and claps that Windows uses for sound effects.

Saving Face:

There are numerous forums and newsgroups on the Net devoted to "animation" in some form. But most of the traffic concerns the hand-drawn cartoon variety, discussions of the art form (including partisan, fruitless comparisons between the U.S. version and the Japanese version, called *anime*) and latest commercial productions, and jobs for illustrators.

Check This Out, Too:

For stills from cartoons in the .GIF format, check out **wuarchive.wustl.edu** and **avatar.snc.edu**.

MULTIMEDIA

And Check This Out:

Video files in the .AVI format (the Video for Windows native format) can be found at **phoenix.oulu.fi** in /pub/avi and in /pub/Windows_AVI, and also at **wuarchive.wustl.edu**.

Check This Out:

There is an entire BBS echo network devoted to MIDI, with about thirty conferences. It's called, predictably, the MIDILink Network, and can be reached through the Sound Management Music/MIDI BBS at 708-949-4301.

alt.binaries.sounds.midi

MIDI files are much shorter than .WAV files, since one byte can equal one musical note. Therefore, files can be uploaded inside one message, instead of spanning two or three dozen, as is seen with the other formats. There is no visible theme to the music that gets posted here, running from Streisand to bird calls. Plus there are the usual technical questions.

alt.binaries.sounds.movies

Here people post (mostly) .WAV files of sound bites lifted from various movies, such as "No fighting in here—this is a war room," from *Dr. Strangelove.* Individual files can easily run across ten messages. But whatever is posted, there is always someone requesting something else.

alt.binaries.sounds.tv

Unlike the people grabbing sound bites in alt.binaries.sounds.movies, the focus here is on theme songs for TV shows. I saw one get posted within hours of someone else requesting it.

alt.binaries.sounds.music

Miscellaneous music is the theme here, although there seems to be a trend toward posting the deathless works of Weird Al Yankovic.

alt.binaries.sounds.utilities

Actually, few if any utilities get posted here. What you do see are endless questions about where to find specific utilities, and streams of technical questions, with some answers.

alt.binaries.sounds.d

This is the discussion newsgroup for the entire alt.binaries.sounds hierarchy, meaning requests and technical discussions are supposed to go here, with the other newsgroups being reserved for actual postings. What happens is that people put their requests and questions in the newsgroup of that genre, and anything that doesn't fit ends up here, including requests for anatomical noises. There are also periodically posted mini-FAQs on various subjects here.

comp.sys.mac.graphics

This is the place to go if you're wrestling with Macintosh graphics software. You see more questions getting actual answers here than you do in the average newsgroup, for whatever reason.

comp.os.os2.multimedia

Hordes of people searching for OS/2 software drivers show up here with their pleas. They appear to draw no solace from the IBM press releases that get posted here as well.

comp.sys.amiga.multimedia

As the name implies, you see people here posting software and technical questions about using multimedia on Amiga systems. The fate of Commodore International is also of intense interest.

alt.3d

If you are seeking radiosity-based rendering software—or even know what it is—then this is the place for you. Here people trade texture maps and dinosaur designs, and post mini-

Check This Out, Too:

An "Audio Files Formats FAQ" is posted at intervals in alt.binaries. sounds.d, and archived as either audio-fmts or AudioFormats in the usual Usenet archives locations. It contains not only a good overview of the recording, sampling, and compression formats used in audio files, but information on audio file archives and the locations of freeware audio editing programs for various platforms.

MULTIMEDIA

FAQs on things like stereograms. This newsgroup is not for amateurs.

alt.graphics.pixutils

Graphics file conversions—how to do them, how not to do them, and where to get the necessary software, is the focus here, and the stream of specific, detailed questions is unending. Anyone who wants to pester the world by inventing yet another file format ought to read this newsgroup and then go to bed.

Other Access Information: There are multimedia conferences on the Intelec and FidoNet BBS echo networks, and MIDI conferences of one sort or another on the NorthAmeri-Net, RelayNet, Intelec, ILink, and FidoNet echo networks.

More Neat Software

While the number of .AVI files online is not great—and you might be loath to download the ones you do find if you had other plans for the evening—there are vast accumulations of multimedia utilities out there. Here are three (almost) random samples.

Vidvue

This media player supports a wide variety of multimedia formats, plus you can write scripts that will present selected graphics in succession, at timed intervals—a slide show, in other words. Also, you step through animation files one frame at a time and save individual frames as pictures. It was able to show the surviving sections of mis-uudecoded Usenet .GIF binaries that even Corel Paint choked on.

CompuServe Access Information: In the Multimedia forum, access the Libraries option, and then use the Browse command, specifying "all files." Then use "Vidvue" as the keyword to find the file vidvue.zip, which you will then need to unzip after downloading.

Like the Windows Media Player, you just load multimedia file, and the software recognizes the format and treats it appropriately. There are, however, conversion and save-frame options not found in the Media Player, plus an extensive help file. The file is shareware, meaning you should send in money if you plan to use it.

ScopeTrax

This DOS freeware program provides some basic waveform file editing functions. Unlike the Windows Media Player, the waveform display is stationary, so you can "zoom in" on the section you're interested in.

Internet Access Information: ftp to **ftp.cdrom.com** and change directories to /pub/simtel/msdos/sound. (Remember, ftp is both the name of the command and part of the host name.) The file is named scoptrax.zip—although you may never get to it as you wade through the tons of other goodies in this archive. Similar archives are located at **ftp.cica.indiana.edu**, at **ftp.marcom.com**, and elsewhere.

The package contains several sample files, including one of Dr. "Bones" McCoy breaking the news to Captain James T. Kirk of the USS *Enterprise* that "He's dead, Jim."

You can watch the waveform of the sound on an oscilloscopelike display, and "zoom" down to the waveform you're interested in—you can narrow it down to the byte level. There you can delete sections or insert material from other

Still frame from an .AVI file converted into a .PCX graphics file by Vidvue.

MULTIMEDIA

Home screen of Vidvue, a Windows shareware multimedia utility that offers advantages over the Windows Media Player.

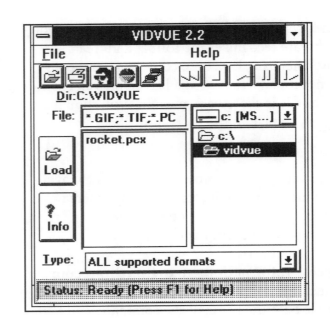

waveform files. You cannot, however edit the waveforms by dragging the lines around—but then, what do you want from freeware?

SOX

ScopeTrax uses files in the .VOC format (plus .SND and Amiga .IFF formats). Your Windows soundboard records files in the .WAV format. But you find sound files on the Internet in scads of other formats. What to do? Check out a sound file conversion facility called the Sound Exchange, or SOX. SOX can handle sound files created by Windows, Sun Microsystems, Digital Equipment Corp., Silicon Graphics, Macintosh, and NeXT machines, plus several types of MS-DOS sound files.

Internet Access Information: Archie for "sox." The latest version as this was written was called sox10dos.zip, although earlier versions (like sox5dos and sox6dos) still circulate. I got it through ftp to **ftp.cwi.nl** in the /pub/audio/ directory. That host is in Holland, and you can probably find the file closer to home.

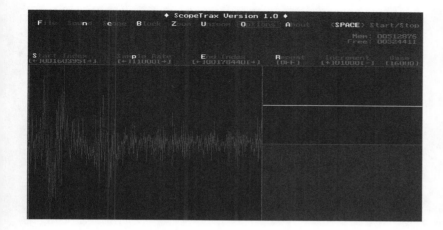

```
                    ◆ ScopeTrax Version 1.0 ◆
 File  Sound  Scope  Block  Zoom  Unzoom  Options  About    <SPACE> Start/Stop
                                                        Mem: 00512876
                                                        Free: 00324411
 Start Index        Sample Rate        End Index        Repeat      Increment    Base
 [→]00160395[←]    [←]11000[→]    [→]00178440[←]    [OFF]    [↓]01000[↑]    [16000]
```

ScopeTrax screen showing with the "He's dead, Jim" sampling loaded. The scope on the left shows the actual waveform of Dr. McCoy's immortal words, while the display at left will show a real-time scattergraph of the sound when the clip is played.

SOX is basically a utility "ported" from Unix, and using it can give you an understanding of the love/hate relationship some people manifest toward Unix. The idea is that you "pipe" a file through SOX, copying it from one file to another while SOX filters it to your specifications. The documentation contains various sample commands. For instance, to convert a file named "file" from .VOC (one of the formats used by ScopeTrax) to .WAV (the Windows waveform format) you'd type **SOX FILE.VOC FILE.WAV**. Once you try anything fancy, you end up listing cryptic options either before or after the first file name. To translate a file named "file" from the **.VOC** format to the Sun Microsystems .au format, you'd type **SOX FILE.VOC -r 8012 -U -b FILE.AU**. Wrestling with such things at the keyboard can be an uninspiring experience, but the approach lends itself to the writing of "scripts" by which commands can be quickly strung together into powerful, handmade systems.

MULTIMEDIA

VIRTUAL REALITY

Virtual reality is the classic cyberpunk dream. With VR, you can immerse yourself in a computer-generated world and construct towering skyscrapers of light, play musical instruments that hang like clouds in the air, or explore dark caverns under the surface of Mars. Reality? We don't need no stinking reality! Yes, VR provides a new way for people to interact and, if that doesn't interest you, to create your own private world and then crawl into it.

If you have a 386 or a Mac, a regular monitor, and a keyboard (or a mouse or joystick) you can download some of the software described in this chapter and get a taste of virtual reality. But VR really becomes an experience when you hook up some custom VR gear to your computer. Some of this gear is military-quality (with a price tag only a military contractor could love). Fortunately, there's a whole underground of "garage VR" activists, preaching cheap VR for the masses. They exchange notes on how to wire Mattel Powergloves and Sega 3D glasses to PCs, or how to build motion trackers and 3D head-mounted displays out of parts you can find at Radio Shack. Others churn out quality shareware VR worlds and/or world-building applications.

Yes, today's powerful PCs, plus all the high-tech goggles and sensor gloves littering the landscape following the eruption of the computer games market, have made home-brew VR a reality. The VR field shows the kind of excitement—

and potential—that the hobby PC field showed in the late 1970s, just before it exploded into an industry.

In case you haven't seen VR in action, here's the deal. The standard approach borrows heavily from the idea of the "architectural walk-through." Through VR software, you create a three-dimensional model of a house, landscape, or whatever that you can walk though, in a virtual sense, using various movement control commands. The computer screen becomes the view that a camera would pick up if it were being held by the person doing the walking. To make the scene react to your virtual walking in real time, the graphics have to be somewhat crude (looking more like cartoons than photorealistic renderings). But they can still be good enough to let you tell exactly what's going on. With the added ability for the user to manipulate virtual objects, and for objects to have animation programmed into them, the potential for games and education becomes obvious.

The programmer's task is to create the necessary objects and define their relations with each other. The result is a "world." To do a world well (to be a VR god) is difficult but worthwhile. It can also keep you sitting alone in the dark for a long time—the 3D house mentioned later in this chapter took three hundred hours to create.

And if some of this still seems like science fiction—well, there is indeed a strong connection between VR and the cyberpunk culture. See Chapter 7.

Saving Face:

Before cruising the VR scene, commit the following jargon to your memory chips:

6d—Six degrees of freedom (pan, zoom, swivel, pitch, roll, and yaw).

Artificial Reality—Where your body movement is sensed and reflected in the computer-generated environment.

Augmented Reality—To use HMDs to overlay images atop real-world scenery.

Cave—Immersion achieved through wall projectors.

CyberMan—A 6d stationary input device made from Logitech.

DataGlove—A gesture recognition device developed by VPL Research.

HMD—Head-mounted display.

HITL—Human Interface Technology Laboratory in Seattle, Washington.

Immersion—The illusion of actually being present, sensing, reacting to, and manipulating the virtual environment.

PGSI—The PowerGlove Serial Interface.

Polhemus—Electromagnetic coils used to provide a 6d input.

PowerGlove—Gesture recognition device developed for the Nintendo.

Presence—The feeling of actually being in an environment.

Projected Reality—Where computer displays give the user windows to the virtual environment, as in cockpit simulations.

REND 386—Previous version of VR386.

Shutter Glasses—Liquid crystal glasses that alternately blink, in sync with the display, to produce a 3D effect.

Spaceball—A 6d device measuring input's magnitude and direction.

Teleoperation—Remote operation of machinery.

Telepresence—Teleoperation with an impressive environment.

VEOS—The Virtual Environment Operating System/Shell, for distributed virtual worlds.

VR386—A real-time polygon renderer for Intel 386s and up—VR on the PC, for hobbyists.

VRD—The Virtual Retinal Display—lasers scan images directly on the retina.

DIASPAR NETWORK— WHY LEAVE HOME?

You can go online and "teleoperate" lunar rover models, or play hide and seek in a VR world called "Poly," using the Diaspar Virtual Reality Network of Laguna Beach, California. The cost is only a dollar an hour, and you get the first five hours free. To use Diaspar, you have to download its special modem software, Dmodem. To use the Poly facility, you also have to download a special program that works with Dmodem, called (of course) Poly. Zipped, both are a little over 100K bytes.

Access Information: You can call direct at 714-376-1234. Or from the Internet you can telnet to diaspar.com. Using the Internet introduces occasional Net lags, but otherwise is said to work fine. However, for uploading Dmodem to your system, Diaspar only provides Xmodem, which rarely works over the Internet, so to get the software you may have to call directly. After logging in, you can follow the directions to get to the Emporium area, where you can search for and download the files dmodem.zip and poly.zip.

Poly Playground

The Polygon Playground is a virtual world intended for two simultaneous users. You'll see stacks of colored blocks (or polygons) scattered around, and the other person appears as a cat face, with an adjacent disembodied hand. You can wave to the other player, do hand signals, play hide and seek or tag, shake hands, or build something with the polygons. You can also type a message and send it to the other player. Users have been known to lose their disembodied hand, and have to ask the other player to help find it. Poly software (for the 386 and higher PC with VGA graphics) is a modem-controlled version of REND386 (explained later in this chapter), that runs at two to ten frames per second. Obviously, you have to line up a partner before getting virtual, although the management will play matchmaker if asked.

LTM1

The LTM1 (lunar teleoperations model 1) is a toy tank with a camera and controls added. The tank sits in the middle of a huge lunar terrain landscape with a painted backdrop. At 2,400 bits per second you get a picture in about one minute, from which you can scout the terrain and plan your move. After moving you can request another image to see if the rover arrived or got stuck in route. At 9,600 bits per second, the time to get an image may eventually fall below five seconds.

Prospective drivers are asked to contact the management for a ten-minute training course before getting full access to the rover. Diaspar uses its own text-compatible graphics format that can be sent as e-mail. The ability to manipulate objects as well as move about may be added later.

Poly and LTM1 are part of Diaspar's efforts to bring cheap VR to the masses, and may have other online VR worlds in operation by the time you read this.

What the operator of the Diaspar LTM1 sees on the screen as the vehicle approaches a man-made structure on the virtual lunar surface it traverses.

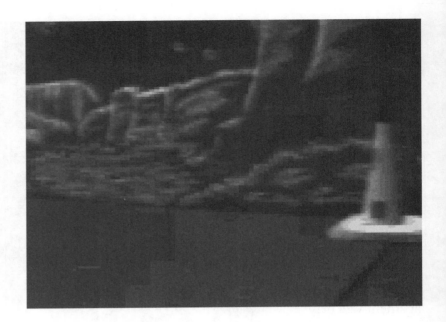

A rocket stands ready in the flat foreground while abrupt hills lie beyond in this screen shot from a Diaspar LTM1 control session.

WHERE TO GET VR386 AND REND386 (VR SOFTWARE)

Ready to download some VR software? There are many programs that you can download and run immediately. There's other software that will let you create your own virtual worlds and fill it with objects. You can even find special display interfaces as well, and software that supports Power-Gloves and HMDs. High-level VR software is intended for Unix machines or Silicon Graphics workstations, or other hardware familiar mostly to people on the *Jurassic Park* special effects team. But there's plenty of good PC stuff if you know where to look.

For instance, VR386 is a stand-alone VR program for 386 and higher PCs, supporting such VR devices as stereo flicker glasses, HMDs, the Mattel PowerGlove, and other VR gear. It replaces the earlier REND386 from the same source, but will run worlds created for REND386.

Internet Access Information: Anonymous ftp to **psych.toronto.edu** and go to directory ftp/pub/vr-386. The file you need is vr386.zip, which is 756K bytes long. (A Cyberscope driver is available as cyber.zip.) When you unzip it, use the -d option to re-create the file structure it expects. (In other words, type **PKUNZIP -D VR386.ZIP** to do it. This assumes you have pkunzip.exe. See the glossary for zipping information.) There are two demos in the version I examined, showing carnival rides and animated rooms. Type **VR386 RIDES.WLD** to run the first, and **VR386 ANIROOMS.WLD** to run the second.

CompuServe Access Information: In Cyberforum, select the Libraries option, select any of the libraries, and then the Browse command. Give it the All option, and then VR386 as the keyword. You'll see VR386, plus some associated worlds. When what you want is on the screen, give the Choices command, and then follow the directions for downloading.

AOL Access Information: You'll see it in the VR Utilities listings of the Virtual Reality listings of the Computers and Software Department. Double click on it, read the notes, and then select the download option. As usual, you'll need to unzip it.

You can move or fly about, and grasp and manipulate things using the mouse cursor. In the rides demo, there's a Ferris wheel, a tilted carousel, and other oddments. You can ride the Ferris wheel by standing under it and letting a car scoop you up. When it comes around to the peak, don't be afraid to move off and fly away. Likewise, you can ride the tilted carousel just by moving onto it—but your view will tilt and turn realistically, reminding you that you don't have to be near the ocean to get seasick. Meanwhile, to catch the four-wheel cart that's constantly circling the fairgrounds, you have to stand on the red carpet.

In the animated rooms demo, where everything keeps changing color and some of the furniture won't sit still, don't get your clothes caught on the dancing polyhedron. Otherwise, don't worry about getting stuck—you can walk right

The carnival ride world that comes with VR386, after "flying" up and away from it to get an overall view.

Pos(x,z): -8608,-53566

Frames/sec: 18

through the walls, which are opaque from the inside but transparent from the outside. But once outside, don't bother trying to catch the circling polyhedral blimp.

VR386 is touted as having the fastest drawing speed of any VR software in its class, exceeding 20,000 polygons per second. The text files that come with it give only minimal documentation, instead referring you to the printed version of the REND386 documentation: *Virtual Reality Creations*, published by the Waite Group Press. However, the C source code modules are included in the zip file and are heavily commented.

THE MOTHER LODE

A central depository of VR stuff seems to lie in the digital vaults of the University of Washington at Seattle, home of the Human Interface Technology Laboratory (HITL or HITLab).

Internet Access Information: Do anonymous ftp to **ftp.u.washington.edu** and cd to either subdirectory/public/virtual-worlds/or/public/VirtualReality/. At press time everything was located in the former, but there are plans to reconstruct the archive and move everything but the FAQ to the latter.

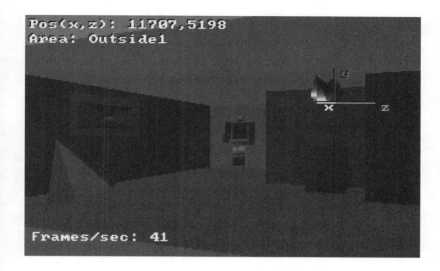

```
Pos(x,z): 11707,5198
Area: Outside1




Frames/sec: 41
```

The playroom of the animated rooms world that comes with VR386, seen from the outside through the transparent wall. Beware the dancing polyhedron on the left.

The cheap-vr subdirectory contains information on modifying SEGA goggles and other hobby projects, and the virtus subdirectory contains walk-through software for the Macintosh. The fly subdirectory contains fly-over software for Unix machines.

Lists of other VR sites was in the file vr_sites in/public/virtual-worlds/faq/other/, and lists of further VR Internet resources are in VRIR.txt file in /public/VirtualReality/HITL/papers/General/. Lists of conventional information sources are included in the file vru-v2n.txt in the directory/public/virtual-worlds/faq/publications/.

MORE SECRET SOURCES AND HANGOUTS

sci.virtual-worlds
These first four listings are the main watering holes for VR gurus, with people in Milan answering questions from people in Alaska. The talk in sci.virtual-worlds tends to get pretty techy, with deep discussions of the fact

that your eyes are constantly darting around and taking in the periphery, so that eye-tracking for HMDs is not as simple as it seems, etc. Basically, it's devoted to theory.

VIRTU-L

This mail list mirrors the traffic of sci.virtual-worlds. Send your request to **listserv@ vmd.cso.uiuc.edu**.

sci.virtual-worlds.apps

Instead of theory, actual events, news, calls for papers, contests, and user reports are the focus here.

VRAPP-L

This mail list mirrors the traffic in sci.virtual-worlds.apps. Send your request to **listserv@ vmd.cso.uiuc.edu**.

glove-list

The glove-list mail list is aimed at hobbyists seeking to adapt the PowerGlove for home-brew, no-budget VR. A FAQ for the list can be found on the Internet at **ftp.u.washington. edu** in the /public/virtual-worlds/faq/other/ FAQglovelist/directory. Otherwise send your request to **listserv@boxer.nas.nasa.gov**.

rend386

This mail list concerns the REND386 virtual reality package for the PC, described earlier in this chapter. Send your request to rend386-**request@sunee.uwaterloo.ca**.

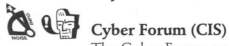

Cyber Forum (CIS)

The Cyber Forum on CompuServe maintains a serious tone, and offers a spaceflight demo and files for VR386 (as noted).

): -5386,-24117   Pos(x,

A REND386/ VR386 world inhabited by a Greek temple and some trees, found on AOL.

virtual.worlds (BIX)

This BIX conference likewise has a lot of technical and semitechnical discussions, plus user reports.

Cyberspace Forum (GEnie)

On GEnie, VR is lumped with multimedia in one forum—Cyberspace. The forum postings are fairly serious, although most people appear to be hobbyists. A weekly Cyberspace Report is also posted, carrying a lot of industry news concerning VR vendors. (Many are just rewritten press releases, but that's an appropriate source of information when you're talking about technical niches.) All in all, it's a worthwhile source of specialized news for the aficionado. There is also gush about GEnie's own developments and file postings, with datelines like "Cyberspace, Earth," which you can skip past without a moment's regret. There are not a few VR files posted, many by hobbyists. I got lost in one called 3DTREK, a 153K-byte DOS game

Check This Out:

There's a BBS echo network called CyberNet that's devoted to VR subjects for PC users and hobbyists. It's hubbed at The Cyber Technologies BBS, at 201-338-1076.

View to the left after walking into the front door of the 3D House, showing the computer alcove and the (functioning) shotgun on the wall.

where you awake in your quarters on the USS *Enterprise* and find that the crew (and most of the furniture) are gone—and the self-destruct timer is running.

Computers & Software Forum (AOL)
AOL has a cool collection of VR material, much of it posted by hobbyists, but there are also free offerings by commercial VR companies. In the Departments area, call up the Computers and Software Forum, and then scroll down until you see the Virtual Reality entry. Pick Virtual Reality from the list, and you'll see several options: VR Presentations, VR Utilities, Worlds, VR386, Text, and others. This part of the Net is still under construction: VR386 and the worlds are in the Utilities area, but there was nothing in the Text and VR386 areas. You can get at the VR collection through the Graphics and Animation selection.

The VR Presentations area is a list of demos, like the famous 3DHOUSE, which is an architectural walk-through of the programmer's house, yard, and tool shed, complete with furniture and storage boxes. The resolu-

Saving Face:

Don't go making gushing comments about cyberpunk books you just read, or ask about the authors or about their connection to VR. Assume everyone has read them, and never, ever admit that you haven't (see the CYBERPUNK CANON entry in the glossary for details).

Initial view of the 3D House from the outside. The front door (site of the other, internal view) is entered from the other side of the building, around the side to the right.

tion is a little cartoonish, but it's easy enough to tell what's going on, and that that thing sitting on the bed in the girl's upstairs bedroom is a stuffed cat. Hint: "Shooting" a door puts you through it. Doing that can also get you through the kitty door in the back of the garage and into the utility room. Don't bother shooting the two cats (in the garage and the storage room)—they don't do anything. But the shotgun hanging in the living room can be fired by shooting the trigger.

There's also a walk-through of a Hollywood studio, located below the famous HOLLYWOOD hilltop sign. Leaving the studio and going behind the sign, you'll see that the hill is itself a theatrical facade. (Some other AOL demos also appear in CompuServe's Cyber Forum.) In VR Utilities there are, as mentioned, several REND386 worlds, which will work fine under VR386.

alt.cyberspace

This newsgroup is more given to noise, the participants agonizing over "What is cyberspace?" and "How can it be set free?" It seems to exist in a netherworld between virtual reality techies and cyberpunk junkies. But these cybernauts do have style. Check out the one-liners in their signatures: "If the government wants people to respect the law, it should set a better example," "Help fight ambient light," "We're upping our standards, so up yours," "Will betray country for food." Gotta like it.

Other Access Information: There are also virtual reality conferences on the EchoNet, NorthAmeriNet, RelayNet, and ILink BBS echo networks.

SCIENCE FICTION

The Net came from science fiction, so it's no surprise science fiction came to the Net in a big way. Most sci-fi groups either exist to discuss a specific science fiction universe or exist to discuss the broader genre of sci-fi itself. You can also uncover thousands of graphics and sound files from *Star Trek*, *Babylon 5*, and other TV shows and movies. I can't cover every popular universe in this chapter—if every sci-fi text, sound, and graphics file were as bright as a match, the Net would light up like a supernova. Besides, the popularity of fictional universes seems to ebb and flow. (The Star Wars universe, for instance, is in a major slump.)

I've organized the material in this chapter into two sections: First you'll learn where to find places that discuss specific sci-fi universes, and then you'll see coverage of sci-fi as a genre.

STAR TREK

On the Net, "science fiction" is almost synonymous with *Star Trek*. Having grown up with Kirk, Spock, and the whole crew, today's cyberspacers treat them like old friends of the family. The

Saving Face:

If, in any posting about a book, movie, or series episode, you are going to give away anything about the plot, put the word "SPOILER" in the subject line or the lead-in text, so that those who want to experience the work in a state of innocence can avert their eyes. Also, on the Internet, when writing about a specific author, it is common to put the author's name in the subject line, like this: "Smith: His Latest Book Is Sexist Gibberish." Readers with kill files that list "Smith" (or "book*" or "sex*") won't have to read your posting or any thread it generates.

official Internet *Star Trek* hangout is a series of newsgroups in the rec.arts hierarchy, plus a mailing list:

rec.arts.startrek.current

To give you the scale of *Star Trek's* online popularity, rec.arts.startrek.current is the busiest Internet newsgroup I've ever visited. And most of these Trekkies are purists—they only like the *original Star Trek.* Many spend their time avidly denouncing the writers of ST:TNG (*Star Trek: The Next Generation*) for being inconsistent in tiny details, or for not doing things the way they themselves would have done them, or for being politically correct, or for being politically incorrect . . . and there's the usual stream of off-color jokes involving different alien races.

rec.arts.startrek.misc

This newsgroup is nearly as busy as rec.arts.startrek.current, but even more directionless, the postings being mostly general observations.

rec.arts.startrek.fandom

The focus here is on *Star Trek* memorabilia for sale and wanted, plus questions about the various actors in the several *Star Trek* series.

rec.arts.startrek.info

This is where you can find online versions of press releases and promotional material from the shows' producers, plus news articles and convention announcements.

rec.arts.startrek.reviews

User-written formal reviews of various *Star Trek* episodes and books show up here, many marked as containing spoiler material.

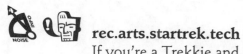

rec.arts.startrek.tech

If you're a Trekkie and an engineer, you'll love this place for its knowledgeable discussions of *Star Trek* technology, including weaponry, warp factors, computers, and aliens. There are even periodic postings of mini-FAQs on various topics.

Trek-Review-L

This mail list is described as a "noise-free forum" for *Star Trek* reviews, covering any of its series, movies, books, or animations. Send your request to **listserv@cornell.edu**.

alt.sexy.bald.captains

While you might assume this newsgroup concerns the commander of the USS *Enterprise* in TNG, it actually has broader coverage, including mooning over the bald captain from *The Love Boat* and several basketball stars who are captains of their teams.

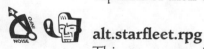

alt.starfleet.rpg

This newsgroup is home to a text-based role-playing game based on the *Star Trek* universe.

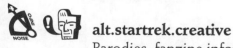

alt.startrek.creative

Parodies, fanzine information, comparisons of *Star Trek* with other sci-fi universes, set design discussion, and directions for making *Star Trek* uniforms are the order of the day here. A rare treat for serious Trekkies.

alt.ensign.wesley.die.die.die

Ensign Wesley has not made a lot of friends. Here they virtually foam at the mouth about the scrubbed-face young know-it-all character

of TNG—they call him "the weasel," and hotly debate appropriately loathsome fates for him.

Saving Face

Where do you begin? Whether you're a recent *Star Trek* convert or a Trekkie who has not yet achieved total mind

Captain Picard

as a Borg alien.

meld with the series, you might want to learn these tidbits and abbreviations:

Bar—The producers have stated officially that the bar on the *Enterprise* in ST:TNG is non-alcoholic.

Censorship—British and German TV elected not to show certain ST:TNG episodes, deeming them unsuitable for children. One episode mentioning Irish liberation somehow never aired in England.

Dates—Stardates are supposed to be twenty-four-hour days. The years are supposed to be part of the Julian calendar. But stringing the date references into a coherent timeline is not for the fainthearted.

DS9—*Deep Space 9*, a spin-off of ST:TNG using some of the latter's walk-on characters.

Online—None of the cast is reported to be online, although a writer or two may be.

Political Correctness—The first interracial kiss on U.S. television took place between Kirk and Uhura on TOS.

ST:TNG—Same as TNG.

Starfleet—Officially, it is not a military organization. It just acts like one.

TNG—*Star Trek: The Next Generation*.

TOS—The Old/Original *Star Trek* Series.

UFP—United Federation of Planets. It has explored 11 percent of the galaxy.

Warp Speed—TOS used a simplistic scale where the warp factor was an exponent of the speed of light. The fastest reported was warp 14. TNG uses a fancier scale where warp 10 is infinity.

Internet Access Information: Besides the Usenet newsgroups themselves, files of *Star Trek* background data appear in the Usenet archives connected with the rec.arts newsgroups mentioned earlier. For instance, you can try **rtfm.mit.edu** in the /pub/ directory. In addition to FAQ files for the various newsgroups (in directories named after those newsgroups) there are files about such subjects as Starfleet ships and bases, and series actors. Articles that have appeared in rec.arts.startrek.info are archived at **scam. berkeley.edu** in the /misc/trek-info/ directory. Examining various read-me files will likely lead you to other collections (or at least mirror sites) as well.

BIX Access Information: There is a *Star Trek* topic in the "sf" conference.

CompuServe Access Information: There is considerable *Star Trek* material in CompuServe's Science Fiction/Fantasy Forum, which you can reach by inputting "go scifi." Browsing the file library will uncover .gif shots and data files, etc.

Delphi Access Information: *Star Trek* is one of the major topic headings in Delphi's Science Fiction and Fantasy SIG, which you can reach through the Groups and Clubs option on the opening screen.

AOL Access Information: There is a Star Trek Club with numerous conference topics, and also Star Trek heading in the AOL Science Fiction and Fantasy Club department. The former had about five times more postings than the latter. Oddly, no overlap is evident. You can reach either by using the keyword command.

GEnie Access Information: SFRT2 (The Science Fiction & Fantasy RoundTable 2) contains 14 conferences devoted to *Star Trek,* including TOS, TNG, DS9, the movies, conventions, and parodies. Select the Entertainment Services item from the main menu, go to SFRT2, select the bulletin board option, and then use the CAT command to view the conference names.

Other Access Information: Any general-interest BBS echo network you can name will have a *Star Trek* conference, including NorthAmeriNet, EchoNet, RelayNet, Intelec, ILink, FidoNet, and Global-Link.

Learn Klingon!

So, you want to speak Klingon? (*vaj tlhIngan Hol Dajatlh 'e' Dane?*) Yes, you, too, can acquire this increasingly valuable skill and converse with the flinty aliens who would have conquered the galaxy were it not for the likes of Kirk and Spock. Not only is there a Klingon dictionary (*tlhIngan Hol mu'ghom*) available, plus language training tapes (*tlhIngan Hol qawHaq*) on "conversational Klingon" and "power Klingon," but the Klingon Language Institute (KLI) offers a correspondence course.

The KLI is involved in an effort to translate the Bible into Klingon, and to restore the text of the works of Shakespeare to its original Klingon form. There's also a writing contest. A Klingon language mailing list is available through **tlhIngan-Hol-request@klingon.east.sun.com**. And there's a Usenet hangout:

alt.startrek.klingon

Klingon-philes can be seen here posing questions to one another about the fine points of the language, discussing the origin of the Klingon mourning howl, complaining about the oppression of the Klingons by the Vulcans, and coming up with recipes for "*qagh*," the main Klingon food (grub worms, served live). Many have sigs in Anglicized Klingon.

Several parties are reported to be working on urgently needed English/Klingon Klingon/English translation software, although it appears to be slow going. Best effort so far: "*gharghmeyqoqraj tIn SuD leghlaHbe' juppu'na'wIj gharghmeyqoqlIj tIn SuD leghlaHbe' juppu'na'wI*" becomes "My definite friends cannot see your supposed big blue serpents."

Access Information: You think I'm making this Klingon language stuff up? Well, the Klingons have a word for you. In fact, it might be advisable for you to leave the galaxy. Or you can absorb the Klingon-language FAQ found in most Usenet FAQ archives (such as **rtfm.mit.edu**, or **ftp.uu.net**). Or you can contact the Klingon Language Institute, PO Box 634, Flourtown, PA 19031-0634. Members get a subscription to the quarterly *HolQeD* (*The Journal of the Klingon Language Institute*).

Saving (Perhaps Much More Than) Face: There are no words in Klingon for "please" or "thank you."

BABYLON 5

Barely a year old at this writing, *Babylon 5* (a science fiction TV series syndicated by Warner Brothers Television Consortium's Prime Time Entertainment Network) has an online following nearly rivaling that of *Star Trek*. Presumably, this is because the founders (especially writer/producer J. Michael Straczynski) are themselves cyberspacers. For instance, the interstellar location of *Babylon 5* is "Grid Epsilon 470,18,22" which matches the original location of the *Babylon 5* topic on GEnie (Page 470, CAT 18, Topic 22). There's a ship named *Hyperion*, after the name of a Babylon ftp site (see later discussion).

Other entities on the show have been named on the basis of suggestions solicited from GEnie participants. Residents of a mysterious place called "Downbelow" are called "lurkers"—the term for nonparticipating conference readers. And the show is a product of the computer revolution—special effects are created with a NewTek Video Toaster and specialized software, rather than scale models.

The concept of *Babylon 5* is simple: Instead of our heroes charging about the galaxy, encountering new aliens, necessitating expensive new theatrical sets and makeup schemes each week, you have one set—a space station, five miles long, twenty-five light-years from Earth—and let the aliens come to you. In fact, you can have batches of them permanently on hand, each with preestablished characters and motives, so that each episode can cut to the chase. (In case you're wondering, *Babylon 5* was in development before *Deep Space 9*, a Trek spin-off based on a similar premise, surfaced.) The station is supposed to be centrally located between five different alien races, and its basic function is to keep the peace between them. Earthbound Net hangouts include:

SFRT (GEnie)

The GEnie forum is no longer at the grid setting mentioned earlier because of the expansion and splitting of the GEnie Science Fiction Roundtable—it's now at Page 471 Category 18 and 19 of Science Fiction RoundTable 2. Straczynski has been there since even before the show began airing, debating the nature of whatever sociological underpinning the *Babylon 5* characters would need. For example, should there be capital punishment, or some kind of high-tech push-button rehabilitation?

rec.arts.sf.tv.babylon5

This Internet newsgroup is extremely active and includes participation from Straczynski. There is a lot of discussion of how to demonstrate support for the show to one's local station, plus questions on extraterrestrial anthropology, who's who among the actors, and future combat speculation. Plus there is a lot of fruitless complaining about the standing rule against posting story ideas.

Outside view of the space station in Babylon 5, found on the Internet.

alt.tv.babylon-5

A smaller incarnation of rec.arts.sf.tv.babylon5, this newsgroup may simply be aimed at those who don't have the rec.arts hierarchy.

B5-Review-L

The Babylon 5 Reviews Electronic Forum mail list is described as a noise-free outlet for reviews concerning *Babylon 5* and any spin-offs (i.e., novelizations). To subscribe, send

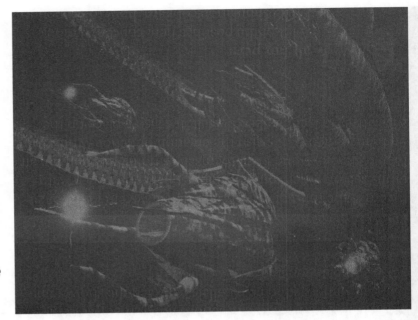

Aliens on the move

in Babylon 5.

your request to **listserv@cornell.edu** and in the body of the message put the string "SUB-SCRIBE B5-REVIEW-L" followed by your name.

Saving Face:

You've got to know the alien races that co-own *Babylon 5*:

Vorlons—Methane breathers who keep to themselves, forming a wild card in the setup.

Minbari—Aliens who fought a war against Earth ten years earlier, were on the brink of victory—and then mysteriously surrendered.

Centauri Republic—Decadent types who were Earth's first contact with aliens.

Narn Regime—Former helots of the Centauri, now independent.

Earth Alliance—Us, represented by a low-level commander, whose presence was mysteriously insisted on by the Minbari.

GEnie Access Information: Go to Science Fiction RoundTable 2, select the BBS option, and then category 18 or 19.

AOL Access Information: Go to the Science Fiction and Fantasy Club (you can enter "scifi" as the keyword in the directory of services menu) and select the TV option from the list.

Internet Access Information: Besides the Usenet newsgroups mentioned so far, you can use anonymous ftp to access **ftp.hyperion.com**, the official *Babylon 5* archive site, in the directory/pub/Babylon-5/. (The material is also mirrored at **ftp.uml.edu**.) You'll find .gif and JPEG stills from the series, episode guides and synopses, archives of the producer's postings from GEnie and alt.tv.babylon-5, electronic press kits the producers have put out, lists of stations that carry the show, plot background, technical background, notes on the characters, notes on the actors, and a history of ancient Babylonia. (They're serious about that last item—there are supposed to be parallels between the show's universe and Babylonia.)

PERN

Pern is the third planet of the Rukbat system in the Sagittarius sector, where human colonist have lost touch with high technology and busy themselves riding through the air on flying dragons. It's also the creation of fiction writer Anne McCaffrey, a Net denizen herself. It's also a place on the Internet:

alt.fan.pern
A lot of the postings here concern various MUD simulations of Pern, how to pronounce

Check This Out:

Do not post story ideas in any of these conferences that are frequented by movie or TV producers, as they may react to it as an attempt by you to expose them to liability. Producers are regularly sued by people claiming to have submitted a certain idea, which was rejected but later turned up on-screen. In fact, Hollywood has a procedure to protect producers and writers, involving registration of ideas with a writers guild before submission. To protect themselves, producers only look at submissions that have been registered or otherwise solicited, sending back all the others unexamined—which is

(continued on page 78)

Check This Out:

(continued from page 77)

probably the "rejection" the litigants experienced. Then, when parallels appear on-screen—wait long enough and it will happen—they decide they've been plagiarized, further stoking the litigation industry.

Saving Face:

Pern simulations can refer to Pern and its characters but for copyright reasons should not be placed on Pern or involve those characters. (Similar restrictions apply to most universes created by individual science fiction authors.)

Pern names, discussions of who's who, and questions along the lines of whether there are lawyers on Pern.

Internet Access Information: You can get the FAQ for alt.fan.pern at the usual FAQ archives, such as **rtfm.mit.edu** in /pub/usenet/alt.fan.pern. It's posted by an organization styled "Nit-Pickers for a Better Tomorrow Afternoon." Read all about dragon sexual behavior and toileting problems, plus details on real-life fan organizations.

MIDDLE EARTH

The epic works of British scholar J.R.R. Tolkien concerning Hobbits and Middle Earth of the Third Age are the center of two Internet hangouts:

rec.arts.books.tolkien

Judging from the postings in this busy newsgroup, Tolkien's followers are like-minded scholars (or would-be scholars), given to Aristotelian debate, textual analysis concerning the race and gender of the Ringwraiths, etc. Do orcs live forever? What are the parallels between Hitler and Sauron? Who is Bombadil?

alt.fan.tolkien

Why didn't the eagles carry Frodo to Mt. Doom? Such questions mark the main difference between this newsgroup and rec.arts.books.tolkien—there are fewer textual and more plot questions here, as you'd expect from the name.

Middle Earth is almost not a science fiction or fantasy universe at all, but a linguistic exercise, with the trolls, elves, and other minority groups speaking full-blown languages—

the "Rohirrim" actually speak Anglo-Saxon. Basically, the books try to give the reader the linguistic experience of the original Hobbit narrators. Tomatoes, for instance, can't be eaten on Middle Earth, since that's a Caribbean word. Tobacco is smoked, but as "pipeweed." Potatoes get by as "taters."

Internet Access Information: There are two FAQs concerning the Tolkien newsgroups: one for those who have read *The Hobbit* and *Lord of the Rings*, and a LessFAQ for less frequently asked questions concerning lesser-known Middle Earth works. They can be found in the usual FAQ archives—I found it at **ftp.uu.net** in the /usenet/news.archives/tolkien directory.

MORE SCIFI UNIVERSES

alt.fan.dune
The desert world of Frank Herbert's Dune novels and the movie treatment is the subject here. The pace is less frenetic than some of the others, as the participants seek historical parallels in the Dune saga, and ponder what religion is practiced there.

alt.tv.prisoner
The old British TV series *The Prisoner* is the topic here. The series was famous for being inexplicable, not only to the central character—who, like all of us, was trapped in an unidentified place by people who would not explain themselves, for reasons that are never given—but to the viewers as well. The newsgroup postings are devoted to pinning down who was who among the actors, where the show can be seen today—and who was #1, anyway?

Saving Face:
   If you can't quote chapter and verse from the Tolkien corpus, better stick to the National Lampoon version "Bored of the Rings" (a hilarious satire which also has a following among the Middle Earthers). And don't ask where you can find the second half of the animated version of *Lord of the Rings* by Ralph Bakshi—it never got made.

This may look like something out of science fiction, but it's really the screen of a thirty-year-old DEC PDP-1 computer.

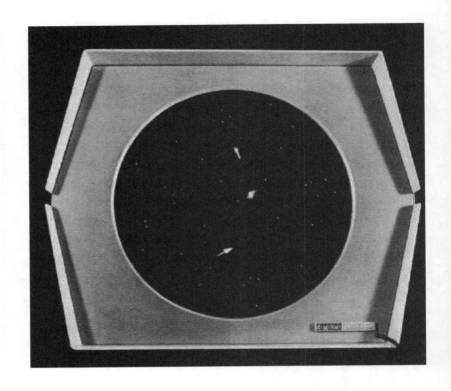

 alt.tv.red-dwarf

Traffic is similar in alt.tv-red-dwarf, which concerns a British science fiction/humor series of that name. Plus there is talk about board games based on the series.

 rec.arts.drwho

Traffic is surprisingly heavy in this newsgroup, which concerns the long-running British *Doctor Who* science fiction series. These fans, however, show none of the awe you can detect in some of the other conferences listed in this chapter. They like to discuss on-screen production bloopers, bashing actors who have played the time-lord doctor, and listing their favorite worst scenes (it's a British thing).

 alt.drwho/creative
The traffic here is about the same as in rec.arts.drwho.

 pkd-list
This mail list is aimed at fans of Philip K. Dick (1928–1982), a science fiction writer who had a reputation for being otherworldly. Send your request to **pkd-list-request@wang.com**.

 rec.arts.sf.starwars
Formerly king of the hill, the *Star Wars* universe has sunk to being just another name on the list. Still, there remain plenty of people out there trying to get plot questions settled, to judge by this busy newsgroup. Whatever happened to this or that actor? For that matter, whatever happened to gravity? What about these parallels with *Star Trek*? What about these continuity problems between the movie episodes? Just how are light sabers

supposed to work, anyway? There's also discussions of the *Star Wars* comics scene, and of
other spin-offs.

alt.fan.eddings

Will Velvet finally get Silk or will he decide to
fall upon his own sword? Will Durnik ever
build his own tower and study in it? What
will Durnik and Polgara's children grow up to
be? Inquiring minds want to know, at least in
this newsgroup.

alt.fan.piers-anthony

There are Piers Anthony fans who start reading one of the author's books and post com-

Good, evil, and light sabers have it out in this Star Wars scene found on the Internet.

ments here every few chapters. In the background, they also talk about time travel paradoxes and speculate on whether any of Anthony's works will get made into a movie.

GENERAL SCIENCE FICTION

 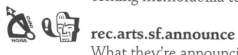

rec.arts.sf.misc
Convention notices and for-sale notices concerning memorabilia turn up here.

rec.arts.sf.announce
What they're announcing is authors' tours, mostly.

Saving Face:

Some sci-fi movie fans seem to be on a quest for a fabled day-long "director's cut" of the movie *Dune* directed by David Lynch—a version that supposedly actually did justice to the novel. The consensus on the Internet: There is no such version, although you can find video versions of varying lengths.

rec.arts.sf.fandom
Science fiction conventions are the subject here, as that's the gathering place of fandom.

rec.arts.sf.movies
This newsgroup is a busy place, with discussions and/or denunciations of most-favorite and/or most-loathed movies. My favorite quote: "It's a shame a fictional character can't sue." Plus there are people searching for video titles, and questions about the release date of rumored future movies. There are even FAQ postings for specific movies.

rec.arts.sf.tv
Much the same description applies to this newsgroup as to rec.arts.sf.movies, except that this one is busier and relates to offerings on the tube. Plus there is talk of ratings and series renewals and cancellations.

rec.arts.sf.written
This is one of the busiest newsgroups that I have lurked in. The participants discuss individual books and authors, plus whole genres, while asking, "What ever happened to . . ." Plus there are lists of book stores by region.

rec.arts.sf.reviews
This newsgroup is entirely devoted to user-written reviews of books.

A "tie fighter" from the Star Wars universe, found on the Internet.

 rec.arts.sf.marketplace
For-sale notices about science fiction material, especially T-shirts, cars, and figurines, show up here.

 **alt.history.what-if**
Here the cognoscenti gather to debate alternate possibilities in history—a common theme in science fiction. The participants mainly talk about what would have happened had there been no U.S. Civil War, or if Hitler had chilled out, but any moment in past time is fair game. Better know your fine points of history before treading here.

 Twilight Zone
The *Twilight Zone* mail list is a quarterly online fiction magazine, formatted in ASCII. Writers are said to be welcome, "as long as they don't like carnivorous plants" (apparently a reference to Terry Prachett—see Chapter 6). If

Drop ship from

the movie

Aliens, *found*

on the Internet.

your plants are all vegans, send your request to **r.c.karsmakers@stud.let.ruu.nl**.

Quanta
Quanta is also an electronic science fiction magazine, sent out monthly in either ASCII or PostScript format. Send your request to **da1n@andrew.cmu.edu**.

sf-lovers
This mail list is a moderated digest of postings from the rec.arts.sf hierarchy. Back issues are archived in **gandalf.rutgers.edu**. Send your request to **sf-lovers-request@rutgers.edu**.

Omphalos
Omphalos is a quarterly speculative fiction review magazine posted in rec.arts.sf.misc and archived in various places. A paper version is also available by subscription.

German World War I fighter found on the Internet.

Saving Face:

Star Trek material shouldn't be posted in the general scifi newsgroups. Otherwise, there are certain background facts that can help you get along better:

Cyberpunk (covered in Chapter 7)—Try to avoid arguments on whether it's a movement or a gimmick.

Deaths—Don't post rumors that this or that writer has died. What if you're wrong?

Filking—Folk singing sci-fi fan music, perpetuating a convention program typo. Check the alt.music.filk newsgroup.

Fruitless Discussion Topics—"Could the Klingons beat the Vulcans?" etc. "Faster than light drive is possible/nonsense." "Writer X was sexist."

The real thing: a space shuttle liftoff, found on the Internet.

FTL—Faster Than Light. Interstellar travel would be tedious without it.

Kilgore Trout—Fictitious sci-fi writer invented by Kurt Vonnegut. Trout's one book was actually written by Philip Jose Farmer.

Steampunk—Alternate reality stories set in the nineteenth century, often with the assumption that Babbage's mechanical computer got built.

Vacuum—Some sci-fi depicts people popping like balloons when exposed to the vacuum of space. Other sci-fi depict the experience as being dangerous and uncomfortable, pending suffocation. The latter is more accurate.

BIX Access: BIX has an extensive science fiction conference, which you can reach with the command "join sf." Fantasy, horror, and mystery are also covered. Along with the usual *Star Trek*, *Deep Space 9*, and *Babylon 5* followings (Straczynski is said to show up there), there are convention calendars, Batman material, and material on the publishing industry. The conference has its own collection of files, including stills from various shows and movies.

CompuServe Access: CompuServe has its Science Fiction/Fantasy Forum, which you can reach by inputting "go scifi." As well as considerable *Star Trek* and Pern material, there are newsletters, fact files, maps of various fictional places, stills from movies and TV series, and fan club information.

Delphi Access: Delphi has its Science Fiction and Fantasy SIG, which you can reach through the Groups and Clubs option on the opening screen. Besides *Star Trek*, there is coverage of conventions, comics, fanzines, movie information, reviews, gossip, upcoming books, writers workshops and the publishing market, and technology. In the attached conference people exult at their freedom to wander off-topic, having gotten their hands slapped in other services.

AOL Access: Under the AOL Science Fiction and Fantasy Club there are headings for *Star Trek,* comics, TV shows, and *Star Wars*. There are fifty conference headings under *Star Trek* alone, with people cataloging ships and comparing Kirk to Picard. There are forty-eight conferences devoted to TV shows, including some nearly forgotten ones like *Starman* and *Battlestar Gallactica*. The files area contained show scripts, episode guides, and sci-fi icons. (The AOL Star Trek Club is described earlier.)

AOL also had a section devoted to the cable Sci-Fi Channel, with show times and other materials—including .gif files from *Plan 9 from Outer Space*, widely hailed as the worst movie ever made in Hollywood.

GEnie Access: As mentioned, GEnie has three highly organized science fiction and fantasy roundtables, which you can reach by selecting the Entertainment Services item from the main menu. In each roundtable, select the bulletin board option, and then use the CAT command to see the categories covered. SFRT1 concerns the written word, covering writing, the market, authors, and science research. SFRT2 concerns movies and TV, plus screenwriting and novelization issues, and the previously mentioned *Star Trek* and *Babylon 5* areas. SFRT3 concerns fandom and conventions, fans by specific author, filking, and, of course, "radioactive materials and mutants."

THE INTERNET SCI-FI CACHE

The premier accumulation of science fiction material on the Internet appears to be the ftp archive at **galdalf.rutgers.edu**. Not only are there guides to most of the topics discussed so far, but lists of science fiction authors and awards, convention information, and information on less-followed subjects, like the Lensmen book series and such old TV series as *Lost in Space*, *The Outer Limits*, and *Space: 1999*. There is even information concerning Godzilla.

Internet Access Information: Do anonymous ftp to **gandalf.rutgers.edu** and go to the /pub/sfl/ directory. In Europe, a similar archive is at **ftp.lysator.liu.se** in the

MRB'89

Godzilla bids you welcome from this picture found on the Internet.

/pub/sf-texts/ directory. World Wide Web users with Mosaic or similar reader programs can try the URL ftp://gandalf.rutgers.edu/pub/sfl/sf-resource.guide.html and http://www.lysator.liu.se:7500/sf_archive/sf_main.html, respectively.

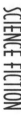

HUMOR

Many people feel trapped in a world they didn't make, and humor helps them cope. Of course, computer nerds like us often feel trapped in a world we *did* make, which demands an even more robust sense of the absurd. So it's no surprise that the Net is a great place to go for humor—especially the Internet.

THE ORACLE

One of the best examples of inspired lunacy online is the Usenet Oracle, a collaborative effort created by some of the most warped minds around. They have two newsgroups:

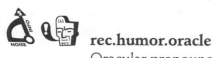

rec.humor.oracle
Oracular pronouncements deemed worthy by the priesthood are presented here.

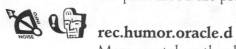

rec.humor.oracle.d
Mere mortals gather here to discuss the pronouncements in rec.humor.oracle.

To participate, you send a question to **oracle@cs.indiana.edu**. The subject line should contain the string "tell me," framed by whatever phrasing seems appropriately groveling:

"Most exalted one, tell me, craven loon that I am, the answer to my question," etc. The body of the message should contain only the question.

You will receive an answer in a couple of days. In the meantime, you may receive a question from someone else, directed to you by the priesthood. Answer it and send it back to **oracle@cs.indiana.edu**. In the subject line, include the word "answer" and the question number. The body should contain only the answer—don't include the question. The pronouncements (called "Oracularities") typically end with an assessment of what the questioner owes the oracle, usually something of metaphorical value representing the oracle's reaction to the spirit of your question, such as "a small green puppet with funny ears" or "the movie rights to the accidental demolition of your building next week."

If the moderators (the "oracle priesthood") like your response, it will be included in the periodic posting of pronouncements in rec.humor.oracle.

Internet Access Information. The priests can be reached through the mail address given earlier, and the pronouncements can be read in Usenet. An archive of pronouncements is available via anonymous ftp at **cs.indiana.edu** in the /pub/oracle/ directory. You can receive pronouncements via e-mail by sending a request to **oracle-request@cs.indiana.edu** with "subscribe" in the subject line (or "unsubscribe" to get off the list).

JOKES

Another humor collection effort is based in rec.humor. funny, whose moderator is actually a paid employee of the ClariNet Communications Corporation, an electronic news publisher. To participate, you send your jokes (one per message) to **funny@clarinet.com**. The moderator judges it by the organization's submission guidelines, may edit it to

```
O Great Oracle, please help me with my difficulty.
>
> I am a personnel manager for a large company. With the recent
> requirements for political correctness I am concerned about my title,
> and the fact that I use a personal computer. The problem is obvious:
> "personnel" has "son" in it as does personal, and "manager" has "man".
> I have therefore sent out a memo which I reproduce below:
>
> From: J. Bloggs, Perpeoplel perpeopleager
> To:   All staff
> Re:   Perpeoplal computers
>
> Henceforth all "personal computers" will be known as "perpeoplal
> computers" in recognition of the potential political incorrectness of
> the former name.
>
> J. Bloggs, chairperpeople, PC committee
>
> Anyway, to my question:
> My analyst has started asking for danger money. Should I pay?

And in response, thus spake the Oracle:

} It'More?
}
} The English "people" comes from the Latin "populus."  While "populus"
} refers to people in general, it is gramatically of masculine gender.
} However, it may be replaced by a gender-neutral term for a
} gender-neutral concept, such as the Tlingit word "makchutep," meaning
} people in general. Unfortunately, makchutep contains the syllable
} "chu," which is strongly reminiscent of the Lahu word "chur," meaning
} one's best friend's uncles. It must therefore be replaced by the Lower
} Middle Late Pidgin Yiddish "Svolbtz," a slang term for collateral
} relatives of any gender. This may be done freely, since LMLPY is
} completely free of gender references (coincidentally, this language was
} only spoken by a group of seven shopkeepers and their families in a
} small village near Gdansk, where it soon passed out of use, since it
} proved impossible to gossip effectively in LMLPY). To sum up, you may
} safely refer to yourself as a
} "Permaksvolbtztepl Permaksvolbtztepger" without fear of offending
} anyone. Other words may be changed accordingly.
}
} Your analyst is a heavily disguised alien from Venus. It is attempting
} to charge you more in order to finance the construction of a
} mind-control network base on microwave oven technology. Kill it. Kill
} it now.

} You owe the Oracle a gender-neutral translation of the Kama Sutra.
```

Typical (?) supplicant-question and oracular answer

from rec.humor.oracle.

make it more concise, assigns keywords and a rating, and then posts it in rec.humor.funny. The moderator is a demanding person: Only two or three jokes make the cut each day.

The jokes are judged on the basis of internal consistency and humor—not subject matter. Warnings are added for potentially offensive material. For *truly* offensive material, the moderator uses the rot(13) encryption method, where letters are transposed 13 places in the alphabet, (*A* becomes *M,* etc.). Your host probably has a rot(13) facility for decrypting the file. (The moderator will not explain the encryption or rot(13)—if you want to be corrupted, you're on your own.) There is apparently no archive of jokes, but annual collections of the material are published in book form. Send mail to **jokebook@clarinet.com** for details on how to order.

Spontaneous Combustion

So you don't want someone censoring your jokes? Well, for a nonstop supply of fresh, uncensored humor, just crank your bandwidth open another notch, logon to the newsgroups listed here, and stand back as the jokes pour in. Incidentally, the creation of newsgroups (especially in the alt hierarchy) is in itself often an expression of wit. For instance, the 1994 Winter Olympics gave birth to the newsgroup alt.fan.tonya-harding.whack.whack.whack, paired with newsgroup alt.fan.nancy-kerrigan.ouch.ouch.ouch.

 rec.humor

This is one of the busiest newsgroups in Usenet. Not only do people post their own jokes and other offerings—some resorting to rot(13), and others that should but don't—but many post requests for genre material, such as puns or answering machine messages.

Figure skater

Nancy Kerrigan,

from a photo

found on the

Internet.

 **rec.humor.d**
Most of the material here is simply slop-over from rec.humor, rather than discussions of the contents of rec.humor (even though the .d suffix usually indicates discussion).

 **alt.shenanigans**
The focus here is on practical jokes, including firsthand reports—real and fabricated—of

practical jokes, and advice on mounting practical jokes. The FAQ files stresses that shenanigans are harmless pranks, devoid of vandalism or rudeness. As for constantly recurring questions along the lines of "What to do about the guy who parks in my parking space?" readers are advised to ask him to move.

talk.bizarre

Talk.bizarre is almost as busy as rec.humor, the main difference being that the emphasis is on purely textual humor. Here people post parodies of poetry and of overcooked short stories, or just snippets: *". . . leaving a wake of dead and injured that will take years to fully identify and recycle. And that's the news, I'm Tom Brokaw, goodnight."* (Rec.humor material is often written renderings of verbal jokes—a subtle difference that leads the writers in completely different directions.)

alt.humor.best-of-usenet

This newsgroup is a moderated compilation of material from other newsgroups—anything from last week that seems particularly funny, witty, weird, or merely inexplicable. The moderator—who can be reached at **best@cc.ysu.edu**—chooses well.

Internet Access Information: Rec.humor.funny and alt.shenanigans have FAQ files, which you can find in **rtfm.mit.edu** in the /pub/usenet-by-group/ directory.

Regional Humour

Notice the spelling—humor becomes humour east of Cape Cod and north of Detroit. Some regional humor offerings on the Internet are:

za.humour

ZA in nearly any online setting stands for South Africa, a tradition derived from British Empire radio call signs. Here you can tap into a stream of mordant, morbid, and cynical comments about "the new South Africa." "What's the problem with political jokes? They get elected."

aus.jokes

If you crave the spectacle of unhinged people pelting each other with the oldest jokes outside Sumaria, commonly of the "why beer is better than women" variety, then this is the newsgroup for you. New Zealanders catch some flak, too.

de.talk.jokes.d

As near as I can tell (it's in German), it's not jokes that they are trading back and forth here, but questions about where to find various genres of humor material, including videos and TV programming times.

fj.jokes

The FJ hierarchy contains material that is "from Japan," and you might predict that the contents would be encoded kanji, impenetrable to anyone who uses an ASCII terminal. And you'd be right. Oddly, many of the sigs are in English.

relcom.humor

The relcom hierarchy is devoted to material originating in the former Soviet Union, and so the focus here is on Russians telling Ukrainian jokes. (This must be one of the few remaining preserves of the endangered ethnic joke genre,

User-generated collection of satirical computer viruses, some slightly dated. Online, you'll run across such collections at intervals, each with slight variations— an "urban folklore" phenomenon that future academics will surely make careers out of studying.

Oprah Winfrey Virus: your 200mb hard drive suddenly shrinks to 80mb, and then slowly expands back to 200mb.

AT&T Virus: every three minutes it tells you what great service you are getting.

MCI Virus: every three minutes it reminds you that you are paying too much for the AT&T virus.

Paul Revere Virus: this revolutionary virus does not horse around, it warns you of impending hard disk attack . . . once if by LAN, twice if by c:\.

New World Order Virus: probably harmless, but it makes a lot of people really mad just thinking about it.

Federal Bureaucrat Virus: divides your hard disk into hundreds of little units, each of which does practically nothing, but all of which claim to be the most important part of your computer.

Gallup Virus: sixty percent of the PCs infected will lose 38 percent of their data 14 percent of the time (plus or minus a 3.5 percent margin of error).

Sears Virus: your data won't appear unless you buy new cables, power supply and a set of shocks.

Jimmy Hoffa Virus: your programs can never be found again.

Congressional Virus: runs every program on the hard drive simultaneously, but doesn't allow the user to accomplish anything.

Kevorkian Virus: helps your computer shut down as an act of mercy.

Airline Virus: you're in Dallas, but your data is in Singapore.

Adam & Eve Virus: takes a couple of bytes out of your Apple.

Terry Randle Virus: prints "Oh no you don't" whenever you choose "abort" from the "abort, retry, fail" message.

L.A.P.D. Virus: it claims it feels threatened by the other files on your PC and erases them in "self defense".

Ross Perot Virus: activates every component in your system, just before the whole damn thing quits.

Ted Turner Virus: colorizes your monochrome monitor.

Star Trek Virus: invades your system in places where no virus has gone before.

Politically Correct Virus: never calls itself a "virus", but instead refers to itself as an "electronic micro-organism".

Ollie North Virus: causes your printer to become a paper shredder.

```
Mario Cuomo Virus: it would be a great virus, but it
refuses to run!

Dan Quayle Virus: their is sumthing rong wit your
cumpewter, ewe jsut cnt figyour out watt!!!

Texas Virus: makes sure that it is bigger than any other
file.

PBS Virus: your programs stops every few minutes to ask
for money.

Elvis Virus: your computer gets fat, slow and lazy, then
self destructs; only to resurface at shopping malls and
service stations across rural America.

Freudian Virus: your computer becomes obsessed with marry-
ing its own motherboard.

Imelda Marcos Virus: sings you a song (slightly off key)
on boot up, then subtracts money from your Quicken account
and spends it all on expensive shoes it purchases through
Prodigy.

Health Care Virus: tests your system for a day, finds
nothing wrong, and sends your a bill or $4,500.

George Bush Virus: it starts by boldly stating, "read my
doc....No new files!" on the screen, and it proceeds to
fill up all the free space on your hard drive with new
files, then blames it on the Congressional Virus.
```

doubtless because the term "politically correct" doesn't translate well for these people.) Some of the material is in English, some is in Russian, and some in a weird amalgam of both.

TV SHOWS

Can't stop staring at your computer screen long enough to go stare at the TV? No problem. Now you can hit the Net to find out what's been happening on most of the 350 (or whatever) channels we now have access to.

The Simpsons

Every show starts with Bart in detention, writing out his punishment on the blackboard—here are some of my favorites:

- ☞ I will not sell land in Florida
- ☞ I will not sell school property
- ☞ I will not grease the monkey bars
- ☞ I am not a dentist
- ☞ High explosives and school don't mix
- ☞ "Bart Bucks" are not legal tender
- ☞ I will not conduct my own fire drills
- ☞ I will not bury the new kid
- ☞ I will not teach others to fly
- ☞ I will not yell "She's Dead" during roll call

The Simpsons (aired on Fox) does not offer up the usual cute characters, goofy plots, and pabulum entertainment. Instead, *The Simpsons'* producers cleave to dysfunctional characters, satiric plots, and gritty entertainment (can anything beat the satire-within-a-satire appeal of *The Itchy and Scratchy Show*?). The backgrounds are often littered with visual wit (such as the contents of Bart's blackboard) which has caused the ruin of many good VCRs. Online, you can follow the show at:

 alt.tv.simpsons
The alt.tv.simpsons newsgroup is busy with denizens posting observations about their favorite moments, discoveries of visual humor, and attempts to trace quotes. Personnel from the show are said to lurk in alt.tv.simpsons, but there is no direct participation by the producers.

 alt.fan.itchy-n-scratchy
Nearly silent, with some slop-over from alt.tv.simpsons.

 alt.tv.simpsons.itchy-scratchy
Again, nearly silent, with some spillage from alt.tv.simpsons.

Simpsons

This is the traffic on alt.tv.simpsons put into newsletter form. Send your request to **simpsons-request@net.bio.net**.

Saving Face:

Bart-heads have some jargon of their own—here's how to walk the walk and talk the talk:

AG—animation goof, found during VCR replays.

Censorship—Said to be routine in Australia and Germany. In the United States, Fox abridges the title sequence. In Canada, it's shown in a pristine state. If scenes show up in promotions that are seen nowhere else, it's because the shows are put together at the last moment.

DYN—Did you notice (some item in the background)?

FF or **FFF**—Freeze-Frame Fun, the finding of visual humor during VCR replays.

Homosexual—Close examination of their behavior suggests (to some) that certain supporting characters may or may not be. The producers won't say.

MG—Matt Groening, the originator of the cartoon (his name rhymes with "complaining"). He is said to have come up with the idea for the show while waiting outside the office of the producer of *The Tracy Ullman Show.*

OFF—Our Favorite Family (the Simpsons).

TRMO—That Reminds Me Of (a particular scene of OFF).

Internet Access Information: Besides the newsgroups, there are ftp archives of *Simpsons* materials at **ftp.cs.widener.edu** in /pub/simpsons, and at **busop.cit.wayne.edu**. Included are ASCII graphic files of

Check This Out:

A fortune-telling program for the PC, based on the show's characters, is reportedly available at **ftp.cs. widener.edu** in /pub/simpsons/, at **wuarchive.wustl. edu** in /mirrors/ msdos/txtutl, and doubtless other places—check archie for a file named simp465.zip.

HUMOR

the characters, liftings from which seem to show up in a lot of online signatures.

Ren & Stimpy

You're lying on your back, thinking pleasant thoughts. Chicken pot pies. Chocolate-covered raisins. Glazed. Glazed? *They'll think you're crazy!* But you know better. It is not *you* who is crazy. It is you who are *mad!* Don't you hear them? Don't you see the crowds? Oh, but your beloved ice-cream bar—not like the others. So nutty. It likes the same things you do. Waxed paper. Boiled football leather. . . .

Ah, *Ren & Stimpy*, the cartoon series shown in adult time slots by Nickelodeon, a cable TV channel that usually aims at younger (easier-to-please) viewers. While most of the cartoons you see there are the classic Looney Tunes with manic behavior and goofy plots, Ren and Stimpy manifest manic behavior along with the deep-seated psychopathology that you'd expect to accompany such behavior in real life. The show has drawn unfathomable amounts of attention, yet the founder ended up getting fired. It's a cold world out there. There are two newsgroups for R&S fans, each of which is (naturally) damned as bogus by adherents of the other.

alt.tv.ren-n-stimpy
Here they talk about what they thought they saw in this or that fleeting scene, post fandom items for sale, and spew vituperation against Nickelodeon for presuming to exert any form of control over the program. Plus they poll each other on the best and worst episodes, and trade rumors about the fate of the creators. Foreigners show up searching for showing times on their local networks.

 **alt.fan.ren-and-stimpy**
Actually, there is little difference between this newsgroup and alt.tv.ren-n-stimpy, save for the lower level of chatter here.

Internet Access Information. There's not a lot online, but then we're talking about fan club members who take an "Oath Of Servitude" to watch R&S until their eyeballs implode, to recite the lines shamelessly in unwelcome situations, and wear unwashed lederhosen for the rest of their lives. But there is an archive of R&S material at **aug3.augsburg.edu**. There is also a FAQ for the alt.tv.ren-n-stimpy newsgroup (anathematizing alt.fan.ren-and-stimpy) in the usual FAQ archives. Try **ftp.uu.net** in the usenet/news.answers/ren-n-stimpy/ directory.

David Letterman

Letterman, the man, the TV god, the ex-Indianapolis weatherman, has joined the Net. Want to check out Dave's newest late-night giveaway, or get the new top-ten list without even reaching for the remote control? No problem. You can hook into Dave's latest jokes and fondly remember his past insanity. Remember when lucky audience members got one of these wonderful gifts from Dave himself?

☞   Collapsible drinking cups
☞   Composters
☞   Edible plunger
☞   French fries
☞   Frogs formerly owned by Glenn Close
☞   Jumper cables
☞   Kentucky Fried Millipedes
☞   Nickels from a bucket
☞   Pounds of hair

Check This Out:
Uncut episodes of R&S are reportedly aired by the national TV network of Iceland. But in reality, the amount of cutting that Nickelodeon does is debatable. And the chills I get watching Stimpy play with his "magic nose goblins" makes me wonder if I really want to risk the psychic trauma of watching an "uncut" episode.

HUMOR

- ☞ Random prescription eyeglasses
- ☞ Single encyclopedia volumes
- ☞ Sod
- ☞ Sponges
- ☞ Toast on a stick
- ☞ Tom Brokaw stationery
- ☞ Watches from a fishbowl

Rumor has it that Dave himself isn't on the Net. (Given the freakish problems he's had with women breaking into his house, I'm not sure I'd make my e-mail address public knowledge, either.) But Dave does have plenty of fans on the Net, and they've collected enough stuff to satisfy even the grumpiest fan from Sioux City, Iowa.

alt.fan.letterman

Rumors about the future of the show, rumors about who is feuding with whom, rumors about who's to be on in the near future, and rumors about the desperation of the other combatants in the late-night TV wars all get spun out here. Plus there's talk about how to get tickets to the show, and speculation about why the show is held in some cities but not others.

Top-Ten

You can get on this mail list to receive Letterman's nightly top-ten list. Send your request to **listserv@tamvm1.tamu.edu**. As usual in such things, the body of the message should consist of "Subscribe Top-Ten yourname," where yourname is your real name, not your e-mail address.

Internet Access Information: The alt.fan.letterman newsgroup has a FAQ file posted in the usual FAQ archives, such as **rtfm.mit.edu**, and posted periodically in the newsgroup itself. Otherwise, there's an archive of Letterman material at **ftp.mcs.net** in the /mscbet.users/barnhart/letterman/ directory. These people have top-ten lists going back to 1987. And don't miss the transcription of the infamous Madonna interview. (The **cathouse.org** site also has some of this material in the /pub/cathouse/television/late.night.with.david.letterman/ directory.) For Mosaic users on the World Wide Web, there's a URL at http://bingen.cs.csbsju.edu/letterman.html. There's even a search facility to probe the top-ten lists. Suggestion: Use "Quayle" as the keyword.

Saving Face:
Read the FAQ file for details on getting tickets to the show. It can't be done online.

Saturday Night Live

A cultural icon and source of timely satire for nearly a generation now, NBC's *Saturday Night Live* has birthed not a few acting careers and at least one newsgroup:

alt.tv.snl
SNL has been around so long that nostalgia is taking over. The retro-Netters here spend a lot of time reminiscing about their favorite skits from years gone by and comparing them (always unfavorably) to the latest crop. Next, will we see historians move in?

Internet Access Information: The alt.tv.snl newsgroup archive includes a general FAQ, plus cast credits and biographies, information about recurring characters, the band, *Wayne's World* (an *SNL* spin-off), song lyrics, and commercial parodies that have appeared on *SNL*. Try anonymous ftp at **ftp.uu.net** in the /usenet/news.answers/snl directory.

More TV Comedies

alt.tv.beakmans-world
Fun and/or suicidal stuff you can do with liquid nitrogen is the focus of the adventurous

Saving Face:
Yes, it really is done live, except for obvious exceptions like the fake commercials. Well, on three occasions the broadcast was delayed because of the reputation of the host, to give the censors a chance to bleep anything. This was done in 1975 for Richard Pryor, in 1986 for Sam Kinison, and in 1990 for Andrew Dice

(*continued on page 108*)

HUMOR

Saving Face:

(continued from page 107)

Clay. The delays were, respectively, five, seven, and seven seconds. And no, no one has been fired from the show for saying dirty words on the air—unless you count the firing of the producer and nearly the entire cast in March 1981, about two weeks after someone slipped. But a long slide in the ratings appears to have been the real cause.

guys in this newsgroup, devoted to *Beakman's World,* a science program disguised as comedy.

alt.tv.beavis-n-butthead

"Sometimes at school I sleep and stuff, and it's pretty cool Beavis. Yeah, he heh hehehehehheh." If that quote from the animated series Beavis-N-Butthead touches your soul, and if trading such quips is your idea of entertainment, then this is the place for you. The show itself is a successful attempt, using hideous animation, to offer entertainment accessible to any viewer, no matter how intellectually challenged. The resulting level of conversation in this newsgroup—concerning favorite episodes, favorite quotes, variations on those quotes, and quests for new euphemisms for self-stimulatory sexual behavior—comes close to that of alt.tasteless. The strong presence of foreign participants was horrifying until I realized that the elementary level of English usage here would make it a good place to practice one's skills.

alt.tv.kids-in-hall

Kids-In-The-Hall is a very funny Canadian comedy group. To judge by their following here, they appeal to a group whose age and general interests are about the same as those in alt.tv.beavis-n-butthead—except they're somewhat more likely to act as if they were raised in a house.

alt.tv.mash

When did Klinger stop wearing dresses regularly? What has become of this or that actor? Mash refers to *M*A*S*H,* the long-running comedy with an unlikely setting: a mobile army surgical hospital during the Korean War. To today's younger viewers the show is as much dusty history as the war it depicts, but the traffic here shows it still has loyalists.

alt.tv.max-headroom

Where and when and how to catch Max is the focus here. *Max Headroom* was a comedy whose title character existed only as computer animation.

alt.tv.mst3k

MST3K is the hip abbreviation for a cable TV "science fiction" series called *Mystery Science Theater 3000.* Joel, a janitor for the Gizmonic Institute, was cleaning out the inside of a rocket ship one day when his bosses decided to shoot him off into space as part of a demented experiment. Every week, Joel's evil scientist bosses force him to watch really terrible B-grade movies (mostly from the 50s and 60s). And as Lucifer dragged angels down with him into hell, so, too, Joel has built a few robot pals to share his cinematic torment. You can see Joel and the robots silhouetted against the big movie screen as they ruthlessly heckle a movie, tearing apart the "acting," the sets, the premise, whatever. Sounds like *Beavis and Butthead Go to the Movies*, right? Guess again! What's really bizarre is the crazy, intellectual, dead-on references that make the show a widely touted wellspring of cultural literacy, with the hecklers citing Melville, Firesign Theater, Spinal Tap, the *Wall Street Journal*, and Buddha *within the same breath.* Both the movies and the heckling are fair game for deep analysis, so this newsgroup is a busy place. The FAQ has information on where to join the fan club, get the fan

Check This Out:

According to the FAQ, you can write for tickets to be in the *SNL* audience at: Saturday Night Live c/o NBC, 30 Rockefeller Plaza, New York City 10112. But your request will be thrown out if it is not postmarked during August. Incidentally, you see so many reruns of *SNL* because the cast—to cut stress—does three shows a month and takes the fourth week off.

HUMOR

newsletter, and find more online fan information. (The fan club's membership card advises you to "keep it close to your heart, because if you keep it in your back pocket it will get all sweaty and yucky and start to come apart and you won't want to show it to anyone.")

alt.tv.mwc

MWC refers to *Married . . . With Children*, a sitcom that gives foreigners an insightful glimpse of American family life. Frighteningly, that's exactly what you see happening here—most of the participants are Europeans, trading favorite moments and tips on where, when, and how to catch the show on the Continent's various networks. Where would we be if we couldn't export our culture?

alt.tv.northern-exp

This TV sitcom concerning life in Cicely, Alaska, has developed a nearly cult following based on its revolutionary reliance on characterization rather than gags or car chases. The moose-lovers here rush to their terminals following each episode to trade analyses of the psyches of each of the show's characters. And also to speculate on the future course of the "Maggie Curse," whereby boyfriends of the main character inevitably encounter "transformational" fates—usually death.

alt.tv.saved-bell

Saved-bell refers to *Saved By the Bell*, a sitcom for teenagers. The fans here moon over the show's various characters and pass around rumors concerning the fate of the show and of some of the actors.

Katey Segal

pinup found on

the Internet.

 **alt.tv.seinfeld**

Seinfeld is a sitcom for adults based on gags and cultural humor. While the participants here carry on the usual talk about favorite moments and story questions, the cultural implications of the action get as much attention. Is so-and-so Jewish? If so, doesn't the action in episode X have deep implications? The Israeli and Norwegian participants who show up here are at least as attuned to the subtleties as the American fans.

 **alt.tv.tiny-toon**

Tiny-Toons are the next generation of the Looney Tune cartoons, using characters who are the avowed offspring of the Looney Tune characters. For whatever reason, the denizens

Daffy Duck, first-generation Looney Tune character, plots the route to Planet X.

here tend to wrestle over comparisons of American versus Japanese (*anime*) animation as if the fate of humanity depends on it. Some of these guys can quote chapter and verse from individual cartoon titles. Sometimes they even talk about Tiny-Toons. People will talk about anything!

alt.tv.tiny-toon.fandom
Here you see people posting unauthorized fiction based on the Tiny-Toon characters, not to mention bearded analyses of the backgrounds and life histories of individual characters. It's a fun place if you can follow all the references.

alt.tv.twin-peaks
Twin Peaks was a TV series inexplicable enough to rank with *The Prisoner*, except that it (apparently) wasn't science fiction. The

Daffy Duck's reception on Planet X, found on the Internet.

Peak-watchers here do talk about the series, but mainly seek to pin down every script detail that might throw light on the fate of Laura Palmer, the investigation of whose death is the purported subject of the whole series. In fiction, as in real life, the official explanation never satisfies some people. Where and how to find pictures of actress Sherilyn Fenn is another focus. There is also a lot of European participation.

FIRESIGN THEATER

Do any of these strange, inexplicable lines sometimes surface in seemingly normal newsgroups discussions?

☞ "You can wait here in the sitting room, or you can sit here in the waiting room."

☞ "You can't get there from here."

☞ "It's just this little chromium switch."

Daffy and Bugs get dressed up in this picture from the Internet.

☞ "Everything you know is wrong."
☞ "I think we're all bozos on this bus."
☞ "Not insane!"
☞ "In the next world, you're on your own."
☞ "Oh, hey, he's no fun, he fell right over!"
☞ "Up against the Wall of Science!"

If any of this sounds familiar, then you have been exposed to the cultural legacy of the Firesign Theater.

Emerging in 1966 with a Los Angeles radio show called *Radio Free Oz*, the four or five guys (they weren't heavy into arithmetic) who were the backbone of the group went on to produce albums with names like *Waiting for the Electrician or Someone Like Him* and *Don't Crush That Dwarf Hand Me the Pliers*. The deeply textured audios would somehow follow bizarre story lines to a conclusion with occasional musical side trips, amid a barrage of whimsical wordplay. Except that if you actually listened to the pitter-patter, you realized it was Zen-direct satire on the time and manners—a cross between James Joyce and the Marx Brothers. Firesign zealots hang out at:

alt.comedy.firesgn-thtre
This is the "official" one, although the intentional misspelling (to keep it short) is hard to master. Mostly, it's a bunch of Fireheads trading information about Firesign reunions and tours, Firesign product availability, trading Firesign material, and trying to track down the source of various Firesign snippets they find rattling around in their heads at three in the morning.

alt.fan.firesign-theatre
This is little different from alt.comedy.firesgn-thtre—it's just easier to spell. Doubtless the four or five crazy guys will find some humor in this matter.

Saving Face:

There's a whole language you need to learn if you plan to be a Firehead. Here are some basics:

Beaners—Fearless people unconcerned about their own refuse.

Berserker—He doesn't have to kill you, but in the back of his mind, it's not a bad idea.

Boogies—Those who take life easy, including Firesign Theater cast members and postal workers.

Bozos—Fat, jobless people who travel in packs, wearing inflatable shoes.

Five Lifestyles of Man—Bozos, Boogies, Beaners, Zips, and Berserkers.

Fudd's Laws—Push something hard enough and it will fall over. Give the people a light, and they'll follow it anywhere. Dig a hole deep enough and everyone will want to jump in.

Nancy—You mean Melanie Haber? Audrey Farber? Susan Underhill? Betty Jo Bialowsky?

Rocky Rococo—Hideous dwarf in F-T's *Nick Danger* album, who gives people gifts and then makes them pay for them through crushing installment plans; subsequently, the name of a pizza parlor chain.

Seeker—There's one born every minute.

Shoes—Recurring F-T motif, representing the loss of innocence, man's search for meaning, or maybe those things you put on your feet.

Shoes for the Dead—Obscure. Existential version of shoe motif? There is actually a mortuary footwear industry.

The Same Old Place—You mean the old Same place?

Tirebiter—Name of several F-T characters. Or perhaps they're all the same character. It's hard to say.

Zips—Those too concerned about their hair.

Internet Access Information: Anonymous ftp to **rtfm.mit.edu**, in the directory /pub/usenet/alt.answers/firesign-theatre. Look for four files, named intro, faq, lyrics, and lexicon. Other Usenet newsgroup FAQ archives are likely to have these files as well.

"LITERATURE"

No matter what your taste in humor, from the British goofiness of Douglas Adams to the dead-on American satire of Dave Barry, you'll find it on the Net.

Douglas Adams

"In the beginning the Universe was created. This has made a lot of people very angry and been widely regarded as a bad

```
> Hello, Dr. Memory.
How do you do? What brings you to see me?
> My name is Ken.
Why do you say your name is ken?
> Well, because it is.
Can you elaborate on that?
> My parents named me Ken.
Tell me something about your family.
> My father was a jelly doughnut.
You seem to dwell on your family.
> Hey, you asked.
Is it because of your plans that you say hey I asked?
```

Compare this quote, from the Firesign Theater album I Think We're All Bozos on This Bus, recorded in 1971, to the output of the Eliza program in Chapter 2. Ahead of their time?

move." Yes, the author of *The Hitchhiker's Guide to the Galaxy* and other science fiction romps has a rabid following on the Net. There are two places you don't want to miss:

alt.fan.douglas-adams
This newsgroup constitutes a typical fan hangout, with people trying to pin down quotes and line up collectibles. Adams himself is said to make occasional postings.

alt.galactic-guide
The newsgroup is a point of contact for people trying to emulate Adams by undertaking something called "Project Galactic Guide." The idea is to put together an online encyclopedia of humorous articles about real things, and real articles about humorous things, all in Adamistic prose.

Saving Face:

There are certain references in the Adams canon that you need to be aware of to hold your own with the Adamites:

42—The ultimate answer to the ultimate question. Unfortunately, the question itself has been lost. Yes, it's also six times nine in base thirteen. But DNA himself denies any hidden numerological meanings.

Bad Poetry—The bad poet named in the original radio version of Hitchhiker's Guide is a real, living poet. DNA found it advisable to alter the name in later renditions to avoid pesky London barristers.

Beeblebears—Teddy bears with two heads, sold at fan conventions.

DNA—Douglas Noel Adams.

Kubla Khan, Second Half—there is no second half to this poem that Coleridge wrote from a dream he was remembering. Unfortunately, a "business caller" knocked on Coleridge's door while he was writing, so he forgot the rest of his dream. The hero of *Dirk Gently's Holistic Detective Agency* must see that the interruption happens, to save the human race from the revelations in the second half.

Lifestyle—"I seem to be having this tremendous difficulty with my lifestyle." Spoken to break up a boring conversation, or as British understatement when catastrophe looms.

Mostly Harmless—The entire entry under the heading "Earth" in the Hitchhiker's Guide.

Panic—Don't Panic!

Safe (alternate meaning)—About to die.

Towel—Indispensable personal accessory of the galactic hitchhiker.

Internet Access Information: The file douglas-adams-FAQ has considerable information about DNA and acquiring Adamsian products. It can be found by rummaging in Usenet archives—I got it at **ftp.uu.net** in the /usenet/news.answers/directory. Accumulated material for the Project Galactic Guide is reportedly available via anonymous ftp at **vela.acs.oakland.edu** through the /pub/guide.project/ directory, with subdirectories for specific computer platforms. Alternately, try **atlas.physchem.chemie.uni-tuebingen.de**, in the /pub/guide.project/ directory.

Dave Barry

Syndicated humor columnist Dave Barry and his satires of modern suburban life have developed a following on the Net in at least one newsgroup:

 at alt.fan.dave_barry.
(The middle initial is an underscore, not a hyphen.) Barry may himself take part in this newsgroup—that the other participants are not sure is probably a good example of the entire Barryan ethos. They also discuss the improbable events (derived, alas, from actual news stories) highlighted in Barry's column, and reminisce about their first "D-B Experience" and the time it took to recover after their sides split with laughter.

Internet Access Information: The FAQ for alt.fan.dave_barry is located in most FAQ archives. I found it as dave_barry.faq.Z in the /usenet/news.answers directory of **ftp.uu.net**. It spells out various D-B facts, gives his Net addresses, and lists papers that carry the column.

Terry Pratchett

Terry Pratchett, author of the Discworld series, falls between humor and science fiction, so we'll include him here for grins. An Englishman who grows carnivorous plants as a hobby, he has a following on the Net in the alt.fan.pratchett newsgroup. A film based on his work may be produced, if he can find an American film producer with more brains than the last batch he tried to deal with. Don't hold your breath, in other words.

 **alt.fan.pratchett**
There are some of the fandom sorts of things in here that you've come to expect, especially

 **Saving Face:**

In case you're wondering (many evidently do), there is no ftp site for downloading Barry's columns. Barry writes for a living, meaning his stuff is not given away. It is online, though, distributed by the ClariNet news service (apparently ClariNet hasn't heard of the "screen capture" mode found in any communications software worth its disk space). If your site gets ClariNet, look for clari.feature.dave_barry.

HUMOR

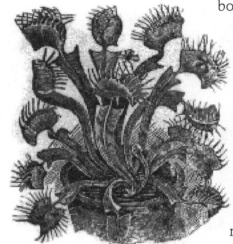

Venus flytrap, a carnivorous plant, found on AOL.

book questions and notices of author signings. Mostly, though, it's a forum for highly British repartee, with Pratchett's work as the (very loose) connecting theme. The participants are not above posting vitriolic comments on their own messages if no one else comes forward to do so.

Internet Access Information. A FAQ for alt.fan.pratchett can be found in Usenet FAQ archives. I found one in **ftp.uu.net** under /usenet/news.answers/pratchett. It includes the usual biography and bibliography. Meanwhile, further Pratchettania can be found archived at **ftp.cp.tn.tudelft.nl** in /pub/pratchett, also at **theory.lcs. mit.edu** in /pub/pratchett/, plus **rincewind.mech.virginia.edu** in /pub/pratchett, and at **ftp.uts.edu.au** in /Mirror/Pratchett/. There's further Pratchett information, song lyrics, games rules, and .gif files of his books' covers.

RANDOM OUTBREAKS OF LUNACY

Delphi offers access to the oddly named "MOFO ex Machina" BBS of Penn and Teller, the comedy/magic team (Teller plays the mute member). AOL has a cartoon section in its General Entertainment department, where you can download .gif files of syndicated cartoons. (Copyright still applies, so you should not circulate them further.) Available is the "Dilbert" strip by Scott Adams, "MacHumor" by Theresa McCracken, "Computoons" by Charles Rodriguez, "Modern Wonder" cartoons by Peter Oakley, and Mike Keefe editorial cartoons. The "Dilbert" section additionally contains a message forum where you can trade quips with Adams, the artist. On GEnie and Compu-Serve, the "comics" forums turn out to be hangouts for comic book aficionados.

Other Personalities

alt.fan.wodehouse
Fans of the English humor author P.G. Wode-house can be found in this Usenet news-group. There are none of the usual offers to trade collectibles and memorabilia. Rather, the tone is tilted toward discussions of whether Wodehouse is addictive, and attempts to nail down the meaning of certain phrases, such as "sponge-bag trousers."

alt.fan.woody-allen
Fans of the New York filmmaker Woody Allen can gather in this Usenet newsgroup. Its denizens search for his movie sound tracks, look for the venue of specific plays, ponder whether the complexity of Allen's produc-tions have increased as he ages—and try to find mirrors of his tortured love life in the plots of his movies.

And Finally, Giving Someone the Finger

And now for something completely different . . . by using the Internet "finger" command, you get a lot of information about someone (like their full name and when they were last logged on). The response can include a "plan" or "project"—a listing of any résumé-style information the person chose to post. For privacy and/or security reasons, some sites refuse fingers.

Saving Face:

Rincewind (the name of a Pratchett hero) rhymes with "mince pinned."

HUMOR

121

Finger response from the vending machine at coke@xcf.berke-ley.edu. There's been a serious run on chocolate candies. And the programmer seems to have developed an aversion to some offerings, slipping the word "death" into the name.

```
Enter target: coke@xcf.berkeley.edu
Login name: coke                In real life: Coke is it!
Directory: /usr/users/coke      Shell: /usr/users/coke/bin/coke
Last login Thu Apr 14 10:26 on ttypd from saturn3.cns.ohio
Plan:
Stock Value: $66.02  Total Balance: $42.96  Loss Percentage: 0.00
Outstanding real debts: stas 24.21  blojo 11.11  mlee 10.25
scott 4.69  grady 0.68
Current Stock List:
 2 Coke            21 Dole Juice          12 Ho-ho (death)
32 Pepsi            4 Minute Maid         26 ETC (death)
 5 Dr Pepper        ? --FOOD--             2 Cup Cake
 4 7-up             0 sandwiches           8 Fruit Gems
15 Dads RB          1 bear claw            0 Reeses Pieces
 8 non-alc bev     18 hansens in a can     0 Twix
 ? Hansens          ? Fruit Rolls          0 Nestle Crunch
 0 belgdeathchoc    2 crystalgey           2 Crackers
 2 Martinellis     41 Frito                1 Granola Bars
 2 Calistoga       10 chocodeath almonds   0 M&M Almonds
 0 ultradeathch     2 Pep Patties
 7 Gatorade         0 Choc Muffin
```

Creative college students have hooked up their campus soft drink or snack vending machines to the Internet, so that the machines respond to being fingered. The machines' "plans" are status reports on their contents. Here are a few of the most creative finger options:

☞ graph@drink.csh.rit.edu
☞ coke@cs.cmu.edu
☞ coke@xcf.berkeley.edu
☞ cocacola@columbia.edu
☞ franklin@ug.cs.dal.ca

So now you can check the contents of a particular Coke machine from across the globe, and in some cases get an estimate on what's warm and what's cold—no small consideration for the caffeine-dependent computer science students who have access to the machines. Graphics interfaces, remote control, and debit payment schemes are evidently in the works at some sites.

CYBERPUNK

He was emaciated. He kept pliers and a wad of telephone patch codes in a leather holster on his belt. He answered the phone, "Center of the universe." When riding an elevator, he would look at the floor indicator and implore, "Open the pod door, Hal." He was a hacker before the media grabbed the term—even before most people had heard the term "personal computer." He had bent the global telex network to his will using an Apple II. At a computer convention in the early 1980s, I worked with him for five days. At the end of the convention, when the booths were taken down, we found ourselves in an empty hall, with a phone on the floor where each booth had been. He and his like-minded employer looked at each other, nodded— and then gathered up the phones, put them in boxes, and mailed them home to themselves. "We have a reputation to uphold," was all he'd say.

Cyberpunks, people who shape their behavior around high technology, existed long before cyberspace. Our friend above took what technology was available (the telex network) and turned it into his private cyberspace. Any cyberpunk would understand why he did it: Technology empowers, so you better make sure it's empowering you as well as Big Brother.

Artwork for the

group Massive

Attack.

Artwork for the group Massive Attack.

Some things change—today there is much more technology to understand, and there are more people pursuing it. And since you can buy a telephone at Radio Shack for eight bucks (or get one free with your paid one-year subscription to *Time* magazine), there are more creative outlets for the technology-driven than swiping unguarded telephones. But the prime directive remains: Understand the technology, and use it, because your psyche won't let you remain with the sheep when you could be one of the shepherds. This drive has resulted in a literary movement and a lifestyle. In this chapter we'll look at both, although especially the latter.

CYBERPUNK: THE LITERARY MOVEMENT

Cyberpunk is a genre of science fiction that examines the situation of underclass members living on the margins of high-tech societies, particularly societies involved in oppressive uses of information technology. Social norms are usually enforced by some Big Brother entity, who may have invaded the lives of the citizens to the point where people are being cloned or having computer brain implants. The protagonist, of course, lives on the edge and has escaped full assimilation. If the protagonist finds he must confront the system, there is no moral uplift in it—the struggle may be for its own sake, as victory does not bring happiness ever after. Meanwhile, the mood and settings are dark, and technical details are thrown at the reader without explanation—rather as the protagonist presumably experiences them. The classics of the Cyberpunk canon are listed in the glossary.

CYBERPUNK: THE LIFESTYLE

If you accept Western society as an oppressive entity based on high technology and think of yourself as an outsider, then you might as well model your life on the cyberpunk genre. (Government and corporate insiders caught in the current frenzy of downsizing may think you're nuts for seeing society as a juggernaut instead of a basket case, but the stance has an appeal to the politically correct. Not to mention Generation X members, who can't get the Baby Boomers—who think they patented the concept of youth—to take them seriously.) The resulting lifestyle involves four main interests:

Cypherpunks—If the evil system is based on information technology, then the main hope of salvation for the man on the street lies in message encryption—encypherment, hence the name "cypherpunk." If outsiders can't read your stuff, then your personal cyberspace is secure.

Raves—Underground dance parties involving music that is manufactured rather than performed, plus computer-generated light shows and other manifestations of high-technology, not excluding "smart" or "designer" drugs.

Hacking and Phreaking—Hacking involves (in this context) overcoming the security features of other people's com-

Saving Face:

Don't expect kaffee-klatsch. You'll see occasional discussions of books in the cyberpunk genre, in the forums listed in this chapter and in the VR ones in Chapter 4. But for genuine cyberpunks the Net is a place that reflects what they do, not a place to reflect on what they've read.

Check This Out:

Back issues of a seminal cyberpunk 'zine *Cheap Truth* are said to be available by anonymous FTP from etext. archive.umich.edu in the /pub/Zines/CheapTruth/ directory.

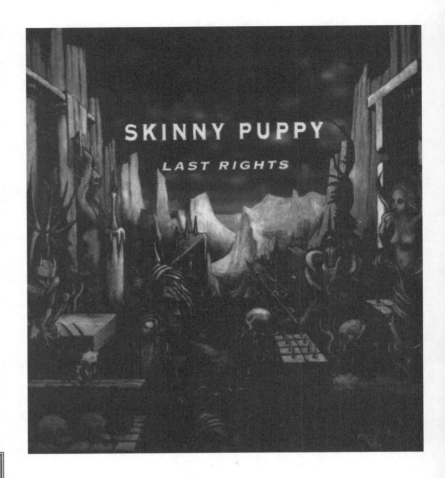

SKINNY PUPPY

LAST RIGHTS

**Check
This Out, Too:**

Further resources and pointers concerning the cyberpunk literary movement can be found in the "Cyberpoet's Guide to Virtual Culture" at etext.archive. umich.edu in the /pub/Zines/Cyber-Poet/ directory.

puters, so you can do unto them before they do unto you. Phreaking means hacking the phone network, either to get free phone calls or to prevent the tracing of your hacking efforts.

Virtual Reality—Where the computer makes it as good as being there.

Virtual reality—which requires a heavier technical commitment than the other interests—is covered separately in Chapter 4. Here we'll look at the other three aspects in turn. First, though, lets look at the main general-interest cyberpunk hangouts:

Nine Inch Nails logo, from the Internet.

alt.cyberpunk

This newsgroup pulses with discussions of the ethics of electrosex and teledildonics, the participants foreseeing the downfall of cultural codes and norms if and when it becomes possible to be intimate with someone without fear of pregnancy, disease, or even the inconvenience of actually meeting them. Gnosticism will be proved under laboratory conditions, some predict. (If only we could prove pragmatism!) Plus there are ongoing discussions of rock groups like Nine Inch Nails and Skinny Puppy, and whether Billy Idol (who released an album titled *Cyberpunk* in late 1993) is a manifestation of the movement or just another peddler of homogenized poodle-rock.

rec.music.industrial

This is where the real action is, culture-wise. The subject lines of the postings (often the names of favorite music groups) by themselves form an elegant dark poetry: Machines of Loving Grace, Death in June, Restless Machines, Blood Axis, Sleep Chamber, Solar Enemy, House of Usher, Blackhouse, Free Contagion.

And Check This Out:

The Cyberforum conference on CompuServe has a selection of 'zines in the CyberLit/Zines section of its file library. Included are titles like *Brain Drain, Crypt, Synapse, Northwest Cyber Artist,* and *Dogma, the Journal of Disbelief.*

CYBERPUNK

Indigo Girls shot,

from the Internet.

 alt.punk

The talk in alt.punk covers much the same ground as in rec.music.industrial, but covers it using harsher language. Plus there is the usual rampant speculation concerning which celebrity is finding inspiration through which recreational substance. This is also a great place to look for concert and tour announcements.

 Escape From Noise

The optimistically named mail list includes articles and reviews on industrial and cyberpunk music, and comes out monthly. Back issues are said to be available via ftp at bradley.bradley.edu. Send your request to **efn@wvolusia.uucp**.

 alt.cyberpunk.chatsubo

Chatsubo is a cyberpunk bar in the novel *Neuromancer* by William Gibson. What's being served in Chatsubo the conference are ama-

Artwork for a group called XDZebra.

teur (¿) cyberpunk short stories. No, not all concern a guy in a suit hiring a cyberpunk to do a megacorp's dirty work, but some participants complain that it seems that way.

alt.cyberpunk.movement

This is the place to go if you want to talk about archetypal forms that resonate in the great psyche of man, especially that of beauty, which gives order to our volition, since it reaffirms that formidable choice we all have between life and death. . . . Right. Enough.

CuD

Chew on this mail list and you'll find it's the *Computer Underground Digest,* a newsletter devoted to discussing the legal, ethical, social, and other issues of the online world, and telecommunications culture, especially "alternate groups outside the conventional Net community." (The Net community must have arrived, if it is spawning alternative, outside communities.) Send your request to **tk0jut2@mvs.cso.niu.edu**.

Skinny Puppy

artwork.

Cyber-Sleaze

This mail list is a moderated newsletter that covers celebrity dirt, edited by an MTV corporate inmate. It covers more than just the industrial music scene—but with a name like that, don't worry about it. What's disturbing is that there is enough material for it to come out five days a week. Send your request to **request-cyber-sleaze@mtv.com**.

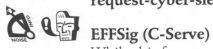

EFFSig (C-Serve)

While this forum appears to be the filing station for the Electronic Frontier Foundation on CompuServe, there is also a lot of general cyberpunk lifestyle material, such as the *Computer Underground Digest*. Plus *Cyanobacteria International*, which turns out to be a newsletter from Finland.

Internet Access Information: Aside from the newsgroups themselves, both the alt.cyberpunk and rec.music.industrial newsgroups have FAQs located in the usual archives—I found them in **rtfm.mit.edu** under the /pub/usenet/ directory. Material concerning industrial music and associated bands can be found at **cs.uwp.edu** under the /pub/music/ directory.

CompuServe Access Information: Either GO CYBER-FORUM or GO EFFSIG and browse in the file libraries.

Other Access: Most commercial services are curiously silent concerning the cyberpunk scene, although there is a cyberpunk conference on the NorthAmeriNet BBS echo network.

CRYPTOGRAPHY

If you live in cyberspace and are concerned about the government's perceived *need* to control technology so that they can watch your every step, then you have allies—the cypherpunks. Cypherpunks believe in the privacy of personal communications and use a variety of methods for securing it against any unintended receiver. Cypherpunks are cryptographers who are dedicated to covering their tracks through the use of message encryption.

Cryptography is a branch of mathematics, but not a new one. Julius Caesar used an encryption method almost identical to the popular rot(13) scheme used by some Internet groups. During World War II, cryptography experts aided our efforts by breaking the Axis codes, opening many of their secret communications to us. But the subject became a topic of serious public scrutiny in the late 1970s with the publication of the U.S. government's Data Encryption Standard, and the subsequent microcomputer revolution has since made the subject accessible to just about anybody.

You don't have to be able to do hexadecimal math in your head or write public key encryption algorithms in a day in order to be a cypherpunk. The technology surrounds us. Anyway, message encipherment looks like the key to online commerce. Material could be displayed online as if in shop windows, but would only be usable to someone who has bought the necessary decryption key. Electronic funds transfers are already protected by encryption, and by a branch of the art called authentication.

Check This Out:

You can get the *Computer Underground Digest* via anonymous ftp at **ftp.eff.org** in the /pub/Publications/CuD/CuD/ directory.

And Check This Out:

AMULET:vc, a BBS devoted to the cyberpunk concerns, including VR, AI, "cybersex," hacker lifestyles, and cyberpunk lifestyles, plus various leading-edge technologies, can be reached at 310-453-7705.

Saving Face:

But the way of the cypherpunk is not an easy one—the encryption field is vast, and to understand it you'll have to learn some serious jargon:

Authentication—Making sure the message came from the right person. Very important when sending keys.

Capstone—Effort by the U.S. government to develop public crypto systems for use internally and by government contractors. Includes Skipjack and Clipper.

CBC—Cipher Block Chaining, where you perform XOR on each 64-bit block using the previous 64 bits as the key, before applying DES.

Clipper—Encryption chip whose development has been sponsored by the U.S. government as part of the Capstone project, using the Skipjack crypto system.

Codes—The use of alternate words to hide meaning, such as calling Ronald Reagan *Rawhide*, as the Secret Service did. It is not the same as encipherment.

Compression—Helpful if done before encipherment, pointless if done afterward, since the cipher text is (or should be) an incompressible string of random numbers.

Cryptanalysis—Attempts to break encrypted messages.

DES—The U.S. government's Data Encryption Standard for nonclassified information. It's a product cipher that operates on sixty-four-bit blocks of data, using a fifty-six-bit key. It was developed by IBM in the 1970s, and involvement of the NSA led to rumors of a secret flaw that government snoops could use. Subsequent analysis has found none. However, its keyspace (10 with seventeen zeros behind it) is no longer considered big enough to resist brute-strength attacks from modern computers—and the NSA had originally told IBM that a longer key was not necessary. The current word is that you should run the message through DES three times using three different keys.

DSS—The Digital Signature Standard, part of the Capstone project, and almost as controversial as the Clipper chip.

Enigma—Electromechanical code machine used by Hitler's armies, compromised by sloppy use, and the U.S. agent who bought one over the counter in the early 1930s. The latter explains ITAR.

ITAR—U.S. International Traffic in Arms Regulations, which define crypto systems and software as munitions. Export must be licensed by the State Department, which defers to the NSA. The NSA frowns on the export of all but the simplest cipher systems (forty-bit keys for export, fifty-six-bit keys for foreign subsidiaries of U.S. companies), and any authentication system that can be used for ciphering.

Kerberos—A secret-key system developed at MIT for real-time authentication of requests for network resources, using the DES. It does not, however, produce digital signatures.

Keyspace—The possible keys allowed by a particular cipher system.

Knapsack—Cipher scheme once in vogue, now known to be breakable.

NSA—National Security Agency, the U.S. government agency involved in cyphers. It is said to be the largest employer of mathematicians and the largest buyer of computer hardware on earth.

PEM—Privacy Enhanced Mail, a proposed Internet standard for message encypherment. PGP and RIPEM are close implementations.

PGP—Pretty Good Privacy, a public domain cipher system used on the Internet, which uses an RSA-like method to extract a session key. Threatened legal action by the holders of the RSA patent makes commercial distribution of end-user PGP software in the U.S. problematic—but seems to enhance its popularity among cypherpunks. Some list their PGP key in their newsgroup signatures, or invite you to "finger" their e-mail addresses to get it.

Plaintext—A message before it's been encrypted.

Practical Cryptanalysis—Attempts to break encrypted messages based on guesses of the messages' contents.

Prime Factorization—The factors of a number are any two smaller numbers that can be multiplied together to create it. Modern crypto systems are based on the idea that any integer has a unique "prime factorization"—two prime numbers that factor it—and that finding those factors for a large number takes ridiculous amounts of computer power. But they may yet find a shortcut. Who knows? Someone may already have.

Product Cipher—a block cipher that performs a string of arithmetic operations on the data to encipher it. DES is an example.

Public-Key Cryptography—You have a private key (a long number) from which a public encryption key is factored. But the decryption key is factored differently and can't be computed without knowing the private key. You can send people the public key, and they can use it to send you messages that only you can read, since only you know the private key. So you no longer need a secure channel to send a key, or a key to create a secure channel.

RIPEM—Riordan's Internet Privacy Enhanced Mail, Internet cipher system used in the United States instead of PGP, since it has licensed the necessary RSA patent and since export is banned, anyway. Uses both RSA and DES.

RSA—a public-key crypto system named for its inventors: Rivest, Shamir, and Adleman. It allows keys that are 2,048 bits long. Now promoted by RSA Data Security, Inc.

Session Key—A cipher key in a message, encrypted with a public-key algorithm. The recipient decrypts it with the public key and then uses it to decrypt the rest of the message using a faster algorithm, usually DES. (Public keys can be slower than DES by a factor of 100.)

Signature—You run a computation using the message and the key to produce a result that could only be generated by that message and that key. If the reverse computation does not work at the other end, the recipient knows the message is not authentic or has been altered.

Skipjack—Recent, classified revision of DES, using eighty-bit keys.

Strong Crypto System—One where security resides in the secrecy of the key rather than in the secrecy of the algorithm, where there are many possible keys, where the ciphertext appears to be random gibberish even under statistical tests, and which has so far resisted attacks.

Tempest—Equipment that prevents your computer screen from being read (via its radio frequency emissions) by those spies parked in a van across the street.

Unbreakable Crypto System—There's no such thing, since any system can be misused, or fall to luck. If a clerk uses a cipher to send the same identical message—"Nothing to report"—every day at noon, the enemy will eventually figure it out and read all the other messages using that cipher. That happened to Rommel's Afrika Korps in World War II.

XOR—Exclusive Or, a binary math operation used in simple cipher systems. If one key was used, breaking the cipher is routine if the text is at least ten times longer than the key.

Where are we now? Well, there was an outbreak of concern (and anger) after DES came out, since it was feared (or assumed) that the NSA had crippled it to facilitate its own eavesdropping. But as far as is known—publicly—no one has ever succeeded in breaking DES. Meanwhile, the NSA got famous for attempting to block certain patent applications and the publication of certain papers in the field of cryptography, lest amateurs give the game away.

Meanwhile, with the power of microprocessors doubling every eighteen months, the U.S. government decided in about 1987 to develop a new generation of crypto systems, and began the Capstone program. The subsequent proposal of the Clipper chip sparked firestorms of concern—orders of magnitude beyond the polite questions that greeted DES. The government openly stated that it wanted to see a public cipher system that the FBI could break at will. Industrial and financial institutions were not thrilled, since they want genuine security, not security that depends on government indulgence. Net denizens were enraged at this perceived intrusion into their use of cyberspace. And cypherpunks were thrilled by this validation of their ideology.

The government proposes that the Clipper chip be used as follows: Messages will be encrypted with an eighty-bit session key, known only to the users. But appended will be a LEAF (Law Enforcement Access Field), which carries the session key. The LEAF is encrypted with a registered "unit key," then a serial number for the unit key and an authentication string is added, and then everything is encrypted again using a "family key." The recipient will decrypt the LEAF to check the authentication string, and then decrypt the message using the private key.

After capturing the message during a wiretap, the FBI would decrypt the LEAF using the family key, where it would find the serial number of the unit key. Armed with a proper court authorization, the law would then go to two separate "escrow agencies," each of which possess half of the unit key, which put together can then decrypt the session key, which they can then use to decrypt the rest of the message.

It almost seems too elaborate a system to abuse, but many objections have been voiced:

☞ How can you trust a classified encryption scheme? The strength of any system can only be established by years of intense expert attack—mathematical proofs can't do it.

☞ Who are you going to trust to be the escrow agencies? How do you ensure their security?

☞ Exactly how are you going to make criminals use the Clipper chip?

Meanwhile, an online effort by Clipper opponents to get input for the congressional hearings on Clipper generated about fifty thousand replies. In response, an NSA official was quoted online as mocking Clipper's opponents, calling them Net-heads, late-blooming counterculturalists, and cybernauts with pocket protectors, while adding (without offering practical details) that Clipper would help crack down on child pornography.

Aside from Clipper, the biggest piece of news in the crypto world was the breaking of an RSA public-key crypto system that used a 129-digit key. It took eight months (part-time) by a network of about six hundred machines in twenty-four countries, so the event did not exactly trigger mass panic. Still, it took less than the originally estimated forty quadrillion years. So, obviously, the crypto world is a happening place. Places where some of the heat gets generated include:

 **sci.crypt**
This newsgroup is the most commonly cited when the subject of encryption comes up. It's mostly devoted to technical discussions—like "factoring N+P*Q when (e,N,d) is known." Anyone with the least touch of math phobia is likely to faint dead away.

 talk.politics.crypto
Nontechnical talk from the sci.crypto crowd gets shunted to here, where legal and social issues are expounded.

 sci.math
This newsgroup touches on the methods used in crypto systems, and is frequently cited in

cipher discussions, but most postings there concern theoretical topics—so inexplicable that math phobics would actually feel safe.

alt.privacy
Libertarian ranting is the order of the day, with Clipper surfacing along with the questions of whether smoke detectors are really government surveillance devices. (What—you didn't know about that?)

alt.society.civil-liberty
The atmosphere here is similar to alt.society.civil-liberty, with added emphasis on whether the state has a right to try to cure your depression, or respect your right to commit suicide, or at least ensure that you use safe and effective methods.

alt.privacy.clipper
As you might have suspected from the name, this newsgroup is a little more focused on the Clipper issue. There may come a time when they don't say, "beat a dead horse." No, they'll say, "rant at Clipper."

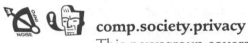

comp.society.privacy
This newsgroup covers some of the same ground as alt.privacy.clipper, with additional discussions of appropriate uses for cyberspace, appropriate uses of social security numbers, etc.

alt.security.pgp
Questions, tricks, and traps concerning the PGP (Pretty Good Privacy) crypto system get expounded here. Most postings are in clear text, but nearly everybody has a crypto key in their sig, or an invitation to finger their address to get it.

Info-PGP

This mail list is a gathering of material from alt.security.pgp, plus PGP-related material from other newsgroups. Send your request to **info-pgp-request@lucpul.it.luc.edu**.

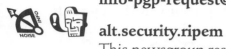 **alt.security.ripem**

This newsgroup resembles alt.security.pgm except it concerns the RIPEM crypto system and (for some reason) draws a lot more theoretical discussions.

 **comp.org.eff.talk**

The Clipper issue in particular and online privacy in general get heavy examination in this newsgroup of the Electronic Frontier Foundation.

 comp.org.eff.news

The Electronic Frontier Foundation uses this newsgroup to pose source material, such as their newsletter, minutes of congressional hearings, and technical notes.

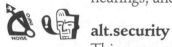 **alt.security**

This newsgroup is populated mostly by site administrators talking about ways to keep hackers at bay and where to buy burglar alarms, but they also touch on crypto systems, especially Kerberos.

 **misc.legal.computing**

Here lawyers can talk openly and without shame about what they do with computers. Legal issues and crypto systems also come up.

 Cypherpunks

This high-traffic mail list covers cryptography and its sociopolitical impact, plus the anarcho-capitalist/libertarian debates you've probably come to expect. Send your request to **cypherpunks-request@toad.com**.

Cypherwonks

A spin-off of the Cypherpunks mail list with less ranting and more ciphering. Send your request to **majordomo@lists.eunet.fi**.

Privacy Forum Digest

This mail list covers both high-tech and no-tech privacy-related issues. Send your request to **privacy-request@vortex.com**.

CPD

The *Computer Privacy Digest* is a newsletter on the effect of technology (plus and minus) on privacy. Send your request to **comp-privacy-request@uwm.edu**.

RFD

The *Risks Forum Digest* moderated mail list is put out by the ACM Committee on Computers and Public Policy. It includes hard information and banter about whatever risks computers offer to the public. Send your request to **risks-request@csl.sri.com**.

EFF (AOL)

This AOL department contains discussion and materials on civil liberties online, plus PGP, Clipper, and other crypto concerns.

Cyberlaw (AOL)

The *Cyberlaw* and *Cyberlex* newsletters occupy the same corner of AOL. The former covers legal issues that concern computer technology, and the latter is about legal developments in the computer industry. Clipper gets covered, plus those intractable "look and feel" copyright issues. There's also enough ranting to avert boredom.

 ### EFFSig (CIS)
This CompuServe forum offers a grab bag of Electronic Frontier Foundation material on Clipper and online civil liberties, plus the *CyberLaw* newsletter and similar items.

Internet Access: Besides the newsgroups and mail lists noted so far, the Cypherpunks mail lists have a ftp site at **soda.berkeley.edu** (alternate name: **ftp.csua.berkeley. edu**) in the /pub/cypherpunks/ directory. There is a wide range of cryptography material, plus the latest version of PGP for various platforms.

AOL Access: Use the keyword command, with either "EFF" or Cyberlaw" as the keyword.

Other Access: There are Clipper forums on NorthAmeri-Net, RelayNet, ILink, FidoNet, and GlobalLink; a Key Encryption conference on NorthAmeriNet; one called Encrypt on ILink; and an EFF conference on RelayNet.

And Check This Out:

RSAREF, a collection of crypto routines in C, is available via ftp at **rsa.com** or by sending e-mail to **rsaref@rsa.com**, for noncommercial use by citizens of permanent residents of the United States or Canada.

RAVES

Raves (sometimes called "underground parties") are dance parties with high-tech light shows and recorded industrial music put on in empty warehouses with or without the necessary permits. For the high-tech DJs at such affairs, the recorded music is merely the raw material they can mix, speed up, or slow down, changing the ambience at will. (The absence of vocals in most of the songs makes sonic manipulation easier.) Some participants seek to enhance the experience by ingesting substances tailored for the occasion, and some have even rediscovered LSD. (You'd think aspirin and Gatorade would be the drugs of choice.)

Saving Face:

Don't post ciphertext in sci.crypt and ask others to try to break it. You might post the details of your cipher scheme and ask the other to poke holes in it. But it is best to study cryptanalysis before trying to design a code system. Do not ask questions about noncryptographic espionage topics, since no one will know (or admit knowing) the answer. Legal and political discussions go elsewhere, too.

CHAPTER 7

The entire environment, in other words, is manufactured via high technology, tying the phenomena closely to cyber-punk culture. The audience, meanwhile, is also manufactured through high technology, as evidenced by the regional rave mail lists shown presently. (The individual rave organizers have their own local resources as well, and the old-style telephone and word of mouth play their parts.)

The end result is a shared intoxication via centrally controlled sensory overload, leading observers to talk about raves in terms of shamanistic religious experiences. As for what the participants talk about:

alt.rave

The cybertribe of alt.rave reflects the general angst of Generation X ravers, frantically

searching for meaning in their lives but also for the titles of songs going through their heads. Such inquiries are generally complicated by the absence of discernible words in the songs. Other participants bemoan/applaud things like chipmunk vocals and gangsta-hiphop samples, dark breakbeats, straight techno/acid beats, and overtly commercial kiddie-raves.

Collage of ravers, raving, from the Internet.

Acid Jazz
The Acid Jazz mail list covers a style of jazz said to be popular at raves, often some other

Logo of the

Aphex group.

dance music genre performed as jazz. Covered are such immortal groups as Straight No Chaser, UFO, Night Trains, Massive Attack, and scads of others. Send your request to **gregbb@uhunix.uhcc.hawaii.edu**.

 AusRave

AusRave covers the Australian rave scene, and it said to have an archive site at **elec-sun4.elec.uow.edu.au** in the /pub/ausrave/ directory. Send your request to **ausrave-request@lsupoz.apana.org.au**.

 DCRaves

DCRaves covers the Washington, DC, area only, and is said to have an archive site at **american.edu**. Send your request to **list-serv@american.edu**.

FL-Raves

FL-Raves covers the rave scene in the state of Florida. Send your request to **flraves-request@cybernet.cse.fau.edu**.

MtnRaves

MtnRaves covers the rave scene in the mountain states of Utah, Colorado, Arizona, New Mexico, Idaho, and Wyoming. You can get the digest version by asking for mtnraves-digest. Send your request to **majordomo@xmission.com**.

MW-Raves

MW-Raves covers the rave scene in the midwestern United States, including Nebraska, Iowa, Minnesota, Wisconsin, Illinois, Michigan, Indiana, Ohio, Kentucky, Missouri, and Kansas. Archives are said to be found at **pasteur.cvm.uiuc.edu** in the /pub/mwr/ directory and at **techno.stanford.edu** in the /pub/raves/archives/mwraves/ directory. Send your request to **mw-raves-request@engin.umich.edu**.

NERaves

NE-Raves covers the northeastern United States, including Maine, New Hampshire, Vermont, New York, Massachusetts, Rhode Island, Delaware, New Jersey, Pennsylvania, and West Virginia. Send your request to **listserv@umdd.umd.edu**.

House of Pain group logo, from the Internet.

"Rave Girl"

found on the

Internet.

NW-Raves

NW-Raves covers the northwestern United States and western Canada. Send your request to **nw-raves-request@ wimsey.bc.ca**.

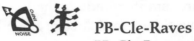

PB-Cle-Raves

PB-Cle-Raves covers the Pittsburgh and Cleveland metropolitan areas. Send your request to **pb-cle-raves-request@tele-rama.lm.com**.

R.U.N.

R.U.N. stands for Raving Up North, and covers eastern Canada, including the maritime provinces. Send your request to **dionf@ere.umontreal.ca**.

Collage of DJ tools, from the Internet.

SERaves
SERaves covers the southeastern U.S., including Tennessee, Virginia, North Carolina, South Carolina, Georgia, Florida, Alabama, Mississippi, and Arkansas. Archives are reportedly available at **american.edu**. Send your request to **listserv@american.edu**.

SFRaves
SFRaves—said to be the original rave mail list—covers the San Francisco Bay area. Send your request to **sfraves@soda.berkeley.edu**.

SoCal-Raves
SoCal-Raves covers southern California, including Los Angeles and San Diego. Send your request to **socal-raves-request@ucsd.edu**.

Technopolis
Technopolis is a daily rave sheet covering New York City alone, and is said to have

INXS collage.

archives at **techno.stanford.edu** in the /pub/raves/archives/technopolis/ directory. Send your request to **laura@soda.berkeley.edu**.

UK-DANCE
UK-DANCE covers the United Kingdom rave and general music scene. Send your request to **listserv@orbital.demon.co.uk**.

V-Rave
V-Rave is a chat line you can telnet to and talk to other ravers, in real time, who happen to be there. Telnet to **techno.stanford.edu** 7283. A mail list synopsis is available from **v-rave-request@gnu.ai.mit.edu**.

WNY-Raves
WNY-Raves covers western New York, plus southern Ontario. Send your request to **v077nk88@ubvms.cc.buffalo.edu**.

Internet Access: Aside from the resources mentioned so far, there's a FAQ on industrial music in the usual FAQ archives. Try **rtfm.mit.edu** in /pub/usenet/news.answers/ music/industrial-faq/ directory. And the /pub/raves/ directory at **techno.stanford.edu** has material on the rave scene. Once you get in touch with your local scene, you'll undoubtedly find other communications channels.

HACKING AND PHREAKING

"Hackers" used to mean really good programmers who came up with creative solutions to difficult problems. Now "hackers" are people who run wild on the Net, trying to get past as many computer security systems as possible. Phreaking refers to using technical tricks to control the phone system, either to get free long-distance phone calls or to prevent the tracing of hacking attempts.

A certain amount of romance has attached itself to hacking, since it is techno-wizardry that only the smart kids can pull—and some of it is. Businesses build elaborate "fire walls" between their computers and the Net to keep out infiltrators. But not all genuine hackers are misunderstood computer geniuses. A lot of hacking is low-tech, even no-tech. All you need to get into most systems is to con some legitimate user out of his or her password. And that's how many hackers operate, as con artists. But refusing to ever give out your password is not protection enough—you'd be surprised what someone can find out about you (or your company) by burrowing through your Dumpsters and looking for discarded computer manuals, especially ones with passwords scrawled on them.

Nine Inch Nails

artwork.

Metallica logo.

In the process these hackers may come across credit card receipts with legible numbers. Hackers, of course, need computer equipment, and those credit card numbers come in very handy when it comes time to purchase some by mail order. Then all they need is some legitimate address where they can have the stuff delivered, while being there to take delivery without arousing suspicion. That's the hard part.

Those who hack into computer systems are actually called "crackers" by cyberspacers.

Phreaking does require genuine technology, plus some skill in electronics. Plus it requires a belief that the phone company deserves to get ripped off, and a blind spot to the fact that the phone company has more technology than you do. Real-world hackers have their own private BBSs, which they take care to keep out of the limelight.

 alt.cyberpunk.tech
This newsgroup has a lot of discussions of the various colored boxes used to phreak the phone system, with sources of information and reviews (mostly negative) of the same. There are discussions of the Clipper encryption scheme, some specific technical ques-

tions about various oddments, and ongoing talk about the forging of false identification documents.

alt.cyberpunk
We'll return to this one because it also contains a lot of hacking talk, including hacker convention announcements. A game commonly held at these conventions is called "spot the fed."

alt.2600
This newsgroup is named after one of the audio frequencies used in phone phreaking. It is more technical than most, with talk of police radar, caller-ID tricks, eavesdropping on cellular phones, etc. Odd how none of the participants seem to use their real names.

alt.crackers
This newsgroup is a special case, being always empty. Even the deadest newsgroup will have chain letters or lawyer ads, so the situation can't be accidental.

hack-1
This mail list is for the *Hack Report*, a monthly newsletter concerning the hacker and pirated file situation on BBSs. Send your request to **majordomo@alive.ersys.edmonton.ab.ca**.

Online Access: Surely, Mr./Ms. Hacker, you don't need *me* to tell *you* anything.

Saving Face:
Get a life. More specifically, redirect your energies into more adult endeavors. For instance, look

into these organizations, which advocate (or, at least, seek to define) responsible behavior online:

Electronic Frontier Foundation—Examines public policy and individual rights in light of the information revolution. They have a presence in the comp.org.eff.talk, comp.org.eff.news, and alt.politics.datahighway newsgroups, and also on AOL (keyword: EFF) and on CompuServe (GO EFFSIG). They have an ftp site at **ftp.eff.org**. Or try 1001 G St. NW, Suite 950 E, Washington, DC 20001, USA, phone 202-347-5400, fax 202-393-5509.

Computer Professionals for Social Responsibility (CPSR)—Seeks to protect privacy and civil liberties, among other things. It's open to the public, despite the name, and has branches in several U.S. cities. The CPSR has several mailing lists, and an ftp site at ftp.cpsr.org. E-mail for the national headquarters is **cpsr@csli.stanford.edu**. Or you might try P.O. Box 717, Palo Alto, CA 94302, phone 415-322-3778, fax 415-322-3798.

Saving Face:

There are several danger signs to watch out for—in yourself. If you begin to experience strange events like these, your friend may be an up-and-coming hacker:

First—"Mike is always busy with his computer. Oh, well. What harm could he get into?"

Second—You hear Mike complain that he can't pay his $600 phone bill.

Third—Mike says his phone bill returned to normal. He's still never around because he spends all his time online, of course.

Fourth—Next time you go over to Mike's he has a room full of brand-new expensive computer equipment. But he says he borrowed it, so it's okay.

Old-fashioned Hacking

Real hacking is the variety that existed before the media got hold of the word: the seat-of-the-pants creation of elegant solutions to technical problems. Without hacking, other pursuits such as programming or engineering would just be dreary deskbound alternatives to shoveling coal. Participants in any conference dedicated to the guts of any system will appreciate real hacking, so half the conferences in cyberspace could potentially qualify as hacker conferences. A good general example of a hacker hangout is:

alt.hackers
Bringing dead machines back to life with WD-40, duct tape, paper clips, rubber bands, and Super Glue is the thing they boast about here. Silly programming stunts to pull on the

Saving Face:

Do not go around posturing like a hacker/cracker/phreaker in front of genuine hackers. They know the difference better than anybody.

boss are also a theme, plus little tricks you can perform with various pieces of hardware or software.

Access Information: Essentially every corner of cyberspace has conferences devoted to specific varieties of hardware and software, many of them moderated by the vendors, where you can thrash out technical minutiae to your heart's content. Cyberspace was created by real hackers for real hackers and they still constitute the bedrock of its population.

MONDO SOFTWARE STASHES

There are gigabytes of software out there, waiting for you to come along and download it. People have gathered vast collections online, either out of calculated self-interest or pure generosity—it doesn't matter. What matters is all that stands between you and it is a quick login and a few minutes of downloading. Almost every location on the Net has some kind of collection of free-distribution software. You'll see a lot of duplication, though, as waves of new stuff supplant the old. The kinds of files you see online fall into several categories:

Public Domain—It's free to use, and you can even write and sell a new version if you like.

Freeware—You're free to use it, but the author retains copyright, so, for example, you can't package and sell it yourself.

Shareware—The author expects you to send him/her money if you are going to use the program. (However, I have yet to see one that would blow up if you didn't.) You should send in something, though, to support the shareware industry.

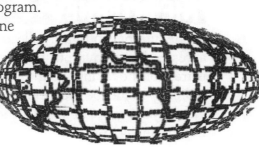

Crippled Shareware—You don't get a fully functional version of the program and/or its documentation until you send in money.

Demos—Versions of commercial software that are not fully functional. Usually the save and print commands don't work, or the package will only run *X* number of times.

Patches—Corrections for bugs in commercial software, usually circulated by the vendors.

Demo Applications—Small programs in a particular programming language demonstrating how to do something, of great interest to programmers, and usually circulated by the vendors.

Game Scenarios—Often circulated as freeware even when the game is not.

Artwork, Sounds, Animations—Files usually for use in a game.

Piracy—Posting copyrighted, commercial software packages to make them accessible for free downloading is a major no-no. Mere rumors of it have gotten BBSs shut down. Meanwhile, attempting to upload commercial software to a repository can get you the wrong kind of reputation, so be sure you don't do it.

In this chapter we'll mostly pay attention to repositories of PC software (DOS, Windows, and Windows NT), although substantial collections can also be found for other platforms, especially Macintosh, Unix, and Amiga.

THE INTERNET

The Internet software collections detailed here can be accessed by anonymous ftp—which means everything there is free for the taking. Your only expense is the up-front one of being online, be that your subscription to an Internet service or your share of a departmental budget at your corporation or university.

But this free access means that you, the user, must show a certain amount of respect and discretion. As long as the software repository can be offered for no particular additional overhead, the site's accountants can write the whole thing off to goodwill. If hordes of greedy file-suckers have brought the computer to its knees, further justification of the repository will be impossible. So don't be greedy, don't camp online, and try to restrict your file grabbing to nonbusiness hours (in the site's time zone, not yours).

SimTel

The SimTel Software Repository is now run by Coast to Coast Telecommunications, Inc., a regional long-distance phone company serving the midwestern United States out of Clarkston, Michigan. About 350 new titles are posted each month, mostly shareware and freeware offered by programmers known to the archivist or referred there by the Association of Shareware Professionals. As is common with online file collections, the postings are scanned for viruses, but practical considerations make it impossible to make any real effort to test the programs. The repository is funded by the sale of the collection on CD ROMs. Online access, basically, amounts to free advertising.

As this was written, SimTel had about ten thousand files, mostly MS-DOS programs, although increasing numbers are in Windows. With some trimming, the collection is sold on two CD ROMs. The collection gets its name because it was formerly located on a TOPS-20 computer belonging to the Simulation Teleprocessing section of the U.S. Army Information Systems Command at the White Sands Missile Range (hence the former site name wsmr.simtel20.army.mil). That site fell victim to post–Cold War military cutbacks in the autumn of 1993 and Coast to Coast took it over.

Internet Access Information: Use anonymous ftp to access **oak.oakland.edu** and go to the /pub/msdos/ directory. A description of the files can be found in the /pub/

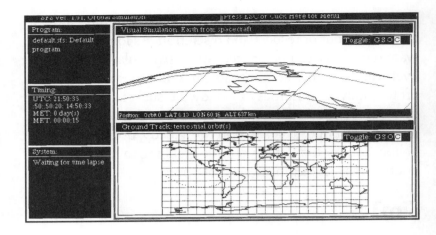

You're high over the Indian Ocean with Japan on the far horizon in this orbital spaceflight simulator, file sfs101.zip, one of thousands of programs available from the SimTel archive.

msdos/filedocs/ directory as either of two large files: simindex.zip, which is a comma-delimited list suitable for importing into a database program, or simlist.zip, a text file.

Mirror Sites: The SimTel collection is mirrored in various sites worldwide. You should try to go to the site nearest you, and thus avoid burdening the Net.

U.S.—**wuarchive.wustl.edu** in the /systems/ibmpc/msdos/ directory, or **archive.orst.edu** in the /pub/mirrors/simtel/ msdos/ directory

Australia—**archie.au** in the /micros/pc/oak/ directory

England—**src.doc.ic.ac.uk** in the /pub/packages/ibmpc/ simtel/ directory

Finland—**ftp.funet.fi** in the /pub/msdos/SimTel/ directory

Germany—**ftp.uni-paderborn.de** in the /pcsoft/msdos/ directory

Hong Kong—**ftp.cs.cuhk.hk** in the /pub/simtel/msdos/ directory

Israel—**ftp.technion.ac.il** in the /pub/unsupported/dos/ simtel/ directory

Poland—**ftp.cyf-kr.edu.pl** in the /pub/mirror/msdos/ directory

Switzerland—**ftp.switch.ch** in the /mirror/msdos/ directory

Taiwan—**NCTUCCCA.edu.tw** in the /PC/simtel/ directory

Thailand—**ftp.nectec.or.th** in the /pub/mirrors/msdos/ directory

Garbo

The "garbo" site at (of all places) the University of Vaasa in Finland has a large collection of MS-DOS and Windows files, plus Unix, Macintosh, and Sinclair QL material.

Internet Access Information: Use anonymous ftp to go to garbo.uwasa.fi. The file index is in a file called /pc/INDEX.ZIP.

Mirror Sites: Garbo is mirrored at a number of sites worldwide. The major ones appear to be:

Australia—**archie.au** in the /micros/pc/garbo/ directory

Germany—**ftp.germany.eu.net** in the /pub/comp/msdos/mirror.garbo/ directory

Italy—**cnuce_arch.cnr.it** in the /pub/msdos/garbo.uwasa.fi/ directory

South Africa—**owl.und.ac.za** in the /mirrors/garbo/pc/ directory

Taiwan—**ftp.edu.tw**, in the /PC/garbo/ directory, and nctuccca.edu.tw in the /PC/garbo/ directory

U.S.—**ftp.cdrom.com** in the /pub/garbo/ directory, and at wuarchive.wustl.edu in the /systems/msdos.garbo.uwasa.fi/ directory

CICA

CICA (The Center for Innovative Computer Applications) has an anonymous ftp site with well over four thousand Windows (and some Windows NT) applications.

Check This Out:

Do not attempt to upload software to any repository without first looking for upload guides at that site. Some will want you to contact the site administrator in advance.

Screen icon of the Elvis Detector, file elvisd10.zip from the CICA archive. One of thousands of Windows applications available on CICA (most of which have narrower appeal than this one), the Elvis Detector is designed to alert you to the presence of Elvis Presley, its animated icon continually showing a radar sweep. Screen windows with song snippets from The King appear when the detectors are triggered. Based on the latest tabloid technology, the documentation includes an unusually full set of legal disclaimers.

And Check This Out:

Mirror sites are always separate operations, with no administrative connection with the site they are mirroring. There is no guarantee that all files will get mirrored, and personnel at a mirror site cannot answer questions about the operation of one of the other sites.

Everything is shareware, freeware, or demos. Areas covered include drivers, utilities, fonts, icons and patches, plus a lot of material of interest to programmers, covering Visual Basic, Asymetrix ToolBook, C++, Windows Pascal, and Windows Paradox, among others. Also, there are games, sounds, and bitmap graphics. The latter are kept online for six months only, to conserve room. The site is said to experience more than sixteen hundred ftp logins daily, and about a gigabyte of downloading. Users, therefore, are advised to try CICA at night, during off-peak hours. But keep in mind that the files are not scanned for viruses—you're on your own there.

Internet Access Information: Do anonymous ftp to **ftp.cica.indiana.edu**, and go to the /pub/pc/win3/ directory. The file index is in a file there, called INDEX.ZIP.

Mirror Sites: CICA is a popular collection to mirror. With directory information included when known, sites include:

Australia—**ftp.cc.monash.edu.au** in the /pub/win3/ directory

Germany—**ftp.uni-stuttgart.de**

Israel—**vmsa.technion.ac.il**

Japan—**ftp.iij.ad.jp** in the /pub/win3/ directory

Poland—**ftp.cyf-kr.edu.pl** in the /pub/mirror/win3/ directory

Switzerland—**nic.switch.ch** in the /mirror/win3/ directory

Taiwan—**nctuccca.edu.tw**

Thailand—**ftp.nectec.or.th**

U.K.—**src.doc.ic.ac.uk**

U.S.—**wuarchive.wustl.edu** in the /systems/ibmpc/win3/ directory, **gatekeeper.dec.com**, **ftp.cdrom.com**, **ftp.marcam.com**, and **polecat.law.indiana.edu**

Games! Games! Games!

The PC Games Archives at the University of Massachusetts at Lowell is an "unfunded, unsanctioned" repository of games that run under MS-DOS or Windows. This includes shareware, freeware, and demos (playable and unplayable), and front-ends for online games—anything that is intended for free distribution. My count shows about 430 files, about which half are games and the rest are data files, scenarios, or scenario editors that support a particular game. Included are scenery and weather files for flight simulators, and bizarre

Check This Out:

A list of the programs that the Garbo site manager (Professor Timo Salmi of the Accounting and Industrial Management School of the University of Vaasa, Finland) thinks is the most useful is labeled bestpr*.zip, where * is the latest version number.

And Check This Out:

A file listing ftp sites offering MS-DOS and Windows materials of any kind is in the /pc/pd2/ directory at the garbo site, and presumably its mirrors. It is called moder*.zip, where * represents the latest version number.

artwork for mah-jongg tiles. Executable files are scanned for viruses.

Internet Access Information: Do anonymous ftp to **ftp.uml.edu** and go to the /msdos/games/ directory. A readme file contains information about the organization of the site, and a master list of files is available as games.idx.

Mirror Sites: The PCGA, as it calls itself, is mirrored around the globe. The major sites appear to be:

Germany—ftp.uni-paderborn.de in the /pcsoft/msdos/games/ directory

South Africa—ftp.sun.ac.za in the /pub/msdos/uml/ directory

Taiwan—nctuccca.edu.tw in the /ulowell/msdos/ directory

Thailand—ftp.nectec.or.th in the /pub/mirrors/games/ directory

U.K.—src.doc.ic.ac.uk in the /computing/systems/ibmpc/ msdos-games/Games/ directory

U.S.—wuarchive.wustl.edu in the /systems/msdos/msdos-games/ directory, and ftp.uwp.edu in the /pub/msdos/ games/uml/ directory

COMMERCIAL SERVICES

Of course, you have to pay to use the commercial services, although they may suspend charges while you are uploading files, or while downloading files needed to use the service. Also, they are not in the business of amassing software for its own sake. Their file collections are there because they are of interest to participants in specific conferences—and in many cases are supplied by those participants.

AOL

You'll see a large file collection under the Computer and Software Department, with more than fifty thousand files organized under more than a dozen headings. For convenience, the staff maintains a "Download Hall of Fame," with popular or useful-looking files organized under various headings. Last I looked, the headings included DOS, Windows, OS/2, fitness, home reference, Internet tools, "toys" (such as a mouse "odometer"), and vacation planning. Through the "Industry Connection" icon you can find vendor-sponsored file collections from various hardware and software makers, offering demos, patches, and other software add-ons.

BIX

BIX is mainly a service of conferences. Some conferences have an attached "listings" topic containing files. Plus there is a shared listings area—for files that are of interest to multiple conferences. But the files you run across have all been put there for a specific purpose or project—BIX does not amass fiiles purely for the sake of doing so. You need to go elsewhere if you want to pan for software gold.

CompuServe

CompuServe is a major source of files. Each conference has a library of files, and you can sort the contents by keywords. Offerings in the vendor-sponsored product-specific conferences are prodigious. For some software companies, "customer support" has come to mean posting patches on CompuServe. Microsoft even supports commercial developers through this medium. A listing of popular and/or notable files available for downloading appears in the monthly magazine that is sent to CompuServe subscribers.

Delphi

While Delphi emphasizes its Internet connectivity, it still has a full slate of in-house offerings, with each SIG or forum having its own "database" area, whose contents you can browse or search. No major theme emerges, although there seems to be more graphics for their own sakes than in other services (see Chapter 11).

GEnie

Each of the various computer-oriented roundtables—found under the Computing Services heading on the main menu—has its own software library, which you can search by keyword. Altogether, GEnie boasts of having 200,000 files available for downloading. Of these, 150,000 are said to be software, as opposed to text or data. Of the software files, more than 23,000 are for the Macintosh, which must make GEnie one of the biggest Mac repositories around.

BBSs

Any BBS worth the name has a file collection. In fact, the "subscription" for some boards is a favorable upload-to-download ratio—they'll let you keep taking files as long as you supply some yourself. (If the board welcomes copyrighted software, hang up and don't go back—you don't want your name associated with it.)

Meanwhile, some of the larger BBSs have huge file collections, rivaling what you see on the Internet. (There is, of course, duplication.) For most users those file collections are their chief attractions. The larger boards, of course, charge a subscription, but you can usually logon and do a certain amount of rooting around with an initial guest membership.

The names of the larger boards are covered in Chapter 14.

GAMES AND MUDS

Is MUDding a game or an extension of life itself with gamelike qualities? The fact that there are those who pose the question in all seriousness should give you some clue as to the power of the phenomena we're dealing with here.

MUD stands for either Multiple-User Dimensions, Multi-User Dungeons, Multi-User Dialogues, or anything else within reason. It connotes multi-user software in which each user controls a persona (usually given names like KillJoy, DeathKnight, or TinyDinosaur) that interacts with the other online player's personae. You can either be playing a win/lose game or exploring a different social setting—*Star Trek* or the Middle Ages, for instance. You can fight, talk, explore, and even define and create online objects.

There have been stabs at graphic interfaces, usually using local area networks, whose speeds always let you pull more stunts than you can with a modem connection. (The Diaspar service, noted in Chapter 4, is, however, is a move in the direction of modem-based graphic MUDs.) But nearly any MUD you'll come across at this writing will be text-based. You enter your commands—go, say, look, etc.—plus anything you want to say to the other characters, from the keyboard, and the system sends you little messages informing you of what just happened: "So-and-so has entered the room."

Some MUDs are glorified chat channels, while some include programming languages that let you define, for instance, your character's attributes and even what your character is wearing and armed with, and what magical powers he or she possess. In some games the idea is to press on through monster-clogged caverns (alone or in groups, cooperating with or slaying other players) to find treasure and solve puzzles, elevating your character's abilities with each victory until you reach wizard or god rank. Some MUDs you can log right into. Some require preliminary steps, usually meaning registering and programming your character, usually by e-mail.

In all cases, though: RTFM. Every MUD is its own universe with its own rules—that, in fact, is the attraction. In this chapter we can only point you in the direction of god status—ultimately every player must find his or her own way. (*Now* do you see why they ask the opening question about life equaling MUDding?) When in doubt, cry (well, actually, type) "help" and read the directions.

I, MUD

If you're a newbie (see the jargon list that follows), you'll have many hard knocks ahead of you. Incorporating the jargon into the core of your being will help, however. You should know that there are two main types of MUD systems, the hack-and-slash adventure MUDs, and the chatty role-playing MUDs.

Role-playing MUD software includes:

☞ MOO
☞ LambdaMOO
☞ TinyMUCK
☞ MUG
☞ TinyMUSE
☞ TinyMAGE
☞ MUSH
☞ TalkerMUD

- TeenyMUD
- TinyMUD
- UberMUD
- UnterMUD

Hack-and-slash adventure MUD software includes:

- AberMUD
- DikuMUD
- DgdMUD
- DumMUD
- LPMUD
- MercMUD
- OxMUD
- UriMUD
- YAMA

Check This Out:

The classifications represent the norm, but there is nothing to stop you from, say, using hack-and-slash software to set up a pacifistic, vegetarian theme.

The original MUD, called "MUD" and dating to 1978, has gone on to its reward, although a variant is used on CompuServe for a game called "British Legends." Except for YAMA, which was written for the PC, most MUD software systems (called servers) were written to run on UNIX workstations. Some have been ported to MS-DOS, but will require a well-decked machine to run.

Saving Face:

Now, let's look at some of that jargon:

Berserk—What happens when two cyborgs get caught in a loop. If your client is told to answer "Hello" anytime another player says it, and another player has done likewise, guess what happens when they meet and one says "Hello"?

Bot—Program that plays one of a MUD's characters. Short for "robot."

BSX—Graphics-based MUD systems, usually LPMUDs with added polygon graphics, using various servers.

Client—Software running on the machine of a player that handles certain tasks. On the Internet you want it to at least handle line wrapping and separate incoming and outgoing text, something telnet won't do by itself. It may also perform tasks specific to a MUD, such as directing the characters through preprogrammed tasks. Most are written for Unix workstations or the equivalent.

Clueless Newbie—You, until you read the directions.

Cyborg—A player who has set up his or her client to perform certain functions automatically, like query every player who walks into the room.

Dino—Player who has been around forever. Or one who is large yet extinct.

F2F—Face-to-face. Players sometimes do meet each other.

Furries—Characters that are animals, similar to cartoon characters.

Gag—Suppression of incoming text by the client, usually from players the user has become sick of.

Gods—Players with the top ratings, who have the power to do as they please to other players and even alter the game database. If you don't like what the gods are doing, you'll have to find a different MUD.

Haven—A room, usually in a TinyMUD, where characters may not kill each other.

Julia—A particularly clever bot, known to have fooled players.

Killing—In some MUDs, it means the character lies there and bleeds to death. In others, the character returns to its "home room" and collects pass-go money. In yet others, "killing" is just a way to get another character's attention.

Log—To save the screen as you play, especially to preserve TinySex moments so they can be studied and/or exposed to public appreciation in an appropriate online newsgroup or forum.

Mave—To make a typo with disastrous consequences, especially to say out loud what you had intended to whisper.

Puppets—Game objects that respond to commands.

Server—The MUD software and the machine it is running on.

Spam—To flood the screen with text, accidentally or in anger.

Theme—The setting of the world your MUD creates. Examples include vampire, furry, Arthurian, Dante's Inferno, Japanese animation, Middle Earth, medieval fantasy, folklore, meditation, *Star Trek*, Pern, and various other specific science fiction and future-combat settings.

TinySex—Interactive erotica between two characters in a MUD. It's all verbal. You may hear jokes about typing with one hand. Ignore them. You may hear references to the log facility. Pay attention to them.

Toading—What happens when the other MUD characters turn against you because of your intolerable behavior, as in "Let's all get this little toad."

Triggers—Events that cause the client to do something, as programmed by the user, such as greet other players entering the room.

Whisper—To send a private message to another character.

Wizards—Players of high ranking, who can do much as they please, but are not as powerful as gods.

INTERNET MUDDING

At this writing there are something over three hundred MUD servers you can reach over the Internet. The telnet command will have to include the specific port number used by the MUD server at that site. If you found that there was a MUD at port 9000 at styx.mud.edu, you probably say "telnet styx.mud.edu 9000" to get connected, although the exact syntax will vary. You may, however, need to contact the sys-

Saving Face:

Ethically speaking, never do anything in a MUD that you would not do in real life. It's good practice, and things can otherwise turn ugly in f2f mode. (You still remember f2f mode, don't you?) Study the directions. Do not be afraid to ask other players for advice, although it may not always be wise in confrontational combat settings. But don't do such things as whine and demand things of other players, or follow them around. And in combat, do not steal from corpses you didn't kill.

tem administrator in advance to get an account and set up a character.

Lists of MUDs, their addresses, and pertinent information are posted at intervals in the rec.games.mud.announce newsgroup on Usenet (see the following list). To avoid Net lag (response time problems) it is always best to try sites nearest your own. Other MUD materials can be found at the following sites:

- ☞ **ftp.tcp.com**   Material and software for various servers and clients, plus general documentation
- ☞ **ftp.ccs.neu.edu**   Server software for various MUDs, client software, documentation, and databases for various themes
- ☞ **nightmare.connected.com**   Client software, including DOS files
- ☞ **ftp.tu-bs.de**   LPMUD material, including documentation
- ☞ **actlab.rtf.utexas.edu**   LPMUD material, clients, FAQs and documentation
- ☞ **ftp.lysator.liu.se**   BSX and LPMUD material
- ☞ **ftp.cd.chalmers.se**   LPMUD material
- ☞ **quepasa.cs.tu-berlin.de**   Material on LPMUD and other MUDs
- ☞ **marble.bu.edu**   LPMUD material
- ☞ **ftp.math.okstate.edu**   Various varieties of client and server software, FAQs, and other material
- ☞ **eskinews.eskimo.com**   LPMUD material

A good way to follow the Internet MUD scene is through the various MUD-related newsgroups on Usenet. The main ones are as follows:

rec.games.mud.admin
This newsgroup contains a lot of general MUD information, with added discussions of how to set up and administer a MUD, and

how to convince the campus authorities that
setting up a MUD is a worthwhile computer
science programming project.

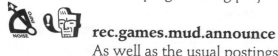 **rec.games.mud.announce**
As well as the usual postings seeking genres
and technical answers, there is a periodic
posting of Internet MUD lists in this newsgroup.

 rec.games.mud.diku
This newsgroup concentrates on DikuMUDs,
with the usual site announcements, technical
notes, bug reports, and sociologists seeking to
survey the population.

 **rec.games.mud.lp**
This newsgroup is similar to rec.games.
mud.diku, but covers the LPMUD variant
of MUDs.

 **rec.games.mud.misc**
Besides the usual technical questions, there
are MUDders here seeking specific genres,
like Middle Earth and *Star Trek*.

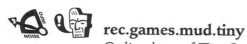 **rec.games.mud.tiny**
Online logs of TinySex encounters appear
here more frequently, for whatever reason.

 alt.mud
Here you'll find a lot of general questions
about MUDding, plus Internet MUD lists that
tend to be dated, and calls for playtesters.

 MUD
The Internet Games MUD-List shows you
where to go to MUD. Send your request to

jwisdom@gnu.ai.mit.edu and include the string "mud list" in the subject header.

tinymush-programmers
This mail list covers the programming language that the TinyMUSH subfamily of MUD servers is written around. Send your request to **tinymush-programmers-request@cygnus.com**.

Other Internet Access Information: Besides the addresses and newsgroups noted so far, a three-part rec.games.mud FAQ is posted at intervals in the various rec.games.mud newsgroups, and can be found at many of the ftp site lists. It gives more specific information on where to find various pieces of MUD software and documentation. Lists of MUDs also appear there.

OTHER INTERNET GAMES

Of course, there are games besides MUDs that are played on the Net, and the denizens talk about all sorts of games, computerized or not.

Saving Face:

Catch up on these gaming terms before you hit the Net:

Action games—Arcadelike, joystick-centered games.

Advanced Dungeon & Dragons—Foundation of the industry and still popular, this FRP system comes from TSR.

Adventure—FRP genre (usually single-player) in which you are in a cave and have to solve riddles and kill monsters.

Amber—Amber is a world taken from the novels of Roger Zelazny, in an FRP system offered by Phage Press.

Arcade—Implies a game that depends on fancy graphics, joystick control, and a lot of action.

Call of Cthulhu—The elder gods drive mortals to insanity in this horror-theme RPG system based on the works of H.P. Lovecraft, offered by Chaosium.

Campaign—An ongoing game in which each session is part of a larger story line.

Champions—Superheroes contending in today's world. Just make sure you use the latest version of this FRP system from Hero Games/Iron Crown.

Character—Gaming personae created for use in a game, within the rules of its system.

Cheats—Playing hints not available from the documentation.

Chill—Horror is the name of the game in this FRP system from Mayfair Games, Inc.

Custom—Where the game master writes his or her own rules and is immediately accused of cheating.

Cyberpunk 2020—If you're not already living the cyberpunk life, simulate with this RPG system from R. Talsorian Games.

D.C. Heroes—You can be Superman, Batman, etc., in this (copyright licensed) FRP system from Mayfair Games, Inc.

Dungeons & Dragons—Preincarnation of Advanced Dungeons & Dragons, making it the granddaddy FRP of them all. The cognoscenti prefer Advanced D&D.

Earthdawn—FASA offers this FRP system concerning magic and its many uses around the house.

Flight Simulators—Graphic simulators of a cockpit, with aeronautical controls mapped to the keyboard. Aerial combat may be involved.

FRP—Fantasy role-playing, an RPG in a setting with dragons, magic, damsels, no lawyers, etc.

Game Master—The person running the game, interpreting the rules, and possibly triggering certain events.

Check This Out:

When setting up a MUD account, never choose a password that is the same as your computer system password.

Gamma World—What to do after a nuclear apocalypse is the theme of this RPG system from TSR.

GM—Game Master.

GURPS—The Generic Universal Role-Playing System is a generic system from Steve Jackson Games, which uses it in games of widely varying themes.

Hero System—This is a generic system for creating your own theme, published by Hero Games/Iron Crown.

Interactive Fiction—Text-based role-playing games, which can take years to play.

Mage: The Ascension—Powerful magicians contend in this FRP system, part of the White Wolf Storyteller system.

Marvel Super Heroes—The Marvel Comics superheroes can live again through you with this (copyright licensed) system from TSR.

Middle Earth—Iron Crown offers this FRP system based on the writing of J.R.R. Tolkien.

Over the Edge—Byzantine intrigue is the subject of this RPG system from Atlas Games.

Paranoia—This RPG system from West End Games is a cyberpunk satire, unless you're paranoid enough to take it seriously.

Role Playing—To control a character within a game setting.

Role-Playing System—An agreed-upon set of rules and procedures for playing a game.

Rolemaster—This is a fantasy system published by Iron Crown.

RPG—Role-playing game, in which your character interacts with other characters in a highly contrived setting. Similar to MUDs, but are usually single-player with a graphics interface.

Shadowrun—Cyberpunk and fantasy coexist in this FRP system from FASA.

Simulations—Build a virtual city, railroad, civilization, galactic empire, or ant colony. War games that emphasize historicity are also examples.

Star Wars—The RPG system is published by West End Games, long ago, in a galaxy far, far away.

Strategy games—Games that involve planning ahead, rather than joystick dexterity. Simulations and war games are examples.

Tales from the Floating Vagabond—Time, space, and humor finally get together in this FRP system from Avalon Hill.

Toon—Anything can happen in a cartoon, and in this FRP system from Steve Jackson Games.

Traveller—Very popular science fiction role-playing game from GDW.

Underground—Mayfair Games offers this RPG system involving grim superheroes in grimmer futuristic settings.

Vampire—An entry in the White Wolf's Storyteller FRP system, for those feeling undead.

Werewolf—You know what this is. Also, it is an entry in the White Wolf's Storyteller FRP system.

Following are some of the more interesting game-related places. Most that relate to online games will have FAQ files posted at intervals indicating where you can play the game, download the software, or both.

comp.sys.amiga.games
This very busy newsgroup is abuzz with talk of games with names like Monkey Island, Frontier and Dune, searches for cheats, and concern for the business fate of Commodore International, maker of the Amiga.

> I presume you've been through the various scenarios you get to by using the IID, to collect the various tools and fluff? One of these scenarios should be inside the whale, where you get the flowerpot in which to plant the four pieces of fluff from which grows the Tree of Foreknowledge which enables you to determine which tool Marvin needs to open the airlock. If the IID never puts you into the whale scenario (as happened with me - for four years or so), you can never finish the game - and if you don't use the real tea, rather than synthetic tea, to activate the IID while the whale and bowl of petunias are falling to the planet, then you never get inside the whale . . . Once you've landed on the planet it's too late, as the whale has been destroyed, so you could sit there for ever and never get anywhere. This is a rather monumentally bad 'feature', as you must use the synthetic tea initially to save the ship (as the Nutrimat is still on making the real tea at the time), and there's no reason for you to consider switching it (apart from not being able to finish the game for several years, I suppose :-)). Unfortunately, the ending when you get out onto the planet isn't worth the wait, I'm afraid - it's quite feeble.

Typical answer in comp.sys.ibm.pc.games.adventure to another user's plea for a "cheat" concerning the game Hitch Hikers Guide to the Galaxy. Getting stumped for years is apparently not uncommon.

comp.sys.ibm.pc.games.action
A lot of PC game aficionados are into hacking the shareware game Doom, as you can see in this very busy newsgroup. Many are involved in a quest to add Barney the PBS kiddie dinosaur to the game for cathartic hack-and-slash practice. You can turn to this place for bug reports (plus reviews) on nearly any PC arcade game you could name.

comp.sys.ibm.pc.games.adventure
Pleas for advice from people caught at some point in an adventure-style game (sometimes for years at a stretch) echo through this newsgroup.

comp.sys.ibm.pc.games.announce

This newsgroup is devoted to newsletters and press releases, especially concerning the availability of shareware games on the PC.

comp.sys.ibm.pc.games.flight-sim

This busy newsgroup covers air and/or space-flight simulators that run on the PC, with participants finding new meaning for the term "system crash" as they swap mission editors, ask unending technical questions, post games for sale, and ponder whether to use the rear turrets of their starship to cover their retreat or just run for it.

comp.sys.ibm.pc.games.misc

This newsgroup covers games-related subjects left over from the other groups, including sound cards, Amiga editors, pinball games, old orphaned games, for-sale notices, and recurring searches for a way to cheat at Windows Solitaire.

comp.sys.ibm.pc.games.rpg

"There are a lot of bit players—kids, beggars and dogs—in the game I'm playing, and I wonder if play would go faster if I was to just kill them all" is a recurring question in this very busy newsgroup. Consensus: Why even ask? Alas, our virtual citizens have no rights that players are obliged to respect.

comp.sys.ibm.pc.games.strategic

In this newsgroup, "strategic" means military history, city planning, or railroad building simulations. Check here to find which computer war game cheats.

comp.sys.mac.games

This one of the more active newsgroups in Usenet—as you'd expect, since it covers the entire Macintosh game scene. Name a Mac game, and it's being talked about here. Plus there's a lot of yearning for PC titles not yet ported to the Mac, and recurring baiting from PC fascists just dropping by for a raid.

rec.games.abstract

This newsgroup covers pure strategy games, meaning there's no joystick, but nothing specific is simulated. There are games under discussion with names I'd never heard of, like Mankala and Abalone.

rec.games.backgammon

Here they talk about backgammon, either in tabletop or computer versions, examining software, reliving tournaments, and challenging each other with special problems.

rec.games.board

Yes, people still play games the old ways, without computers, and those who do it gather here. Most topics are map-based war games, but classics like Scrabble and Risk get their day, too.

rec.games.board.ce

"The Terrorist is attacking the Bully's planet on an Inverted Cone with the Bully having allies. The Terrorist loses the fight and the defensive ally lands exploding the planet. Can the Bully use power on the defeated Terrorist?" Obviously, this person is playing a game called Cosmic Encounter.

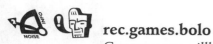

rec.games.bolo

Can you use pillboxes to take bases? Can you put mines in deep water? I don't know, either, but it all relates to an online strategy game called Bolo.

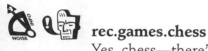

rec.games.chess

Yes, chess—there's no escape. It's discussed here, along with computer chess programs from all over.

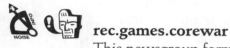

rec.games.corewar

This newsgroup forms a point of contact for those interested in Core Wars. The ultimate computer war game, Core Wars involves two or more programs written in a virtual assembly program (called Redcode) running on a virtual computer (called MARS, for Memory Array Redcode Simulator) trying to tear each other to pieces. Last one to terminate wins.

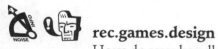

rec.games.design

How do you handle multiple joysticks? How do you incorporate AI? How important is ambidexterity? If these questions haunt you, check out this newsgroup.

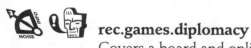

rec.games.diplomacy

Covers a board and online multi-player negotiation game called Diplomacy, where you conquer Europe—if you can convince the other players to let you.

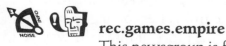

rec.games.empire

This newsgroup is for discussion of an online multi-player war game called Empire.

 rec.games.frp.advocacy
How to inject reality, and whether the presence of combat is realistic, are among the flames and counterflames amid discussions of various role-playing systems.

 rec.games.frp.announce
Check this place out for convention announcements and club listings in the fantasy role-playing world.

 rec.games.frp.archives
Be careful not to actually read the postings here, or you may go nuts. Logs of online Internet fantasy games are posted here for the reference of the participants. To nonplayers they are largely inexplicable.

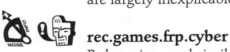 **rec.games.frp.cyber**
Rules gripes and similar material on cyberpunk-related role-playing games are hashed out here. Should sniper rifles be allowed? Always a good question.

 rec.games.frp.dnd
Yes, there's nothing like slaughtering a few score orcs and trolls after coming home from a hard day at the office. If that's the way you feel, you must be into that granddaddy of FRP

A maiden battles a dragon in this Dungeons & Dragons fantasy artwork.

games, Dungeons & Dragons, and should check out this newsgroup.

 rec.games.frp.live-action
If you can get into a combination of hiking, orienteering, fencing, and character acting, then you could get into live-action role-play games, which are the subject of this newsgroup.

rec.games.frp.marketplace

This is the place to go for posting wanted or for-sale notices concerning FRP games and figurines.

 rec.games.frp.misc

General discussions of role-playing games take place here, with the participants swapping code, looking for other gamers and game sites, looking for discount games prices, flaming each other's freely offered opinions, and marveling at the Canadian government's game censorship efforts.

 rec.games.hack

This newsgroup covers Hack—the online game, not the lifestyle. "Until I got killed, I was having a really good time with my level 13 Valkyria. I had +6 Mojo, +5 GDSM, +4 SoR, +4 HoB, +5 Speed boots, +4 Hawaiian shirt, +4 GoP and :+0 CoP, all blessed and fire/rustproofed." If you understand that, maybe you can Hack it.

 rec.games.int-fiction

The participants here are into "interactive fiction"—single-player text-based adventure games with names like Leather Goddesses of Phobos.

 rec.games.mecha

Talk here centers around games that involve combat between player-designed virtual robots. Participants trade designs and debate about whether taking prisoners is worthwhile.

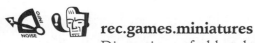

rec.games.miniatures

Discussions of old-style tabletop war gaming, where you use tiny figurines, often hand-painted to frightening levels of details. The participants largely wrestle over rules and boast of their Tables of Organization and Equipment.

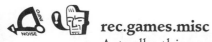

rec.games.misc

Actually, this appears to be a collection of random cross-postings from the other games-related newsgroups.

rec.games.netrek

Netrek is a sixteen-player (two teams) graphical real-time *Star Trek* war game. Participants discuss things like the best way to conquer planets or, failing that, destroy them.

rec.games.pbm

PBM means Play By Mail. In this case, they usually (not always) mean e-mail, so they are really talking about online games that are not played in real time.

rec.games.programmer

If you seek land generation algorithms, fast square root solvers, or the fine points of 3D graphics programs, camp out here. The place is awash with techie pointers. Hacking the Doom PC shareware game is a big topic.

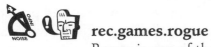

rec.games.rogue

Rogue is one of the original single-player, hack-and-slash, dungeon-exploring computer games, usually found on Unix, using simple graphics. It has since spawned descendants with names like AngBand, Moria, and NetHack, plus multi-player variants like CrossFire. At this writing Rogue was also covered by the newsgroups rec.games.roguelike.announce, rec.games.roguelike.angband, rec.games.roguelike.misc, but there was a move on to reorganize.

crossfire

This mail list is for those interested in the development of Crossfire, an arcade and adventure game for Xwindows descended from Rogue. Send your request to **crossfire-request@ifi.uio.no**.

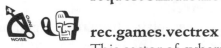

rec.games.vectrex

This sector of cyberspace is inhabited by cult followers of a self-contained vector graphics game machine called Vectrex, which lived and died in the early 1980s.

rec.games.video.3do

Discussion of 3DO video game system and the games that run on it, and the companies behind them.

rec.games.video.advocacy

How much freedom of movement ("rails") should a player be given? If such questions excite you, this is your newsgroup.

rec.games.xtank.play

Xtank is a multi-player game involved player-designed and controlled virtual tanks that run around in virtual mazes, usually shooting at each other. Some AI is generally built into the tanks. If you're not a programmer with access to a workstation, forget it.

rec.games.xtank.programmer

Technical discussion concerning Xtank, as described in rec.games.xtank.play.

alt.games.doom

Participants discuss a popular hack-and-slash video game for the PC called Doom.

alt.games.frp.dnd-util

If you're interested in software for drawing D&D maps, check this place out.

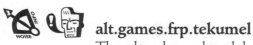

alt.games.frp.tekumel

The place has rules, debates, and for-sale announcements for miniature figurines concerning a role-playing game based on a universe called Tekumel and/or Empire of the Petal Throne.

alt.games.gb

Discussion of a game called Galactic Bloodshed. Who's naming these games, anyway?

alt.games.lynx

This is the place if you follow the Atari Lynx game system and the games that run on it.

alt.games.mk

Mortal Kombat aficionados fight here merely with words.

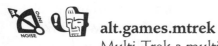

alt.games.mtrek

Multi-Trek a multi-user *Star Trek*–like game, and this newsgroup offers the usual wrestling matches over fine points in the rules.

alt.games.netrek.paradise

A version of Netrek called Paradise is the topic here.

 alt.games.vga-planets

VGA-Planets is an eleven-player e-mail computer-umpired PBM war game between galactic empires, using player-designed starships, with heavy emphasis on economics. You need shareware client software to play. This newsgroup forms a contact point for the players.

 alt.games.whitewolf

If "Triat symbolism in Xtian mythology" is what you talk about at breakfast, go no further than this newsgroup, devoted to the WhiteWolf line of gothic/horror role-playing games.

 Ars Magica

This mail list is devoted to the Ars Magica role playing game from WhiteWolf. Send your request to **ars-magica-request@soda.berkeley.edu**.

 vampire

This mail list is devoted to the Vampire role-playing game from WhiteWolf. Send your request to **vampire-request@math.ufl.edu**.

 alt.games.xpilot

Xpilot is a sort of air/space warfare simulator that runs on Unix and Xwindows workstations, with user-designed ships and terrain. Participants swap ship designs and favorite maps.

CZ

The Convergence Zone mail list concerns Harpoon naval war game series and related naval topics, plus pointers on what to do when those cruise missiles start converging. Send your request to **cz-request@stsci.edu**.

Nero

The Nero mail lists concerns a commercial live-action role-playing game with a medieval theme, in New England. Send your request to **Isonko@pearl.tufts.edu**.

pd-games

Is there an advantage to being nice to people? If so, when does that advantage end? That's the gist of the so-called Prisoner's Dilemma line of game theory inquiry, which is the subject of this mail list. If you've hammered out a sound scientific basis for mutual social cooperation, let's hear it. Meanwhile, send your request to **pd-games-request@math.uio.no**.

RuneQuest

This mail list concerns the commercial role-playing game RuneQuest and associated fantasy world of Glorantha. Send your request to **RuneQuest-Request@Glorantha.Holland.Sun.com**.

ShadowTalk

This mail list is devoted to ShadowRun, a role-playing game set in Seattle in the year 2054. Where else? Send your request to **LISTSERV@HEARN.nic.SURFnet.nl**.

Cheats, solutions, and hints for many popular games are available via anonymous ftp at **risc.ua.edu** in the /pub/games/solutions/ directory, at **ftp.uu.net** in the /pub/games/solutions/ directory, and at **nic.funet.fi** in the /pub/doc/games/solutions/ directory.

SFB Tacticsline
This mail list is a point of contact for players of an e-mail game called Star Fleet Battles. Send your request to **hcobb@fly2.berkeley.edu**.

torg
"Torg, the Possibility Wars" role-playing game from West End Games, is the subject of this mail list. Send your request (with "HELP" in the subject line) to **torg-request@cool.vortech.com**.

traveller
This mail list covers the Traveller series of role-playing games from Game Designers' Workshop. Send your request to **traveller-request@engrg.uwo.ca**.

Existential Note: "Life is an RPG, run by an idiot, full of badly designed mechanics, signifying nothing." From a games newsgroup sig.

GAMING ON COMMERCIAL SERVICES

Adventure, role-playing, and MUDlike games are offered by the commercial services, but there's a difference: The caustic, gritty verve you see on the Internet is unapologetically suppressed. You see constant warnings that everything is supposed to be G-rated. The sponsors figure that Mommy and Daddy will not pay to have Johnny corrupted by foul-mouthed, gutter-minded MUD players. Forget TinySex. Forget those scatological metaphors you've fallen into the habit of using. For that matter, forget every epithet stronger than "gosh darn that dungeon master." If you can't live that way, this is not the place for you. If that's what you actively want, then read on.

AOL

After choosing the Games and Entertainment Department on AOL, you are presented with a list of options—most show business features—and an icon for the On-Line Gamers Forum. Under it you'll find the following forums:

 Free Form Gaming Forum
This forum in devoted to role-playing games—both discussion and online play. Supposedly it's for all genres, although there is a trend toward fantasy themes.

 Game Designers Forum
This forum is aimed at professional designers of noncomputer games, and is the place to go if you want to gossip about publishers. The future direction of gaming is a popular subject.

 Gaming Company Support
More than two dozen game publishers offer varying kinds of support here, and there's an invitation-only area for play-testing unreleased games.

 **GIX**
The Gaming Information Exchange is a general discussion forum covering most areas of games, especially role-playing games.

 PBM & Strategy
This forum is the contact point for people playing play-by-mail through AOL, especially chess and war games but also sport and Adventure games. Many are multi-player games with self-appointed game masters. There are also associated discussion forums and a Wargame Club.

 **RPG Forum**

This forum is a contact point for people playing fantasy role-playing games online through AOL, either by live chat, e-mail, or through a message board. The place is highly organized, with updated descriptions of joinable games-in-progress.

 **FOG**

This is the private forum for members of the Fellowship of On-Line Gamers, AOL's branch of the Role-Playing Game Association.

 PC Games

Talk here is specifically aimed at PC games, from war games to flight simulators to golf.

Neverwinter

An Advanced Dungeon & Dragons campaign called Neverwinter Nights is played here. It requires downloaded software and an investment of $14.95.

 **MasterWord**

You need downloaded software to play this Broderbund games, which involves the manipulation of vowels and consonants.

 RabbitJack's

At RabbitJack's Casino you can play various casino games online, including multi-player poker and slot machines. The money is virtual.

BIX

BIX does not offer online games per se, but there are several organized areas devoted to the online play of adventure and role-playing games, using the BIX chat facility, called CBIX. The conferences are for rules and schedule notices, plus general discussion, while the games themselves are played via CBIX at appointed times, usually weekly. There are also several general game and game-design conferences.

amiga.games

Anything concerning games and entertainment on the Amiga is fair game here, with topics added and removed as games come out to interest that flares and then wanes. There is also a library of shareware games.

chess

Professional chess and chess software is followed here, along with Chinese chess.

d.horizons

Distant Horizons is the point of contact for playing futuristic role-playing games on BIX. Aside from the organized games, you can trot out ad lib characters at any time in the conference's Nexus Bar & Grille. Any historical period is permissible there, but the bouncer will throw you out if you stoop to vulgarity, flaming, or virtual brawling.

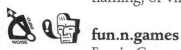

fun.n.games

Fun 'n Games is the point of contact for parlor-style games (such as Trivia and Crazy Eights) played at scheduled times via CBIX.

games

Rather than play games, here they talk about the designing, publishing, and marketing of games, and sometimes the playing of games. Anything from checkers to arcades are fair games. Be sure to check out the tense after-action reports in the war games section.

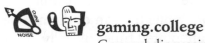

gaming.college

General discussions of role-playing games (rather than the playing of those games) takes place here. Dungeons & Dragons, space gaming, play-by-mail, and game designing are all covered.

the.realms

The Realms is the point of contact for playing online fantasy role-playing games on BIX, either live by CBIX or by e-mail. Most games use Advanced Dungeons & Dragons rules, which you're expected to already know, although there are sections for questions and general discussions.

CompuServe

In the CompuServe Entertainment/Games Forum (where you can go by typing "GO GAMES") you'll find some "basic" offerings like Hangman and Adventure games, apparently put there to whet your appetite for the "extended" offerings. Besides forums on game play and game design, there are actual games in the following forums:

Advent

This area includes fantasy, Adventure, and role-playing games, including British Legends (the original MUD), Island of Kesmai, a role-playing game forum, and a play-by-mail game forum.

Wargames

The war/simulation games here include Sniper, MegaWars I and II, and Air Traffic Controller.

TTgames

Parlor and trivia games are offered here. The derivation of the acronym is obscure.

MTMgames

MTM means modem-to-modem. You can hook together two commercial or shareware modem-to-modem games through Compu-Serve. This will be cheaper than long-distance (especially international) calling in many cases, and CompuServe also stresses the potential of anonymity, although why that's an advantage remains obscure. There's a listing of interested players and specific instructions for hooking up more than a dozen different games.

Entertainment Center

Here CompuServe offers several multiplayer games that use graphical interfaces on the PC, requiring EGA graphics or better. The interface software is available there for downloading. Included are chess, checkers, backgammon, and a space combat game called StarSprint.

Delphi

On Delphi there's an entry on the main menu labeled "Entertainment and Games." Choosing that gives you a list of games and forums, including:

Adventures

Here you are offered several Adventure-style includes, including Colossal Cave, Dungeon, Quest, and something in French.

Board/Logic Games

The possibilities here include single- and multi-player Othello, Super Wampus, and the opportunity to crash on the moon with Lunar Lander.

Modem-to-Modem

This facility lets you play a modem-to-modem games through GEnie, which should often be cheaper than long-distance calling to do the same thing. Instructions are available for pulling this trick with about a dozen commercial games, plus several shareware games that you can also download here.

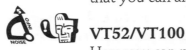

VT52/VT100

Here you can play games that rely on the cursor position commands used by VT52 or VT100 terminals, which are emulated by most PC telecommunications software packages.

GameSig

Reached through the Games and Clubs selection on the main menu, this forum covers talk, hints, reviews and product information on most kinds of games, including Adventure, arcade, sports, strategy, and war games, plus Dungeon & Dragons and board games. There is also live playing of adventure games and Stellar Conquest.

GEnie

There are several games-related round tables on GEnie, each with its own discussion bulletin board and library of files. These include:

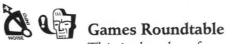

Games Roundtable

This is the place for general talk about games, with reviews, calls for opponents, after-action reports, and technical questions.

MPGames
GEnie offers more than a dozen multi-player games in this roundtable, with names like Cyberstrike, Hundred Years War, and Stellar Empire. There's an attached bulletin board for announcements and general talk.

JCGD
The *Journal of Computer Game Design* Roundtable, run by the professional journal, encourages the users to trade ideas on "how it ought to be done."

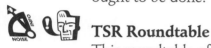
TSR Roundtable
This roundtable offers support for role-playing games from TSR, Inc., plus periodic online live playing through the associated chat channels.

Classic Games
The online games offered here include Adventure, Black Dragon, Castle Quest, Dor Sageth, and Showbiz Quiz.

BBS GAMING

While many BBSs carry games you can play remotely (usually called "doors"—see Chapter 14) the limited number of call-in lines makes village-sized MUDs out of the question. Therefore, most are Adventure-style games played solitaire.

On the other hand, BBSs are conducive to games played by e-mail, and you'll be hard put to find a BBS echo network without a conference devoted to chess and role-playing games.

CHATTING

Chatting is the Net's version of a conference phone call. Anybody can communicate with anyone else in the group simultaneously. You can "tune in" to a chat channel and talk/listen to everyone else on that channel. With CB radio or conference calling, it is as if you are talking in a dark room. But with online chatting, it's as if you can see a blackboard that invisible people are writing on, except that the blackboard can (usually) prevent the users from overwriting each other. Details vary, but chatting online offers advantages unheard of in conference calls:

☞ You can get the ID of the other people on the channel.
☞ You can devote specific channels to specific topics.
☞ You can (usually) pass private messages to another user.
☞ You can log the conversation.
☞ It's (sometimes) possible to disconnect abusive users.

The drawback about chatting is that it has to take place inside one network, due to its real-time nature. While e-mail can travel from one network to another, this is not commonly done with chatting (although, doubtless, it could be rigged). In this chapter we'll focus on the Internet chat facility, since it's the most visible. But nearly any other system will also have some kind of chat facility, usually much less elaborate, each with its own wrinkles.

INTERNET CHATTING

The chat facility on the Internet is called IRC, for Internet Relay Chat. You login to an Internet server that supports IRC, perform whatever commands it expects, and get connected to the IRC server. It uses the Internet to hook itself to all other IRC servers, so that you can converse with any other IRC chat user on earth. Usually your input is at the bottom of the line, and incoming text takes up the rest of the screen, so your typing does not collide with that of others.

IRC became famous during the Persian Gulf War when cruise missile attacks and other events were monitored in real time by users around the globe huddled in single channels. During the 1993 coup attempt against Boris Yeltsin in Russia, IRC users in Moscow were giving live accounts of what they were seeing, and IRC has also been a source of information during various natural calamities in California.

IRC is used from more than sixty countries at this writing. The predominant language remains English. (English of a sort, anyway—no one seems to remember how to spell "meant," for instance.) Many conversations are carried out in other languages, however, and if a channel is named after a German university town the conversation there is probably in German.

 ## Saving Face:

Now commit the following jargon to your wetware before proceeding:

Nick—Your online nickname, the name the system refers to you as.

Bot—Intelligence added to your connection to automate responses—a practice widely damned (see below).

Luser—a chat user. Don't take it personally.

@—A channel operator.

Alias—An abbreviation of a command that can substitute for the full command word.

Channel—A self-contained gathering place where a group conversation is held. IRC channels have names, either several digits, or an alphanumeric string preceded by a + or a #. The name is usually followed by a string that indicates the intended subject of the channel—which may or not be the subject actually under discussion when you join.

Channel Operator—The person who has the power to change the mode settings of a channel, or eject users. There can be more than one per channel.

Channel 0—The null or "limbo" channel that you are in by default. Everything said on this channel is lost. It's a place to park when you don't want to converse but don't want to leave IRC.

EU-Opers—European version of Twilight_Zone.

IRC Operator—Operator at an IRC server site, with much more power than a channel operator.

Private Channels—Those channels whose names are shown as "Prv" in the /NAMES and /LIST listings, preventing those who don't already know the name from joining. Public channels can be turned into private ones using the /MODE command. Those with numeric names of 1000 or higher are private by default.

Public Channels—Channels with numeric names between 1 and 999, and those whose names have the + or # prefix. Anyone can see the channel using the /NAMES or /LIST command, and anyone can join.

Secret Channels—Channels with numeric names lower than zero. Secret channels do not show up in the /NAMES or /LIST listings, and the users are not counted by the /LUSERS command. A public channel can be turned secret with the /MODE command.

Twilight_Zone—channel habituated by IRC site operators.

Wall—A message sent to everyone on IRC.

Wallop—A message sent to IRC system operators.

At any given moment, you're likely to find something over twelve hundred channels in existence, with more than three thousand users, of whom up to a third will be in private channels. (This doesn't count the secret ones.)

At any moment there is usually a channel called #Hottub and one called #initgame that you can join and see immediate action. The users in #Hottub are pretending they are lounging in a communal hot tub, while #initgame is the home of a non-stop game of initials. As indicated, IRC operators are usually joined to #Twilight_Zone, or, if they are in Europe, #EU-Opers, so you can go there with questions, complaints, or demands that someone be /KILLed immediately.

At this writing, IRC is clogged and painfully slow in the afternoons and evenings, while free-flowing at night and morning (as clocked in North America.) Net-lags can be several seconds long, and there are long moments when the system dies altogether. An alternate Internet chat network, called Undernet, has been set up in response. Otherwise, close study of the IRC user commands are your best bet for happy Internet chatting.

IRC Commands

All IRCII commands (assuming you're connected through the commonly found IRCII server software) begin with a "/" character. Anything that begins otherwise is assumed to be a message to the channel at large, or to the person you are currently QUERYing.

```
/list
***       Channel: Users  Topic
***       Private:    1
***         #edo:     3   we are hungry for LOVE
***      #deutsch:    1   Hier spricht man Deutsch..
***       #lemurs:    1   Furry critters with BIG eyes. Whooo!
***       #emacs:     1   For fans of big hairy editors.
*** #Manhattan:       1   Bike to Work Week!
***      #Werner0:    3   You only live twice
*** #neighbour*       1   gorgeous >>>>>>>>>>>>>>>>>>>>>>>>>
***      #halley:     2   Once bitten, twice shy...
***      #sweden:    10   SWEDISH OR ENGLISH *ONLY* ON THIS CHANNEL-PLEASE RESPECT THAT!
***    #SE-Opers:     1   Swedish Users help Channel
***     #kleenex:     1   A-A-A-CHOOOOOO!
***        #ash:      1   Are you asleep? No. Dead. Leave the flowers and get out.
***      #Hotsex:    18   synched ?
***      #ZAGREB:     2   Zagreb, the capitol of Croatia^G^G
***#^[$B$o$;$@*        1
***      #bipbip:     1   Ze Channel Of Me Tout Seul ... And Of The Other ... Too
***    #altmusic:     3   THE ALTERNATIVE MUSIC CHANNEL
*** #Demon's_L*       1   What evil lies in the hearts of Men? The DemoN knows!
***      #anime!:     4   Lonely Otaku starved for attention
***       #USPN:      1   Discuss the Utterly Deeper Meaning of Life With Me
***        #box:      4   The imagery is in the box...
***      #koala:      7   Koala Project, Bull research - private work channel
***       #essi:      4   Tous des pedes sur ce channel !
***     #Azatoth:     2   Azatoth's hiding place.
***    #topmodel:     1   TSATSARES
***     #Sverige:     2   Vi skulle ha behallit Norge !! Norrmannen klarar sig
                          inte utan sverige
***        #ms1:      3   We're playing a cool cardgame!
***      #zivot:      6   Uz iba 45 min do session   (A)
***    #Catholic:     2   THE FAMILY, CELL OF CHRISTENDOM
***    #Phalange:     1   Monarchy Yes! Judeo-Masonic Democracy No!
***     #amigaFr:     7   aujourd'hui est un jour de netsplits
***     #polonia:     6   Uwaga! Nikt na #polonia nie ma nic wspolnego z obora na #polska
***      #lesbos:     1   Your first Lover: remember or forget?????????
```

**This is about 5 percent of the IRC channels shown one morning by the
/LIST command. Most channels did not show a topic, and here I
included most of the ones that did, plus other channels that did not
but had evocative names. Note that the languages include English,
Swedish, Polish, French, German, Greek, and Spanish, and the text with
the dollar signs and uppercase letters is encoded Japanese. Sex, sports,
ranting, and idle gossip remain favorite pastimes online as well as off.**

If you can't remember the spelling of a command, type /
and the first few letters, and then press the ESC key twice.
You'll get a list of commands that start with those letters.

Note that while all the commands that follow are shown
uppercase, that is just to set them apart. IRC commands (and
their abbreviated aliases) are actually case-insensitive, and so
can just as easily be given in lowercase (which, if you're
used to struggling with Unix, is a relief).

☞ /ADMIN xxxx   Give administrative details about
the server with name xxxx—usually the e-mail
address of the administrator. If no name is given, you
get details about your own server.

☞ /AWAY xxxx   This tells the server that you have
stepped away and to reply with the message xxxx to
anyone who sends you a message in the meantime.
Inputting /AWAY without a message tells the server
that you are now back from the bathroom.

☞ /BYE   Same as /QUIT, /EXIT, or /SIGNOFF.

☞ /CHANNEL   Same as /JOIN.

☞ /DATE   Same as /TIME.

☞ /EXIT   Same as /BYE, /SIGNOFF, or /QUIT.

☞ /HELP xxxx   Calls up a help screen on topic xxxx.
When in doubt, try /HELP HELP.

☞ /IGNORE xxxx –T   Suppresses input of type T from
the user with the nick xxxx. The input type can
include MSGs, NOTICEs, PUBLIC messages,
INVITEs, ALL, or NONE. If you suspect the miscre-
ant will sneakily change nicks, you can use a full user
name (a user@hostsite name) for xxxx. Using –
(minus sign) instead of the + prefix removes a previous /IGNORE setting.

☞ /INVITE xxxx yyyy   Invites users with nick xxxx to
join you on channel yyyy. If you don't include yyyy,
your current channel is the default. The recipient will
get a screen message saying something like "lwood
invites you to channel yyyy."

☞ /JOIN xxxx   Changes your current channel to one with the name xxxx, as shown by the /NAMES or /LIST command, complete with the + or # prefix. A message is displayed on the channel that you have joined. If channel xxxx does not already exist, it is created and (congratulations!) you are now the moderator, with /KICK privileges, etc. Your name will appear with an @ in front of it, automatically making you the enemy of certain lusers. /JOIN with no parameters gets you the name of your current channel.

☞ /JOIN –INVITE   Joins you to the channel to which you were last invited.

☞ /JOIN–NICK xxxx   Join whatever channel that the person with the nick xxxx is on.

☞ /KICK xxxx yyyy   Now we're getting to the fun stuff. This command kicks the user with nick yyyy off channel xxxx. You have to be a channel operator before you can /KICK.

☞ /KILL   A procedure available to IRC site operators (not channel operators) to purge berserk bots and/or temporarily remove offensive users from IRC. (The user can thereafter return, hopefully chastened by the experience.) It is not supposed to be used to settle spats between channel operators.

☞ /LEAVE xxxx   Causes you to leave the channel with the name xxxx. You can also do this with /JOIN 0.

☞ /LINKS   Shows all of the servers currently connected to the Internet chat network. If a server name is specified (you can use wildcard characters) /LINKS will show any server names that match.

☞ /LIST   Lists all current IRC channels, their topics, and number of users.

☞ /LUSERS   Gives you the number of users, servers, and operators online with IRC at that moment.

☞ /MODE xxxx +m p   Changes the mode settings of the channel, where xxxx is the channel name, m is the mode setting character, and p is any parameter you need (usually a nick). You have to be a channel operator to use /MODE, meaning you set up the channel, or were given channel operator status by the person who did or his or her heirs. Using a – (minus sign) instead of a + removes a previously set condition. Possible mode settings include:

☞ m—Moderated channel, meaning only the channel operators can speak

☞ s—Makes channel secret

☞ p—Makes channel private

☞ l xxxx—Limits the number of users in the channel to xxxx

☞ t—Only the channel operators can now change the topic

☞ o xxxx—Makes the user with the nick xxxx a channel operator

☞ i—You can join only after an /INVITE from someone on the channel

☞ n—The /MESSAGE feature is disabled in this channel

☞ b xxxx—Bans the user with nick xxxx from the channel

☞ /MOTD xxxx   Get the message of the day from the server with the name xxxx. The default is your own server. It may be anything from a cheery greeting to a notice that your site and all its users have been banned en masse from all IRC use because of their notoriously abusive behavior.

☞ /MSG xxxx yyyy   Send the message yyyy to the person using the nick xxxx. No one else on the channel will be able to see it. You can usually use the alias /M. The message will appear on the recipient's terminal preceded by your nick. Using a comma instead of xxxx means "to the last person who sent me a message" and is used to reply to messages. Using a period instead of xxxx means "to the same person to whom I sent the last message," and it used to continue a private conversation.

☞ /NAMES   Shows the nicknames of all users on each channel. Since the list might be lengthy, you can say

/NAMES –MIN 20 to see only channels with twenty users or more.

☞ /NICK name Changes your nick to "name." The nick can be no longer than nine letters. Your default nick is the same as your logon name, but the server will not let you on if someone else is using that as a nick at the moment. You can register your nick, as described later.

☞ /NOTICE xxxx yyyy Sends a private message to the person with nick xxxx. You can include a channel name after the nick. /NOTICE differs from /MSG in that no automated responses will be generated. Used by bots.

☞ /QUERY xxxx After using this command, all text you thereafter type will be sent as a private message to the person with nick xxxx. This is so you can carry on a private conversation without resorting to the /MSG command each time. Using /QUERY by itself ends the private connection.

☞ /QUIT Same as /BYE, /SIGNOFF, or /EXIT.

☞ /SIGNOFF Same as /EXIT, /QUIT, or /BYE.

☞ /TIME xxxx Displays the local date and time on the server with the name xxxx. The default is your server. You can use wildcards—*.de should get the times on all servers in Germany.

☞ /TOPIC xxxx Changes the topic for your current channel—as it appears when using /LIST, etc.—to the string xxxx.

☞ /USERS Gives you a list of the users currently logged on your server.

☞ /WHO xxxx Lists users in channel xxxx. If no channel is given, the default is your own channel.

☞ /WHOIS xxxx Displays information about the user with nick xxxx, including what channel he or she is on.

☞ /WHOWAS xxxx Displays information about the user who last used the nick xxxx, even if he or she has left IRC or changed nicks.

Results of using

the /LUSER com-

mand on IRC,

showing the

number of users

and conferences

then online.

```
/lusers
*** There are 2780 users and 1382 invisible on 117 servers
*** There are 95 operator(s) online
*** There have been 1263 channels formed
*** I have 46 clients and 1 servers/list
```

This list only scratches the surface—IRC server software includes a respectable programming language, which some people use to create "bots," (discussed later in this chapter). But, obviously, when you get on, you might want to do /LIST to see what channels are available, or perhaps /LIST –min20 to see the ones with the most users. Then you would use /JOIN to enter one.

The Good, The Bad, The Bots

Bots (from "robots") are software programs pretending to be IRC users. The fancier IRC commands (see the IRC Primer, mentioned later) can be used to do things like respond automatically to certain messages or give channel operator status to someone. A nick with such software—and no user—behind it is a bot. (Other Unix programming facilities, such as C and perl, can also be used to make bots.)

Bots trigger odd emotions—the cognoscenti will begin a paragraph denouncing the use of bots and end it with a description of their pet bot. But with the spectacle of hordes of bots chirping hello at each other, passing around operator status like a football, cloning themselves into infinity, and /KICKing everything in sight, many sites have begun to ban all bots. Some go so far as to threaten to ban all users from any site where a clone bot originated.

Should you nevertheless want to proceed with bot tinkering, keep these rules in mind:

☞ Build in some way to kill the bot with a message or notice.

☞ Use a nick for it that indicates its bot status: MyBot, HelpBot, Server01, etc.

☞ Have it use notices, not messages, since the results are more predictable.

☞ Never have it send channel-wide messages.

☞ Go easy on the /MODE commands.

☞ Make sure someone else can't get at your system files by taking over the bot.

NickServ

If you have a favorite nick, and logon to IRC one morning to find someone else is using it, you have no recourse except to politely ask them for it back. (IRC operators will not /KILL over nick ownership.)

To ease this problem, there is a sort of super-bot, located in Germany, called NickServ. If you register your nick with NickServ, it will send a warning to anyone else who signs on with your nick. The registration expires if you don't use IRC for ten weeks.

To register, you send a message to NickServ while online on IRC. Send:

`/MSG NickServ@service.de register ppp eee aaa`

In this case, ppp is your NickServ password, which you will need if, in the future, you want to change your registration; eee is your e-mail address, and aaa is "additional information"—generally, your real name. Do not use your logon password as your NickServ password. And keep in mind that the NickServ password is case-sensitive—Smith and smith are different passwords.

To query NickServ about a registered nick, you should send:

`/MSG NickServ@service.de whois xxxx`

where xxxx is the nick you are interested in.

Check This Out:

If you have channel operator status, do not share it on a whim. People have been known to take over channels in lightning coups by sweet-talking themselves into channel operator status and then /KICKing out all doubtful parties (including the original channel operator), then issuing "/MODE +ib *!*@*" to set the channel to invite-only and ban all nonjoined users everywhere. Those /KICKed cannot get back in. But they can always set up a new channel, so the point of this stunt remains elusive.

The Undernet

The ever-more-clogged condition of IRC has led (besides to bickering) to the formation of additional, separate networks, of which the chief is the Undernet. The operators all know each other, and etiquette by the users is enforced. There are about thirty servers, and about 5 percent of the users you see on the main IRC.

If your access provider does not offer a choice of IRC chat networks, you can reach Undernet from the main IRC network by using, after you're online in the usual way, the /SERVER command. That connects you to another server, and if you select a server that's on the Undernet, suddenly you're chatting on the Undernet. All the same IRC commands apply, except that things should now run smoother. The protocol for using /SERVER is:

```
/SERVER servername port#
```

However, you need to give the port number only if it is listed as part of the server address. Other than that, you should try to use the nearest Undernet server. Undernet server names in North America include:

- ☞ Montreal.QU.CA.undernet.org 6667
- ☞ Pasadena.CA.US.undernet.org 6667
- ☞ Norman.OK.US.undernet.org 6667
- ☞ Boston.MA.US.undernet.org 6667
- ☞ Albany.NY.US.undernet.org 6667
- ☞ Manhattan.KS.US.undernet.org 6667
- ☞ Milwaukee.WI.US.undernet.org 6667
- ☞ Ames.IA.US.undernet.org 6667
- ☞ StGeorge.UT.US.undernet.org 6667
- ☞ Tampa.FL.US.undernet.org 6667
- ☞ Davis.CA.US.undernet.org 6667
- ☞ Puebla.MX.undernet.org 6666

A fuller, updated list can be found in the undernet-faq file, archived with the alt.irc.questions FAQ in the usual FAQ archives, such as rtfm.mit.edu.

Saving Face:

We covered the negative aspects of online behavior in Chapter 1, but there are other things specific to chatting you should avoid:

No jingoism—Speak the language of that channel. Otherwise, find another channel. If the channel has a group of Finns speaking Finnish, they are not going to switch to English just because you entered the room. The topic may give you an indication, before entering, what language is being used.

No glad-handing—One hello upon entering a channel is sufficient. The others will not think you rude for not greeting them personally by name. If you must, use /MSG. Meanwhile, using a bot to greet everyone automatically is very poor form.

Easy on the beeping—Sending Ctrl-G causes the terminals of the other users to beep. Perhaps I shouldn't have told you that.

Harassment—Dumping big file blocks into chat channels will get you /KICKed and perhaps even /KILLed, as will any other purposefully annoying behavior.

Handle with care—Do not do anything that would overload or otherwise reduce the functionality of IRC.

IRC Newsgroups

Not only do people chat on the Internet, they talk about chatting in Usenet newsgroups. If you're serious about IRC chatting, you'll probably want to check out the action here as well.

Check This Out:

All responses from NickServ should be prefixed with -service.de- except in cases where you're sitting at certain graphics server terminals, in which case the response will be in an information window. Hackers have been able to get account information by posing as NickServ.

Users at English-speaking terminals may occasionally be mystified by gibberish strings of the {}[]/| characters. This is because there are a lot of Scandinavian users on the Net who use alphabetical characters foreign to American equipment. (IRC is supposed to support the Latin-1 ISO alphabet, but there is no guarantee your terminal can display all its characters.) For instance, it turns out that [, { represents Ä,], } represents Å, and \, | represents Ö or Ø. Meanwhile, Japanese users employ ANSI escape code sequences to transmit kanji symbols. The strings include a lot of { and $ symbols and upper-case letters, and there is no simple translation.

alt.irc

Anyone who doesn't like his or her server comes here to vent: "It needs to spend two hours with me and a chain saw." Anyone resenting the way they were /KICKed by the channel operator for using one or more (many more, usually) naughty words comes here to complain, to complain about the people who complained about the original complaint, and to wage unending flame wars with those who complained about the anticomplaints complaint: "I know where you live and I know your name." Sermons against Net-sex, bot use, and bot abuse also show up here: "I bury the chassis of sexually molested bots under my bed." It's fortunate this newsgroup exists, lest these troubled people resort to kicking puppies or something.

alt.irc.ircii

This newsgroup is much calmer, being devoted to technical questions concerning version 2 of the IRC server software. Being only human, the users still grumble about "every newbie wanting a bot." Best comment: "If you want to establish voice contact, please yell into the keyboard."

alt.irc.questions

Icy calm reigns here, the users having achieved catharsis in alt.irc. Instead, they trade questions and answers about site listings, access problems, and software updates.

Internet Access Information: An IRC primer is available via anonymous ftp at various sites, including: **nic.funet.fi** in the /pub/unix/irc/docs/ directory; **cs.bu.edu** in the /irc/support/ directory; and **coombs.anu.edu.au** in the /pub/irc/docs/ directory.

OTHER CHAT NODES ON THE NET

All the commercial services have some kind of chat facility, usually with "chat rooms" devoted to each conference, forum, or roundtable, plus a system-wide one. The conference chat rooms will sometimes have celebrities as invited guests at scheduled times, so that anyone can logon for a moderated discussion with them. Some groups hold meetings online via chat.

On BBSs, the situation is more restrictive since they have fewer dial-in lines—rarely more than a couple dozen. On smaller boards the chat line may only be suitable for signaling the sysop—although that can be invaluable.

CHATTING

NETSEX

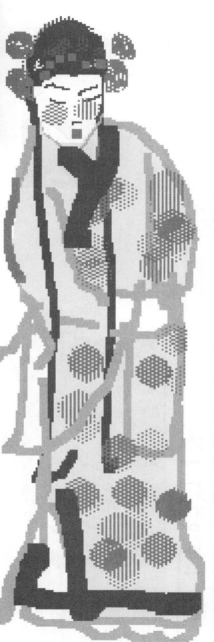

It's rumored that what originally launched the videocassette industry was not the availability of Hollywood movies. Huh-uh. Hollywood jumped in after the waters had been tested by filmmakers of, shall we say, nonmainstream reputations, peddling, y'know, porno flicks. Likewise, in the Old West, it was the social outcasts who showed up first, to be chewed on by Indians and coyotes. After they demonstrated a locality's viability, some sheriff cleaned up the town, school boards were set up, sewers dug, and the place settled into banality.

So it should be no surprise that some of the initial pioneers of cyberspace devoted quite a bit of attention to sex. Once cyberspace becomes an accepted part of the body politic, we may expect eruptions from prudes and self-designated authorities announcing that the place needs cleaning up. (In fact, there are already rumblings in that direction.) But for now, the Net remains a place where you can find friendly solace on those long, dark nights.

On the Net you can either talk or look at pictures (although creative Net-heads blur the barriers by talking about pictures). The pictures involve the usual themes of people who managed to misplace their clothes and/or be overcome with passion just before a photographer happened along. The talk runs from postings of amateur erotic fiction and poetry to e-mail postings where people talk about what turns them on.

Life in the raw is especially evident on the Internet, where there is no central authority to take offense when the users admit that sex exists. Some BBSs and BBS echo networks exist only to explore the subject. The commercial networks are more circumspect, not wishing to run afoul of any Bible Belt sheriffs or be accused of corrupting little Johnny with naughty pictures. Yet the subject manages to surface even there.

Saving Face:

Before we go on, there's the usual jargon you'll need to absorb—in this case, code words used by Net insiders:

Adult—Contains sexually explicit material not suitable/legal for exposure to minors.

Boink—Face-to-face gathering of soc.singles denizens.

LJBF—Let's just be friends. (You'll hear it a lot—sorry. Increasingly used as a verb, too.)

LO—Lust/love object.

MOTAS—Members of the appropriate sex (you decide).

MOTOS—Members of the opposite sex.

MOTSS—Members of the same sex.

NG—Nice Guy/Gal.

NIFOC—Nude In Front Of Computer. (It happens.)

PDA—Public Display of Affection.

POSSLQ—Person of Opposite Sex, Same Living Quarters.

RI—Romantic Interest.

RL—Real Life.

RP—Romantic Partner.

SNAG—Sensitive New-Age Guy.

SO—Significant Other (e.g., boyfriend, girlfriend, spouse, betrothed).

Check This Out:

As with any part of the Net, you should never give someone your phone number, address, social security number, password, dog's name, or anything else that would help him or her find you. Don't mention it while chatting, and don't send it in e-mail.

Multicultural sensitivity! Oriental couple found on the Internet.

TL&EH—True Love & Eternal Happiness (opposite of RL).

WFYITBWNBLJO—Waiting For You In The Bathtub Wearing Nothing But Lime Jell-O. (It happens. The recurrence of the lime flavor remains a mystery.)

THE INTERNET

In the Light Breathing section we'll look at R-rated hangouts on the Internet. In Heavy Breathing we'll take a tour of the Internet's hardcore X-rated hangouts. You'll get a good

NETSEX

215

Check This Out:

In case there was any doubt in your mind: Some of the material covered here is *not politically correct.* Some may not even be suitable for minors. My encapsulations of it, however, are multiculturally sensitive and suitable for all audiences (we'll say).

idea of what's out there for the mainstream, and what's out there for the, well, broader-minded. And some sources of erotica will be revealed to you. Then we'll look at what's available on the commercial services and in the BBS world.

Light Breathing

Let's start with the relatively tame stuff. (No sense in burning out early.)

soc.singles

How do you meet women in supermarkets? How do you meet anyone in big cities? What do you hate most about the opposite sex? Are women intimidated by tall men? The point in this very busy newsgroup is not to arrive at an answer, but to keep talking about the question. The posting of personal ads, incidentally, is verboten.

alt.hi.are.you.cute

The protocol here is to go online, announce that you're cute, and flirt with others who agree with you (on whatever basis, since they can't see you). The participants seem to like it. Depending on where you're coming from, this is either the most innocuous place in cyberspace or the most unendurable.

alt.sex.movies

Here you'll see questions like: Who was Divine? What was Linda Lovelace's first video? How do I get hold of certain videos? What ever happened to the Italian Stallion? You know that one scene in *Debbie Does Dallas*, well, do you think they're really doing it? Basically, this is like any other movie discussion forum, except for the ongoing sexual themes.

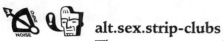

alt.sex.strip-clubs

The quest never ends: Are there girlie clubs in Denver? How about in Toledo? No conurbation on the planet goes unexamined, and users often complain about sporadic police raids. Touchingly, you also see people asking etiquette questions before making their first club trip.

alt.polyamory

Intense discussions rage here as the participants attempt to reinvent the whole birds and bees phenomena from first principles. Amid all the concern about the acceptance of triple relationships and the definition of marriage, there's little evidence that anybody ever gets around to consummating anything.

alt.amazon-women.admirers

If you want to be a lady bodybuilder, this is the place. If you want to talk to lady bodybuilders, or find binary pictures of them, ditto. If you're worried about the progress or effects of your bodybuilding hobby, you can find support here. But first, consider: It may not be your muscles that are intimidating your boyfriend. It may be the fact that you use the Internet and he doesn't.

Amazons International

Physically and psychologically strong, assertive women—in fiction, fact, art, and literature—are the honored subjects of this mail list. Female athletics are also popular. Send your request to **amazons-request@math. uio.no**.

Check This Out:

Some of these newsgroups (you'll probably be able to guess which ones) contain anonymous postings, made through an anonymous reposting service called anon.penet.fi. Replies made to anonymous postings will also end up being anonymous. To find out more about the anon service, send e-mail asking for help to **help@ anon.penet.fi**.

HEAVY BREATHING

They say that, at some point in the training of a Jesuit, he is locked alone in a room full of pornography, lest in the real world his strength ever be compromised by ignorance. Along those lines, the following Net resources can certainly be recommended. However, such lessons are likely to be harder and harder to come by in the future, as the trend (especially, lately, in Canada) is to not carry the alt.sex hierarchy at all. Here's some of the things you could be missing.

alt.sex

What you have here is a locker room without the lockers—without the room, even. Does it matter how big it is? What are the advantages/disadvantages of doing it a certain way? If you think people shouldn't be talking about such things online, then you're in the minority because this is one of the busiest places on the Internet.

rec.arts.erotica

Here people post their erotic fiction and verse. Anything goes—but no pictures. Some of the writers seem to be trying to show that you can write erotica without mentioning sex. Where can this trend end?

alt.sex.wizards

People here frenziedly trade sex manual material. As for the information itself, members of the target audience of this book will find little they didn't already know.

triples

If you're into "polyfidelity," this is the mail list for you. Hint: They're not talking about stereo equipment. Send your request to **triples-request@hal.com**.

alt.sex.stories

People write sex stories and post them here, with appropriate descriptive notes in the subject header (male/female, domination, etc.). And they post requests for repostings, and questions about ongoing stories, and more. Such activity is doubtless therapeutic to somebody—a lot of somebodies, since this is a very busy newsgroup.

alt.sex.bondage

Looking for a new way to keep those endorphins whipped up, eh? Here they trade information about where to find the necessary equipment, and post after-action reports (real or imagined). Personal ads, however, are supposed to go in the next newsgroup.

alt.sex.wanted

Surely you can predict what this newsgroup is about from the title? (Actually, a lot of what goes on here is just banter, but there are some dead-serious personal ads.)

alt.personals.bondage

"Midwest Master Seeks Sensuous Submissive." "Dominant female in NJ seeks submissive." "I'm an aggressive master and am looking for the right submissive female to dominate totally via e-mail." Candy-and-flowers romance appears to be out of the question.

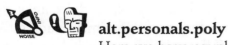

alt.personals.poly

Here we have couples seeking couples, or at least that special third person. Since the people here describe themselves by weight and height, and indicate whether they want someone who smokes or not, this must be a serious place.

alt.sex.masturbation
There's not much two-way discussion here, just people posting random comments that rarely draw replies. Not surprising, considering the subject.

alt.sex.exhibitionism
Some like to watch. Some like to be watched. There are more of the former, judging from the traffic here. Actually, the place tends toward personal ads, plus after-action reports of doing it on trains and planes, where the thrill is to risk being seen, evidently.

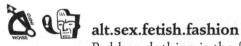

alt.sex.fetish.fashion
Rubber clothing is the focus here: where to get it, how to wear it, how to alter it, how to lubricate it (¿), and what's fashionable. Yes, there are fashion trends to watch out for. They also post graphics—of clothes, you understand, not people.

alt.sex.fetish.feet
The word *foot* by itself can drive some people batty, and if you're one of them, you'd better approach this newsgroup with caution. Yes, there are graphics here of enticing starlets with their shoes brazenly exposed. Excitement reverberates here every time a leading lady takes off her shoes in a movie. And if she then starts painting her toenails for the camera . . . well, let's not get into it.

Example of an encoded picture found in the alt.sex.fetish.hair newsgroup.

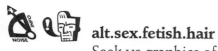 **alt.sex.fetish.hair**
Seek ye graphics of young ladies with luxuriant hair? Yes? Really? No kidding, huh? Well, anyway, here it is.

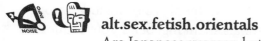 **alt.sex.fetish.orientals**
Are Japanese women better? Do Asian men prefer white women, and if so, why? No answers are forthcoming, but discussing such questions is very important to the people here. Beyond that, you'll see personal ads whose contents you can probably predict in advance.

 alt.sex.fetish.watersports
Careful study leads me to believe that these people are not talking about waterskiing. You'll find the usual personal ads and questions about techniques. Plus there's an ongo-

NETSEX

ing search for movie coverage of the conference's point of interest (with much less success than the similar quest of the alt.sex.fetish.feet people).

alt.sex.spanking

Aside from some personal ads, you see a lot of memoirs of pain and humiliation in early life posted here. That some of this is outright fiction was a relief to me.

alt.personals.spanking

"Seeking smart, interesting, SWF for spanking" is the theme here. The dearth of flaming in this newsgroup and in alt.sex.spanking is amazing, but perhaps predictable—they know the consequences.

Spanking

The subscribers of this mail list send in articles, letters, stories, and memoirs of and about spanking. These are collected and sent out weekly. Material is also included from alt.personals.spanking. Send your request to **an5548@anon.penet.fi**.

alt.sex.bestiality

There is a lot of general sex talk and general political ranting here, evidently by people who assume that, in this newsgroup, they're safe from pursuit. As for animal sex partners, yes, there is some mention of that, plus short fiction on the subject. There's also an ongoing debate on whether to use the term *bestiality* or *zoophilia*, although the alt.sex.zoophilia newsgroup appears to be bogus.

Exploring Otherness

In the previous material in this chapter, readers might have noticed an underlying assumption that the people involved were of the opposite sex. In the real world this is not always the case, and that fact is reflected online as well. Below are some Net resources that apply.

 ## Saving Face:

The code words mentioned previously still apply. Plus:

GLB—Gay, Lesbian, Bisexual.

Lambda—The Greek letter (or, in printed material, the letter itself) denoting some GLB thing.

Gay—Still used, but appears to be inching toward obsolescence.

 alt.sex.homosexual
Here you can find anything connected with the lifestyle: hot clubs, where to find paraphernalia, arguments over whether AIDS is a gay disease or just a disease, discussion about whether some of the characters in *The Simpsons* animated cartoon series have homosexual overtones, media coverage of the lifestyle, the movie *Philadelphia*, and installments of amateur fiction. There are also announcements of social events: "South Asian Lesbian and Gay Association Social in NYC," for instance. Doubtless attracted by the newsgroup's name, homophobes also drop by with intelligent, touching messages like "Die Homos Die!"

 alt.homosexual
This group is substantially identical to alt.sex.homosexual (well, there may be a trifle

more baiting) and evidently exists for the benefit of those whose sites have shut out the alt.sex hierarchy.

soc.motss

This newsgroup (discounting the inflated totals of the binaries hierarchy) is one of the busiest newsgroups I have found. In stark contrast with alt.sex.homosexual and alt.homosexual, there is little evidence of raids by gay-bashers and homophobes—the use of the code-word title (Members Of The Same Sex) is apparently enough to confound potential perpetrators. So, left to themselves, you see the alternate lifestylers here talking about their inner concerns: How to act at a wedding where you're uncomfortable. How to cook lobster. How to rate wines. How to wear earrings. Etc. As for physical sex, a man from Mars reading this forum might never guess there was such a thing.

alt.sex.motss

The situation here is pretty much like that of soc.motss, except it's less busy, there is more genital involvement, and there are a lot of questions about where to find "action." More questions than answers, in fact.

alt.politics.homosexuality

The various anti-gay and anti-anti-gay initiatives that have risen and died in various municipalities around the United States are agonized over in this newsgroup. Plus there's talk concerning the legality of gay marriages, the place of homosexuals in Christianity, police treatment of gays in various locales, the level of gay-bashing in various locales, and online wrangling with gay-bashers. Plus there are announcements of GLB social events in various urban areas.

Mail.alternates
This mail list is intended for those advocating an "open" (meaning, in this case, bisexual) lifestyle. Send your request to **alternates-request@ns1.rutgers.edu**.

Mail.bears
Bears, in this instance, are large, bearded homosexuals. Send your request to **bears-request@spdcc.com**.

qn
QN stands for Queer Nation, a gay rights group. Send your request for this mail list to **qn-request@queernet.org**.

dont-tell
This mail list is concerned about the societal implications of the U.S. Army's don't-ask, don't-tell policy concerning homosexuality. Send your request to **dont-tell-request@ choice.princeton.edu**.

alt.transgendered
There is a lot of talk about hormone therapy, and some (less than you'd expect) about plastic surgery. Plus there's an ongoing search for cross-dressing episodes in the media. Otherwise, you see the usual wrestling over gay issues.

alt.personals.bi
There's a little bit of everything here, from those seeking explicitly described sexual contact with explicitly described individuals, to people seeking platonic relationships with

members of the opposite sex. "Yo Bi M in NY looking to meet of similar age" is pretty much the average.

Pictures

If you grow tired of mere talk, there are other secret passages to travel on the Net. One of the largest is alt.binaries.pictures.erotica hierarchy.

alt.binaries.pictures.erotica

Based on raw traffic, this is the busiest newsgroup in Usenet that I have come across, beating any others by at least 50 percent. However, figures are deceptive, since many of the binaries posted here run across several consecutive messages—five to ten for most color shots, with .AVI files running into dozens. Most have elementary headers: "full-figured blond," or simply the name of the model/actress/whatever. Plus there's constant background noise from people denouncing each other for posting dirty pictures, for being prudes, for going to hell, for being so bigoted as to tell people they are going to hell, and so on. All such talk is supposed to be restricted to alt.binaries.pictures.erotica.d, but the rule is honored largely in the breach.

alt.binaries.pictures.erotica.d

This place, too, is pretty busy, with constant requests for repostings of pictures that appeared in alt.binaries.pictures.erotica (after they screwed up the uudecoding procedure) or requests for pictures of a certain genre, or of a certain comely young celebrity. (Incidentally, anytime a newsgroup ends in .d, that means its is intended for discussions, rather than binary postings.)

Pinup of Connie Sellecca, found on the Internet.

alt.binaries.pictures.erotica.blondes
As the name implies, here you'll find pictures of attractive people (usually female) with light-colored hair. This newsgroup has mini-

mal traffic compared to alt.binaries.pictures.erotica, and is not carried by many sites.

alt.binaries.pictures.erotica.female
As the name implies, there are encoded binaries here of young ladies caught in the act of dressing, etc. This is another newsgroup that is not widely carried.

alt.binaries.pictures.erotica.male
At last! Material aimed at heterosexual women! Or, on second look, maybe not. Some of these photos are explicit in a way that pictures of women just can't be. This is another newsgroup that is not widely carried.

alt.binaries.pictures.erotica.orientals
Here you can find pictures of Asian ladies who neglected to get dressed that morning. Plus there are the usual requests for repostings, and talk about who is prettier than whom. This newsgroup is likewise not widely available.

alt.binaries.pictures.supermodels
Tame stuff compared to the others—most of the traffic, incidentally, is actresses rather than models.

Meanwhile, you'll run across snide comments from observers about "gigabytes of copyright violations." In practice, the participants show no concern about copyright. There are several reasons:

☞ You'd be crazy to claim ownership of some of these pictures.

☞ Careful study shows that many come from erotic-oriented BBSs on the West Coast and can be consid-

Actress Christina Applegate, a pinup found on the Internet.

ered publicity for them (sorry, that phone number in the picture belongs to a BBS, not the girl).

☞ Others are movie stills and can be considered promotional material.

☞ The files are only online for a limited period and would be gone by the time someone decided to take legal action.

COMMERCIAL SERVICES

Outwardly, the commercial services act as if certain things did not exist. But if you look around and maybe pry under a few rocks, you will usually find that they have made concessions to the real world. Here we'll examine some of those brushes with reality.

CompuServe

You can input GO HSX to enter the Human Sexuality Forum, which has an open and a closed area, plus a dictionary of sexual terms, a FAQ file, and other background literature. The general rule is that you have to use your real name, show respect, and use tasteful language.

The open area is barely R-rated, with a singles and a gay forum, Q/A from counselors, plus material on shyness, nudism, and living with AIDS. There's a database you can search for information on a wide variety of topics, with constant reminders that online answers are no substitute for the care of a physician. The closed area, meanwhile, has wide-ranging, frank, and explicit forum discussions, as they try to define orgasm and establish how to do spanking right. If that's too tame for you, read the files under the Announcements menu item to find out how to get enrolled in the several by-application-only areas, covering things like "water sports," "adult babies," information on the BBC's guidelines for depicting gays, fiction with themes like "obedience school," and message threads with headers like "You want me to eat *what*?"

Saving Face:

Don't badger everyone asking about ftp archives of erotic pictures. The postings in the alt.binaries hierarchy remain online for two weeks or a month, depending on the site, and then are gone, and you'd suspect that someone, somewhere, is gathering them into a huge permanent archive, especially as the task could easily be automated. Officially, no, no one does that. Unofficially, yes, people do it all over the place—*but you didn't hear that from me.* And if you run across such an archive, keep it to yourself. Sites have been overwhelmed and shut down under an avalanche

(continued on page 232)

CHAPTER 11

MARTIAN
INFORMATION
NETWORK

MINF0023
BETTY
PAGE

Venerable Betty

Page pinup found

on the Internet.

For those with children in the house with access to the terminal, CompuServe has an option whereby you can shut off access to the entire HSX forum.

Delphi

Under the Groups and Clubs item on the main menu you'll see a listing called Close Encounters, open to those eighteen or over. Here, explicitly sexual material and talk is permitted, although abusive material is not. Topics include "playground," "lifestyles," "art gallery," and "fantasy." There's also poetry, nudist material, and a general discussion forum with topics that range across the landscape.

Saving Face:

(continued from page 230)

of ftp callers when word got out of an erotic archive (ten thousand calls within hours of the address being posted, according to one story). Likewise, when you come across an archive, don't camp online for days in a mindless frenzy of downloading. Moderation is always a test of character—make sure you pass.

There's also a personal ads section with some wide-open categories. Also under Groups and Clubs there's a MensNet forum, which, among other things, deals with sexual issues, including gay issues. The list of user-run custom SIGs under the Groups and Clubs menu includes several that deal with sex in one way or another, including a recovery forum for the love/sex addicted, and "Men Against Circumcision."

Hidden in the Gallery of Graphics in the Graphics SIG on Delphi, you can find graphics files of young ladies in various stages of undress. The text descriptors for the pictures don't even try to be coy, with lists of searchable keywords like NUDE, NAKED, SEXY, and BEHIND. There is also a "model of the month" contest.

AOL

After all the hard-core hangouts on the Internet, AOL is refreshingly coy and old-fashioned. There are chat channels called the Flirt Nook and the Romance Connection. Other than that, about the only thing that fits into this chapter would be the gay and lesbian forum in the Lifestyles and Interests Department. Plus, the Better Health and Medical Forum there has sex information, and the Issues in Mental Health area has a conference on relationships.

Meanwhile, if you turn to the Graphics and Animation Forum and pick the GIF Images option, and then the Faces and Bodies option, you'll see a Pinups entry. You could probably show any of them to your grandmother.

Otherwise, the National Geographic On-Line is about as explicit as it gets on AOL.

GEnie

At first glance GEnie is one of those places with a censorship conference, but nothing to censor. But if you invoke the Symposiums On Global Issues item in the main menu you'll

```
*********************************
*   New Classified Ad(s) Posted   *
*     Type CLASS at ENCOUNTER>     *
*********************************
* DA GA PE NU SW FR GR NA SU OT *
* -1  2  1     -1        -1      *
*********************************


*********************************
*       Currently Available Ads       *
*********************************
* DA GA PE NU SW FR GR NA SU OT *
* 46 49 36  7  9 13  9 69  2  1 *
*********************************
```

Directory of personal ads in Delphi's Close Encounters Forum. The abbreviations stand for, respectively, dating, gay, personal, nudist, swapping, friends only, group sex, naughty but nice, support groups, and other.

see, on the subsequent list, the Family and Personal Growth Round Table. Amid material on home management, overeating, and alcoholism, you'll note references to closed topics. The main screen on the roundtable has a option for applying to the closed areas, which include adult issues, adult sexuality, "transgendered" issues (i.e., cross-dressing), and bondage, and there are male-only and female-only conferences. Should you turn out to be underage or otherwise operating under false pretenses, you can be thrown off GEnie. It takes about two days for your request to be processed and for you to be granted access.

Refreshingly, there are also conferences open only to children (twelve and under) and teenagers (thirteen to nineteen).

THE BBS SCENE

There are hardly any major BBSs without an "adult" area of some sort. Experienced sysops say you have to offer some kind of adult area on any BBS; if not, naughty language and discussions would end up in areas that should remain pure as the driven snow.

NETSEX

Aside from that, BBSs that offer naughty pictures have become an industry. Pay money and you get to use them, just as in the oldest profession. They can and do pay for their own advertising, and if you are interested, that's where to start. (Hint: Pick up several computer and online magazines and flip through the back pages. Or get hold of the BBS lists mentioned in Chapter 14. If the name is something like "Purple Palace of Bondage" or the word "adult" appears in the descriptor, you've found what you're looking for.) For those who prefer talk, there are several adult BBS echo networks, with names Like Sexsation, ThrobNet, ErosNet, and After Dark. You'll find them and more on many of the adult BBSs you call in to. Sexsation Network has a stronger focus on women's viewpoints, and includes a recipe forum. ThrobNet includes conferences on Monty Python and Rush Limbaugh.

But I've told you enough. Youths should be encouraged to shun the false stimulation of mere pictures, turn off their terminals, go out into public places, and meet real girls. (Anyway, almost any adult BBS requires proof that you're eighteen or older before you can get full access.)

DON'T BE FOOLED

You say you went online for reasons too personal to be shared? That's okay—we understand nevertheless. But as you pursue your quest you'd be advised to avoid the following Internet mailing lists, since you'll be wasting your time and annoying people whose minds are elsewhere.

dirt-users
Yes, children, dirt is also a programming language. Just don't mix it with perl, at least not before they come out with one called swine. In the meantime send your request to **dirt-users-request@ukc.ac.uk**.

tinymuck-sloggers

TinyMUCK is a MUD programming language (see Chapter 9). Not all MUD players have dirty minds, but they sure are mired in that acronym. Send your request to **tinymuck-sloggers-request@piggy.ucsb.edu**.

exhibitionists

Exhibitionists discuss what they do openly and without shame in this mail list, which is no strain—they're movie projectionists. Project your request to **exhibitionists-request@jvnc.net**.

porschephiles

Invented another perversion, have they? Gosh, it's getting to the point where the Greeks *don't* have a word for it. But it turns out that porschephiles are fans of Porsche automobiles. Send your request to **porsche-philes-request@tta.com**.

undercover

This mail list actually has something to do with Rolling Stones fans. The derivation of the name is a mystery. Or maybe it isn't. Hmmm. Anyway, send your request to **undercover-request@snowhite.cis.uoguelph.ca**.

two-strokes

Sorry to pop your bubble, but smaller motorcycles use two-stroke engines, so their users can refer to themselves as two-strokers. Send your request to **2strokes-request@microunity.com**.

wetleather

Calm yourself. You see, it rains a lot in Seattle, so if you ride a motorcycle there a lot, you end up wearing wet leather. Send your request to **wetleather-request@mom.isc-br.com**.

can-stud-assoc

Of course, this mail list could only concern members of the Canadian Students Associations. Send your request to **can-stud-assoc-request@unixg.ubc.ca**.

NET FRINGES:
UFOS, ALIEN POSSESSION, DARK CONSPIRACIES, AND OTHER MADNESS

FACE ON MARS

You've seen them on the covers of the supermarket tabloids—pictures of what appears to be a gaping face sculpted out of a large mound on the surface of the planet Mars. (Some tabloids put the face on Venus, Jupiter, or in some other solar system—but, for them, anything outside Hollywood or Las Vegas *is* another solar system.) The face turned up in two Viking Orbiter pictures taken in the 1970s. People have written whole books about this one phenomenon—while other inky wretches toil thanklessly on nonspeculative tomes, dodging the issue whenever their children ask embarrassing questions about food, clothing, and shelter.

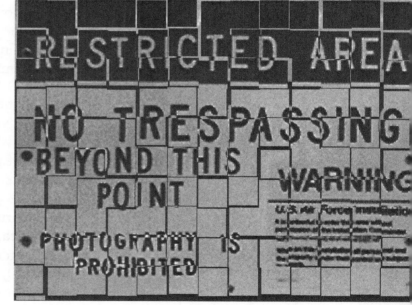

Should you be in the vicinity, the mound is at nine degrees west, forty-one north, right there between Arabia Terra and Acidalia Planitia. It's about a mile and a half wide—just follow the road signs, you can't miss it.

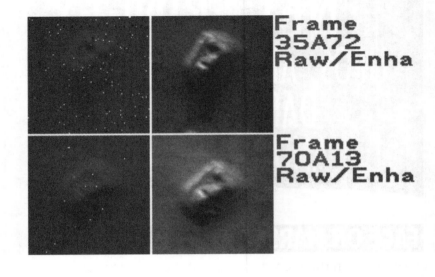

Frame
35A72
Raw/Enha

Frame
70A13
Raw/Enha

The standard liftout you see floating about the Net (and the tabloids), easily spotted by its curtated captions.

If you're temporarily Earthbound, a GIF rendition showing both shots is widely available-—run archie on the string "marsface" and it will show up on a dozen places on the Internet. Filtered from the original NASA tapes by a woman who worked for LucasFilms, it shows both shots enhanced and unenhanced—four images in one file.

But why settle for a little GIF liftout when you can examine the original images? NASA has them—plus the rest of the Martian surface and whatever other mysteries it may contain, assuming you yearn to spend the rest of your life downloading large graphics files.

Internet Access Information: On the Internet, do anonymous ftp to **nssdca.gsfc.nasa.gov** (that's the National Space Science Data Center at NASA's Goddard Space Flight Center in Greenbelt, MD) and cd to the cdrom.dir/image.dir/ viking.dir/raw.dir directory, where you'll see the "selected high res. image" files **f035a72.img** and **f07a13.img**. Those two are, in fact, the only files in that directory. After getting them, go to the software.dir directory, where you will see a list of subdirectories with various kinds of viewing software. WINVIEW.ZIP in the dos.dir directory gave good results for viewing the files in Microsoft Windows, although you need

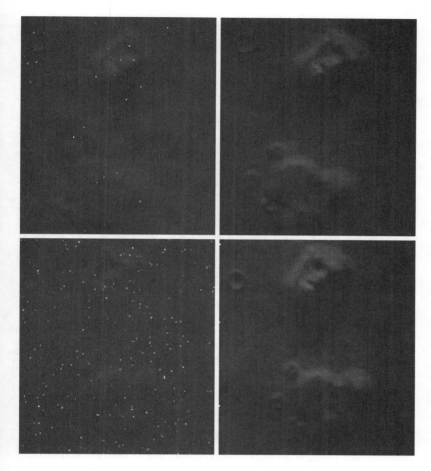

Both Mars faces, before and after author's enhancement of original graphics data. Your mileage may vary—but at least, with the original data, you can appreciate the overall geography.

a 256-color display. To "decompress" the software file, you'll need the PKZIP utility, which is also present if you don't have it. Also get the WINVW_11.ZIP file, which upgrades the viewing software.

CompuServe Access Information: Select the Libraries option in the Space Forum, and then the Browse command, using the All option. Use Mars as the keyword, and you'll get a list showing the zipped NASA shots and the necessary viewing software. There are also GIF files uploaded by hobbyists zeroing in on other surface "anomalies," like the "fort," the "city," the "ramp," and the "tower." (You have to pay attention to the shadows.) Plus the usual canyons and caldera.

Another Mars Viking photo enhancement, found on the Space Forum on CompuServe, of a formation (not far from the face) called the "fort."

Check This Out:

The rest of Mars (and for that matter, the universe) can be found on NASA's CD ROM jukebox at **explorer.arc. nasa.gov**.

AOL Access Information: There are several versions of the face in the Space Images section of the Graphics and Animation Forum.

Downloading the original image file is a serious project if you're connected remotely—both image files are about 1.3 megabytes long, uncompressed, meaning it will take more than twenty minutes to download one even at 9600 bps. Check and see if your access provider has any compression facilities you can use before diving into downloading. The CompuServe versions are already compressed.

In fo35a72 you'll see that the face is in about the middle of the picture, and in f070a13 the face is near the bottom toward the left. You'll also see that in these original, unenhanced versions of the photos the features are almost flat gray, looking like ghostly reflections on a slate. And in both the face is turned almost upside down.

But then you can play with the contrast. If you downloaded the WINVIEW file and its update, invoke Image Histogram Modify and change the contrast to "uniform

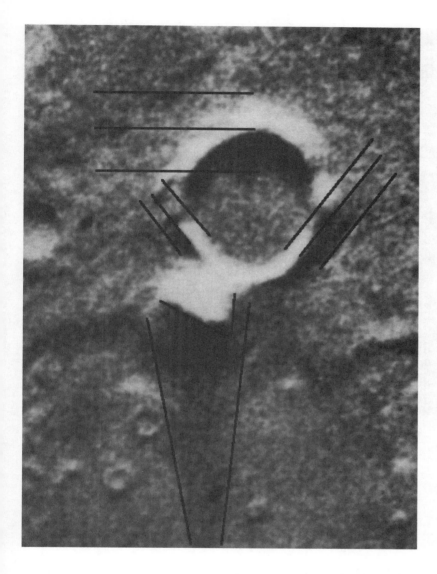

Reference marks have been added to his enhanced Mars Viking photo in an effort to gauge the height of the central cone, a formation called the "tower." The file was found in the Space Forum on CompuServe.

equalize." Or you can use the software to convert the file to the Windows .BMP format and then tinker with the gray scales using a graphics package. Either way, the features should then leap out at you, and you'll see that the face is one of several eroded mesas/city sites on a plain creased by numerous watercourses/interstate highways.

In fo35a72 the sun was ten degrees above the horizon and the features are more defined—that's the image the tabloids

The Pentagon as seen from orbit in a photo found on AOL. For comparison purposes, it's about one-sixth the size of the Mars face.

like to use. In the second the sun was twenty-seven degrees above the horizon, and the affect is not as convincing. Also, the "chin" is flawed by a large black spot. In the GIF liftout this dot appears to be a crater, but in the original you can see it's an imaging system artifact.

Why should a face be gaping at us from the planet Mars? Shouldn't it be squinting? After all, think of the distance.

NASA merely shrugs. It did, however, send out the Mars Observer, which was supposed to provide spy satellite resolution of the Red Planet, the kind that lets them count the number of cats in your backyard, by gender. It went dead as it approached Mars in 1993.

Certain people weren't surprised. Read on.

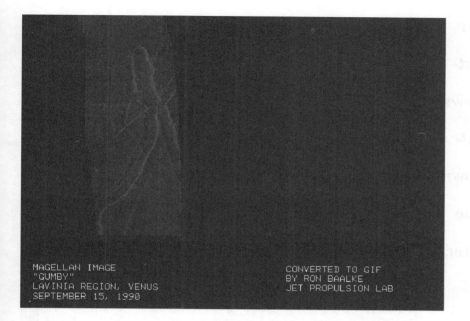

MAGELLAN IMAGE
"GUMBY"
LAVINIA REGION, VENUS
SEPTEMBER 15, 1990

CONVERTED TO GIF
BY RON BAALKE
JET PROPULSION LAB

Even plate tectonics on Venus are not immune to the affects of pop culture, as this NASA shot, titled "gumby.gif" shows. Found on the Internet at explorer.arc.nasa.gov, its official caption says: "These fault-bounded troughs were imaged by Magellan on orbit 147 on September 15, 1990. The image is of part of the Lavinia Region of Venus at 60 degrees south latitude, 347 degrees east longitude. The image is 28 kilometers (17 miles) wide and 75 kilometers (46 miles) long. This region is at the intersection of two tectonic trends. An extensive set of east-west trending fractures extends to the west (left) and a second set extends down to the south-southeast (lower right). The lines of pits suggest some igneous or volcanic activity accompanying the faulting. The prominent trough trending diagonally across the image is 5 kilometers (3.1 miles) wide and is 100 to 200 meters (300 to 600 feet) deep."

Map of Area 51 found at ftp.rutgers.edu. It shows the Tikaboo Valley, with the town of Rachel in the upper left center, the Black Mailbox at right center, and Groom Dry Lake at bottom left.

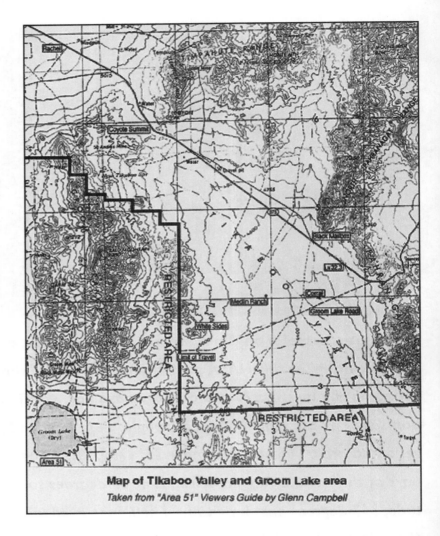

Map of Tikaboo Valley and Groom Lake area
Taken from "Area 51" Viewers Guide by Glenn Campbell

UFOS

Yes, they've been trooping out there, along Nevada State Road 375, in the vicinity of the tiny town of Rachel (or a storied "Black Mailbox" on the road southeast of town). The spot is about 120 miles north-northeast as the saucer flies from Las Vegas (where the skies are safe from attention). About 20 miles south of 375 lies Groom Dry Lake, whose officially nonexistent yet visibly active airstrip is the center of intense interest by UFO-ologists.

Mapping satellite photo of Groom Dry Lake taken in 1968, found at ftp.rutgers.edu.

UFO pilgrims come out along the road at night to gaze longingly at the mysterious lights, especially "Old Faithful" at 4:50 A.M. every Thursday. And if its lights exactly resemble the landing lights of a Boeing 737, they're not fooled. After all, if you take telephoto pictures of the lights and blow them up, they look like mysterious, shimmering orbs. After a bracing breakfast at the Little A"Le" Inn Café in Rachel they head for home, satisfied that they have been in contact with superior consciousnesses.

What does it all mean? Well, that depends. To even begin to approach the subject, you'll have to ingest some background material. Then we'll cover some of the explanations that seek to explain the data, and the online sources of more data.

Area 51—The area around Groom Dry Lake north-west of Las Vegas, Nevada. Areas 50 and 52 remain obscure.

Aurora—Secret U.S. Air Force project to replace the SR-71 high-altitude spy plane, or perhaps a cover for some other project, or perhaps a rumor.

Bill Cooper—UFO lecturer whose latest gig involves saying that JFK was assassinated by bodyguards because he chafed about MJ-12 and wanted to go public with the truth about UFOs.

Blue Book—U.S. Air Force project in the 1950s and 1960s to examine UFO sightings. Nothing came of it and true believers say that it suppressed creditable reports.

Blues—Small-statured UFO race with translucent skin and large almond-shaped eyes, some of whom advised the U.S. government not to deal with the Grays and then went into hiding on a Hopi Indian reservation.

Cash/Landrum Case—UFO sightings by three people in Huffman, Texas, in December 1980. They later showed signs of radiation sickness.

Channeling—To receive extrasensory communications.

Close Encounter of the First Kind—To get within five hundred feet of a UFO.

Close Encounter of the Second Kind—To find UFO ground impressions, debris, etc.

Close Encounter of the Third Kind—To encounter occupants of a UFO.

Close Encounter of the Fourth Kind—To be abducted by a UFO.

Close Encounter of the Fifth Kind—To communicate with a UFO occupant.

Condon Report—A 1969 report that said all UFO sightings were explainable.

Disinformation—Everything put out by the government that does not support your pet UFO theory.

George Adamski—UFO lecturer enlightened by the Venusians in 1952.

Grays—Reportedly the most common UFO occupants and most avid abductors, sporting a short, slender stature but humanoid appearance with slits for mouths, no real nose, and dark bug-eyes. Some say they are responsible for the creation of humanity and its subsequent history.

Gulf Breeze Case—Repeated sightings by a couple in Gulf Breeze, Florida, in 1987 and 1988, of a UFO they thought was trying to abduct them but never succeeded.

Hill Case—Under hypnotic regression, Betty and Barney Hill accounted for their lost-time experience while driving home in New Hampshire in September 1961: They had been abducted by aliens and given a physical exam.

Hypnotic Regression—A technique whereby a person is hypnotized and brought backward in time to the point of the "lost time" and then asked to describe what happened.

John Lear—UFO lecturer who formulated the "dark side hypothesis."

LGM—Little gray men, formerly little green men.

Livestock Mutilations—Grazing farm animals found dead, drained of blood, with certain soft surface organs (eyes, tongue, genitalia, rectum) excised. Sinister UFO pilots might be responsible. Or there might be some involvement from heat, insects, and birds.

Lost Time—The unnerving inability to remember, later, what happened during a previous span of several hours.

Purported photo of a UFO involved in the Gulf Breeze incident, found at phoenix.oulu.fi.

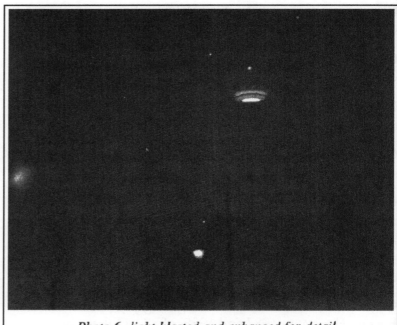

Photo 6, light-blasted and enhanced for detail

Men In Black (MIBs)—Well-dressed individuals who show up around the time of a UFO sighting (before or after, it doesn't matter) telling the witnesses to keep it to themselves.

MJ-12—Purported 1953 briefing document for President Eisenhower that described dealings with "EBEs" (extraterrestrial biological entities) by the U.S. government, overseen by a committee of twelve, code-named "Majestic" or something else that starts with m-a-j, who are now secretly running the world in partnership with the Grays, or something. It is now considered controversial even by UFO believers.

Nordics—Blond humanoids who work with or are controlled by the Grays.

Pleiadians—New Age aliens from the Pleiades, or from our own distant future, or both, whose hobby is to teach Earthlings empowering forms of personal and social metaphysics. They prefer channeling over physical travel or face-to-face communication.

Telescopic view of the Pleiades, star cluster visible (as a blurry patch to the naked eye) in the northern hemisphere, whence come certain space brothers.

Reptoids—Alien race who may be controlling the Grays, breeding them with humans for food and as part of some overall scheme to destroy all humanoids in the galaxy.

Robert Lazar—Person who claims to have worked at a top-secret facility in Area 51 in 1988 and 1989 reverse-engineering nine captured UFOs, apparently near Papoose Lake, about fifteen miles south of Groom Dry Lake, deeper into the desolate mountains, presumably at a spot called Kelly Mine.

Roswell Case—The crash of a weather balloon and/or UFO near Corona, New Mexico, in July 1947, so named because it was investigated from Roswell Army Air Field. Today it is said that besides shreds of balloonlike material they also found a smashed UFO with four aliens: two dead, one injured, one unharmed.

SETI—Search for Extraterrestrial Intelligence, a U.S. government project to search for radio signals from alien civilizations, defunded in 1993, now partially operational with private funding.

Spectral Evidence—If you dreamed that a certain woman is a witch, that's evidence she's a witch. Spectral evidence was banned in Massachusetts in the autumn of 1692 after certain events in Salem.

Travis Walton Case—The person in question was a tree-trimmer reportedly knocked to the ground by bright light from a low-hovering UFO in November 1975. He turned up five days later and under hypnotic regression described a trip to a hospital that was not a hospital, run by robed semi-humans who ignored his questions.

UFO—Unidentified Flying Object.

Zeta Reticuli—A star in the southern hemisphere linked to the Hill Case based on a star map the victims remembered seeing while in the UFO. Lazar also said the UFOs he saw came from there.

Swamp Gas Hypothesis

It's all mass hysteria. Parallels between UFO watchers and South Pacific cargo cultists should not be dismissed lightly. Lost time is just another term of "being preoccupied," and accounts of UFO abductions that emerge under hypnotic regression are confabulations. Channeling is just the modern version of "spectral evidence," and/or saying whatever pops into your head. UFOs are just weather balloons or the planet Venus, etc. Some, of course, may be "black" research projects.

Dark Side Hypothesis

The U.S. government recovered dozens of crashed flying saucers over the years and made contact with the aliens. In

Large sign where Groom Lake Rd. crosses into the Restricted Area. Groom Lake is ~10mi (~16km) past this point. Photo taken on 3/20/93

exchange for technical information and help with reverse-engineering the UFOs hangared in Area 51 (now said to be under alien control), the aliens were allowed to abduct people for their private purposes. But the aliens exceeded the terms of the abduction arrangement, leading to a confrontation in the late 1970s, with casualties among Area 51 scientists and Special Forces troops. The government has been forced to rethink its alien relations and may be leaking distorted UFO facts to prepare the public for the truth. Superficially, things have been patched up with the aliens, except they have since gone hog-wild, abducting as many as one American in ten and fitting them with mind-control implants (Got a BB in your ear, mister?), preparing the country for a complete takeover by the MJ-12 supra-government organization. And if the implants don't work, there's always drug addiction.

Picture of the warning sign on the road to Groom Dry Lake, taken in March 1993. It was found at ftp.rutgers.edu.

Space Brothers Hypothesis

Channelers tell us that the abductions are all part of a battle between good and evil energy forces, represented by the various races of aliens. Some believers, like members of the Aetherius Society (headquartered in Hollywood, natch) gather together in prayer circles to absorb the cosmic energy beamed down from alien spacecraft. The Universal Articulate Interdimensional Understanding of Science (UNARIUS) Academy of Sciences in El Cajon, California, teaches us that a coalition of thirty-three planets are sending thirty-three cojoined spaceships to descend to Earth in 2001 on a tract to be bought for the purpose in southern California, to form a city where seekers can come and learn Cosmic Awareness. And there are other variations on this theme—little of which involves investigations of sightings of unidentified flying objects.

Of course, your mileage may vary. Following are some of the places you can pursue the matter further, if the MIBs haven't convinced you otherwise:

 alt.alien.visitors
Some serious discussion of UFOs seeps through in this newsgroup, despite an ongoing background roar: pontifications from self-styled space and/or time travelers; breathless questions about this or that TV show with a paranormal theme; and fruitless talk about any science-related news story in which the sources involved are still scratching their heads.

 alt.paranet.abduct
This carefully moderated newsgroup covers things like repressed memory research, and features book reviews and conference coverage. Yes, the subject is extraterrestrial

abduction, but the tone is dead serious—to the point of being a news service. If you want to float your private theories, go to alt.alien.visitors.

alt.paranet.ufo
This conference is far more freewheeling, with people reporting UFO sightings in their hometowns, and others floating all sorts of speculation about the nature of UFOs. Grand conspiracy theories draw mostly groans. Announcements of lecture tours by people who claim to see monuments on the moon and Mars also draw groans.

Ground shot of Groom Dry Lake taken in 1978, found at ftp.rutgers.edu. (The lake wasn't dry that day, evidently.)

Saving Face:

Don't post blathering questions about the "germ of truth" behind this or that TV show. The cognoscenti know better than to pay attention to the likes of *The X Files*, a TV show about how the government covers up paranormal happenings and keeps them off TV. If one of them is nice, you might get a tired response pointing out the millionth use of dusty cliché, or perhaps explaining what the word *fiction* means. Or you might get fervent answers from true believers, thus raising the noise level further. (There are those who accept as truth the TV series *Alien Nation*,

(continued on page 255)

CUFON BBS

A BBS run by the Computer UFO Network can be reached at 206-776-0382. It offers e-mail for UFO researchers, files of sightings and a conduit for making your own reports, and files of "verified documents" and "others." The documents include one from the FBI saying MJ-12 is bogus (or at least not a classified document whose leakage requires investigation). To cut down on the noise level that any discussion conference threatens to produce, they don't offer any conferences.

S KEPTIC

The Mail.Skeptic list examines claims of the paranormal—of which UFOs are merely one facet. Send your request to **listserv@ JHUVM.HCF.JHU.EDU**, unless you trust some mystic to conjure it up for you.

Skunk-works

The skunk-works mail list is devoted not to UFOs, but to leading-edge aviation developments, especially those at Lockheed, whose secret development labs used to be called the "skunk works." Reading it might drain some of the romance out of those lights in the sky. If you're willing to do that, send your request to **skunk-works-request@harbor.ecn.purdue.edu**.

Trepan-L

If you feel that phenomenology should have a broader basis than mere sky-gazing, try this mail list, which is a moderated compilation of weird news stories. Send your request to **list-serv@brownvm.brown.edu**.

 Trepan-D
This mail list is for unmoderated discussions of weird news stories, especially those in Trepan-L. Send your request to **listserv@brownvm.brown.edu**.

 Omni (AOL)
AOL's online version of *Omni* magazine includes *Omni*'s Antimatter section, which covers paranormal stories without editorializing. (Running it in a section called Antimatter is editorialization enough.)

 Space Forum (CIS)
There is some UFO coverage in this Compu-Serve forum, although it's strictly a sidelight to hard science.

Internet Access Information: For a large archive of UFO material, try anonymous ftp to **ftp.rutgers.edu** in the /pub/ufo/ directory. The alt.alien-visitors FAQ (called a.a.v.-faq) contains a long list of UFO organizations, plus archived threads from that newsgroup covering various topics, Groom Dry Lake pictures, and other material. Additionally, there's file called ufo-guide in several formats containing an updated compendium of UFO folklore. Meanwhile, the /pub/ufo_and_space_pics/ directory at **phoenix.oulu.fi** contains some purported Gulf Breeze UFO photos, while the /Library/Fringe/Ufo/ directory of the wonderfully named **wiretap.spies.com** contains general Paranet material (including conspiracy and occult material). Remember, if the file you want ends in a .Z, it's in a Unix file compressed format, and you'll have to decompress it before downloading it to a PC.

 **Saving Face:**

(continued from page 254)
about extraterrestrials living openly in Los Angeles. But maybe that's not as crazy as accepting *Leave It to Beaver* as truth.)

NET FRINGES: UFOS, ALIEN POSSESSION, DARK CONSPIRACIES, AND OTHER MADNESS

Telephoto shot of Groom Dry Lake facilities taken in 1978, found at ftp.rut-gers.edu. The airplane in front of the hangar appears to be a captive Soviet model. Of course, that couldn't possibly account for the secrecy surrounding the place. . . .

THE OTHER EXTRATERRESTRIAL INVASION

Of course, it is self-evident that the Grays are acting at the bidding of some Superior Intelligence—one pursuing a cosmic scheme of psychic conquest. Alas, my lips are sealed concerning the Ultimate Truths the MIBs impressed on me while researching the previous section, but any *comprehending* citizen can read the signs—especially if he watches TV with anyone under eight. After all, what tall, purple, all-pervading Presence was not even around a few years ago? Suffice it to say the MIBs were tall, and wearing not black, but some other dark color.

If you still need a hint, scan this list of conferences:

 **alt.tv.barney**
See below.

 alt.satannet.barney
See below.

 alt.tv.dinosaurs.barney
See below.

 alt.christnet.dinosaur.barney
See below.

 alt.sex.bestiality.barney
See below.

 alt.tv.dinosaurs.barney.die.die.die
See below.

 alt.barney.dinosaur.die.die.die

All these newsgroups carry about the same traffic. And what traffic! To fill you in: Barney is a seven-foot purple dinosaur and star of the PBS children's show of the same name. He prances and sings and leads a troupe of impossibly cherubic youngsters in feats of the imagination. For Barney's target audience, the formula works: Fanatic two-year-old fans can wear out the heads on their parents' VCR in less than a month. But adults have proven harder to win over, especially the busy members of the Santa Cruz Anti-B'Harne Task Force, the Texas A&M University Anti-B'Harne Genocide Division, the Minnesotans Against Ugly Lizards (MAUL), the Jihad to Destroy Barney on the World Wide Web, and the like. They tend to refer to Barney with terms like "spawn of hell" and "twisted purple

 **Saving Face Generally:**

Remember, news stories are almost never about events—they are about people saying they experienced an event. The reporter shows up later, or calls in from an office. And in the nineteenth and earlier centuries, news accounts were often third- or fourth-hand. (In this century, Ronald Reagan began his career as a radio announcer, taking stats from real baseball games and making up a play-by-play commentary—listeners never knew.) Yet you see some people calmly accepting as established fact everything that appears, or has ever appeared, in print.

NET FRINGES: UFOS, ALIEN POSSESSION, DARK CONSPIRACIES, AND OTHER MADNESS

While all the rage on children's television, Barney seems to trigger negative emotions in certain adults.

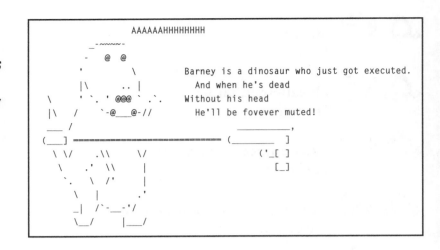

```
                        AAAAAAHHHHHHHH
         _~~~~_
       -  @ @
     '         \           Barney is a dinosaur who just got executed.
     |\      .. |              And when he's dead
   \    ' `. ' @@@ ` '.        Without his head
    |\   /   `-@___@-//        He'll be fovever muted!
    ___ /                     _____,
   (___] ======================= (_____ ]
    \ \/    . \\    \/                     ('_[ ]
     `.  .'  \\ \\   |                      [_]
        \   \ /'    |
         \   |    .'
         _|  /`-_-'/
         \__/   |__/
```

pustule from Pluto" and unite to shout down anyone who points out that "caring is sharing" or otherwise speaks anything but ill of the Purple Savior. Perhaps they should sing the theme song a few times: "I love you, you love me. . . ." Of course, that takes on disturbing new meaning in the alt.sex.bestiality.barney newsgroup.

EARTHBOUND PARANOIA

For others, it is not necessary to invoke sappy purple dinosaurs or lights in the sky. They see fiendish, globe-strangling conspiracies going on all the time—right here on earth, conducted by conventional humans for mundane ends like money and power. Well, they don't actually *see* these conspiracies, you understand—but they find evidence of them going on just outside their field of vision. Not that you can disprove these theories (you can *never* prove a negative statement). Not that you should listen to me—I might be *one of them!* But instead of quibbling, try these conference forums:

 **alt.illuminati**
The thing you'll learn here is that paranoia can't grow to its full potential without some-

Saving Face:
Before downloading the superficially cute ASCII artwork, handing it around at the office, or posting it in the kids' room, be sure to study it for hidden messages.

Partial CAD rendering of the car President Kennedy died in, used by hobbyists for ongoing analyses of the event, found in the JFK Forum on CompuServe.

thing relatively solid to attach itself to. The participants here wander in circles, searching everywhere (everywhere!) for the "unseen hand" in politics, quibbling about whether the Armenians were bad guys, how libertarian Lyndon LaRouche's jury refused to look him in the eye as the verdict was read, the ethics of killing plants, who invented AIDS, and whether the Holocaust is a proven fact. (Odd—you never hear quibbling about the reality of Pearl Harbor, the *Lusitania*, or Fort Sumter.) (*Illuminati*, incidentally, refers to a secret political movement within the secret Masonic Order, whose suppression two centuries ago has not slowed down the rumors about it.)

alt.conspiracy

Except that it's much busier, you can barely tell this conference from alt.illuminati, although at times the balance of power, rhetoric-wise, shifts toward the skeptics. Also, there is a lot more general fringe-politics theorizing, not all of which hinges on conspiracies. Will gun control spark a secessionist rebellion in the United States? Wasn't that tried once before with mixed results? Should that stop anyone?

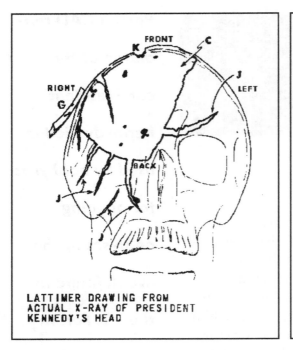

LATTIMER DRAWING FROM
ACTUAL X-RAY OF PRESIDENT
KENNEDY'S HEAD

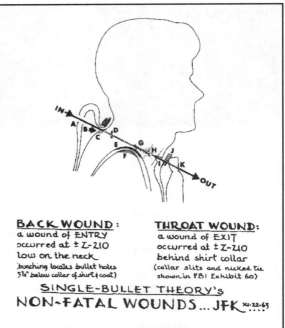

BACK WOUND:
a wound of ENTRY
occurred at ± Z-210
low on the neck
bunching locates bullet holes
5¾" below collar of shirt & coat)

THROAT WOUND:
a wound of EXIT
occurred at ± Z-210
behind shirt collar
(collar slits and nicked tie
shown in FBI Exhibit 60)

SINGLE-BULLET THEORY's
NON-FATAL WOUNDS... JFK ¹¹·²²·⁶³

CompuServe's

JFK Forum offers

amateur forensic

pathologists

plenty of mate-

rial to play with.

alt.conspiracy.jfk
Before you join in here, be warned—you can't hold your head up unless you can display a frame-by-numbered-frame familiarity with the Zapruder film, speak knowledgeably about the Umbrella Man, and know that LHO stands for Lee Harvey Oswald. Conspiracy theories are discussed, but no one gets hypnotized by them—and in any event the theories hatched here lack the breathtaking, cosmic sweep and geologic time spans of the UFO-related theories. (Although, as we saw in the UFO section, there are those who would connect the two.) Anyway, the participants here are more inclined to expound endlessly on why JFK's head jerked backward when he was hit, rather than explain the origin of life on earth.

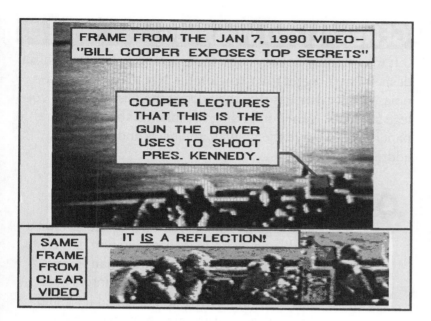

FRAME FROM THE JAN 7, 1990 VIDEO—
"BILL COOPER EXPOSES TOP SECRETS"

COOPER LECTURES THAT THIS IS THE GUN THE DRIVER USES TO SHOOT PRES. KENNEDY.

SAME FRAME FROM CLEAR VIDEO

IT **IS** A REFLECTION!

Self-explanatory artwork found in the JFK Forum on CompuServe, concerning the theory that President Kennedy was shot by bodyguards whose true allegiance lay elsewhere.

 **JFK Forum (CIS)**

The JFK Assassination Research Forum on CompuServe hosts a conference whose tone is comparable to alt.conspiracy.jfk, plus there's a wealth of background material—transcripts, diagrams, scanned photos, old new stories. Wade through it all and you'll be a one-person Warren Commission. Just don't end up espousing the Single Bullet Theory—people will think you're a kook. The satirical comic strip "Doonesbury" must have had this forum in mind when it postulated a conspiracy to cover up the absence of a JFK assassination conspiracy.

Internet Access Information: As mentioned, you can find assassination and general conspiracy material at **wiretap.spies.com** in the /Library/Fringe/Conspiry/directory. (Note their misspelling.)

 **Saving Face:**

Don't think your pet theory is original, or proven by you personally. As for theories based on poor reproductions of individual frames from the Zapruder film, the cognoscenti aren't impressed.

GENERALIZED WHINING

It may or may not say something ominous, but total, black despair has a bigger following on the Net than does paranoia. What's worse is that the bulk of the despairers are college students. If their unending complaints about tests and papers doesn't give them away, their sigs and/or mailing addresses will.

alt.destroy.the.earth

The saga floating around about the founders of this newsgroup is that they first named themselves the Society for Human Immigration from Terra, and then went into a near-terminal funk when they realized it should be Emigration, not Immigration, ruining the acronym.

alt.nuke.europe

While the denizens struggle mightily with the proposition, they keep coming back to the realization that they'd just as soon nuke the United States. "Now quit arguing and start flaming. Endeavor to reach some neural activity within your minuscule crania and provide some enlightenment and humor to the bored masses," they rebuke each other. "Ratings are dropping." At least somebody, somewhere, isn't taking themselves seriously.

alt.drunken.bastards

Those depressed by alt.destroy.the.earth have obviously fled to this one, a forum devoted to recounting lengthy, pointless drinking stories and to rooting out the many euphemisms currently in circulation for vomiting. Scholars a couple millennia from now will doubtless pour over this material with interest.

alt.my.head.hurts

Can you put socks on backward? Do clothes have gender? If toasters are equipped with the latest microprocessors, will they be able to do seventy-eight slices a second? "Anything to avoid studying," is the name of the game here.

alt.shut.the.hell.up.geek

If everything else in your life has gone to pieces, you can always hang out in this newsgroup and, like the other inhabitants, wait patiently for some newcomer to post a message—any message—and then leap at him or her with the eponymous rejoinder. And gratuitously savaging someone does appear to have a calming effect in many cases.

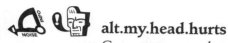

alt.geek

This newsgroup has a lot of traffic devoted to put-downs of computer users less sophisticated than the humble message poster. (For our EASL readers, *geek* means "nerd," which means "drip," which means "anyone suspected of being willing to do homework for its own sake.") If people who actually look for the "any" key when told to "push any key" give you the hives, you'll finally feel comfortable here.

alt.grad-student.tenured

How long does it take to get tenure as a graduate student? Consensus: You're tenured when you can't remember life outside graduate school. What to do if your professor goes on a sabbatical or just disappears from the face of the earth is also a big topic.

alt.life.sucks

You want sob stories from students? You do? "By the time I graduate next year, I'll have more than $45,000 in college loans to pay off, mainly because my parents have been giving my two younger brothers everything that I never had," etc., etc., etc. Some things never change. But why does this have to happen online? Don't students hang out in a physical sense anymore? What ever happened to those glorious evenings when a guy could lounge around the dorm lobby, watching Fred feed crickets to his caged praying mantis, waiting for someone to roll out the projector and show the night's "study break" film (invariably either *Methods of Rat Extermination*, *Advanced Methods of Rat Extermination*, or *VD Attack Plan*, these being available free from the health department).

alt.pave.the.earth

The question before the floor is not why, but how. "Asphalt is holy and must be worshipped for the truly magnificent material that it is. Any other paving material is worthless to the Holy Order for any purpose other than to show the greatness of asphalt. Concrete is a mess to drive on, it is brittle and cracks and is not pleasant at high speeds because of these cracks that inevitably form. We will pave with asphalt and nothing else will do." Others disagree. "I urge you to choose concrete so that future generations may enjoy a paved earth with minimal maintenance."

alt.stupidity

Arguing over what to argue about is as good a way to kill time as any, and that's certainly what goes on here. Does 1 plus 1 equal 3 or 1.99999? They can't decide. The newsgroup actually has a FAQ file, stating that the place exists to provide a forum for those who "take a distinctly unnatural and prurient interest in rug-making, stitchery, and other handicrafts. The group is unmoderated; vituperation is open to all." The FAQ file also advertises the newsgroup as a great place to post chain letters, as the participants are all dupes.

alt.whine

If it's possible for a newsgroup to be more obtuse than alt.stupidity, this is it. At least they've decided on what to argue about: silly TV shows, and each other. Which is better: Pepsi with Jack Daniels? Or Coke with Jack Daniels? Consensus: After the first few, you won't care.

WAY OUT THERE

When the going gets weird, the weird get going. And after the weird have gotten up and gone, what's left over can defy description. I swear that I am not making any of this up.

alt.slack

Time for some scripture: "J. R. 'Bob' Dobbs, the Living Slack Master of Mystick Training, the Bridge between Heaven and Hell, the wordless Bobhead, the naked Dobbs, All-knowing, All-prevailing, All-just, All-true, All-none, ALL-ONE, DOBBS is the ONE TRUE WAY by which we will finally achieve that elusive SLACK which has been denied us. Science and religion each prove totally different things, yet they both appear

Saving Face:

Do your homework first. Then whine about it. Should you be doing your whining online in these newsgroups, standard practice is to take someone else's posting that particularly displeases you and dissect it as if it were a doctoral dissertation. If the posting was just a jumble of four-letter words, so much the better.

to be true. So, by divine logic, the answer must be 'Bob.' He IS his own self-fulfilling prophesy."

Welcome to the Church of the Subgenius, where adherents rant about the "Zen of Terror" and debate which online services exhibit slack, or the opposite quality, "pinkboy." Meanwhile, they venerate their clip-art deity, Bob, and seek slackness within themselves. Actually, once you learn to look for it, you'll see that a lot of the alt hierarchy exudes Subgenius rhetoric. Some say you can judge the inroads of the cult (or whatever it is) in your community by yelling "Slack!" in a dark theater and seeing how many people respond "Bob!"

Counterev-L
The people behind this mail list are serious about reestablishing monarchies in Europe. Oddly (predictably?) it's based in the United States. Send your sovereign request to **ae852@yfn.ysu.edu**.

new.country
This mail list is concerned with establishing a new "sea/city" nation in the Caribbean, to be called Oceania. It is not known if they are in contact with the people on the Counterev-L list. Anyway, send your request to **oceania@ world.std.com**.

CP
CP stands for "carnivorous plants." Be warned if a participant invites you over "for dinner." Otherwise, send your request to **listserv@hpl-opus.hpl.hp.com**.

alt.basement.graveyard

"I've spent hours chasing echoing voices about in the blackness, but when I get to there, there's nobody there." If you understand such sentiments, if you need a discreet venue for talking about the best method for digging in spaces with limited head room, if you don't blink at veiled references to "the bottom of the food chain," then go no further. (Just don't move into my neighborhood.) Others may not wish to read this newsgroup when alone, in the dark, late at night.

 alt.devilbunnies

If you think alt.basement.graveyard is weird, you ain't seen nothing yet. Because the Armies of Fudd *need you.* Bunnyhunters are the only thing that stand between a disbelieving human race and a horrible, inescapable fluffy doom. Yes, they're cute. Yes, they look just like regular bunnies—but they can gut entire towns at will. The part war game, part role-playing game carried out in this newsgroup reflects mankind's confrontation with this scourge. Alas, last I checked, the wittle waskels had the upper hand.

Internet Access Information: Extensive technical notes on weaponry and devilbunny history are contained at **xmission.com** in the /pub/users/snowhare/ directory. Read the FAQ file before engaging in battle.

 corpse/respondents

This is a gothic genre fan newsletter. That's all I know about it. Given the title, that's all I want to know about it. Send your request (diffidently, I'm sure) to **carriec@eskimo.com**.

This must stop!

Join the Armies of

Fudd today!

alt.kill.the.whales

A surprising large and vocal Norwegian contingent turns out in this newsgroup to do things like celebrate the first kill of the whaling season. Other than that, there is a lot of fruitless arguing among eco-warriors over whether to argue over whether Greenpeace is boring, or what. If this newsgroup is truly developing in a battleground between the Norsemen and the eco-warriors, it's clear that the Norsemen are better organized, and they're bitter.

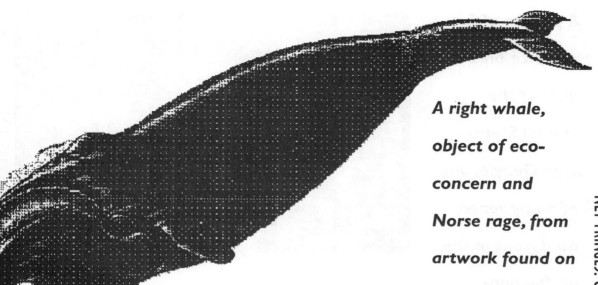

A right whale, object of eco-concern and Norse rage, from artwork found on the Internet.

alt.fan.dan-quayle

Extremism in political rhetoric is no vice here, as long as it's amusing. Building on one of the published quotes from the tanned, rested, and ready former vice president of the United States ("I didn't live in this century," September 15, 1988), while noting that Shakespeare, too, couldn't spell, the crew here is ready to accept Quayle as the author of Shakespeare's plays and therefore a centuries-old undead British resident alien not qualified to be president under the U.S. Constitution. By now you've probably figured out that the hangers-on here are not really fans of J. Danforth Quayle and that those posting pro-Quayle material here (or simply notices of his book-signings, describing mothers standing over Quayle to make sure he spells the name right as he autographs books for their children) are voices lost in a hurricane. Actually, pay close attention and you'll see that the situation is

A picture of former vice president of the United States Dan Quayle, one of many venerated icons in the alt.fan.danquayle Internet archive.

worse even than that—the denizens are, under the veneer of Quayle-bashing, pursuing some kind of naval-theme role-playing game carried out through the medium of political argument. The Snapple-tossing liberal crew of the corsair *Ayeffdeeque* (flying the "Jolly Danoe") accompanied by conservatives in the HMS *Burke* (the two ships seem to need each other at some deep level) launch occasional raids against the Good Ship *Lollypop* (alt.fan.ronald-reagan), the *Garbage Scow* (alt.fan.rush-limbaugh), and the *Decaying Hulk* (alt.society.conservatism).

Internet Access Information: An ftp archive of Quayle pictures and sound bites is located at **vaxa.crc.mssm.edu** in the /quayle/gif/ and the /quayle/sound/ directories. Mosaic users of the World-Wide Web can access URL http://www.pitt.edu/~dejst5/quayle.html for a "home page" on Quayle information. Meanwhile, the group has a periodically posted FAQ file, which should not be read by anyone recovering from abdominal surgery.

alt.bigfoot

This appears to be a nonpolitical version of alt.fan.dan-quayle. I say "appears" because it's difficult to make sense of all the non-stop manic flaming and moose poetry that goes on here. Apparently the newsgroup has a membership roster, and all nonmembers are flamed until they go away. Or so I gathered from the FAQ file, with its uuencoded flag, its anthem sung to the Canadian National Anthem (ending "God keep our group / Offensive as can be / Alt-Dot-Bigfoot / We stand on guard for thee"), its sign-off

notes from victims they claim to have driven to suicide, its research efforts to protect itself from more powerful newsgroups, its feud with the certain people in alt.suicide.holiday, its proposition that power is everything and is best derived by flaming people mercilessly, and its proposal to use ThighMasters as legal tender. Members report spotting bigfoot (a mythic humanoid forest-dweller of the Pacific Northwest) walking the land in various guises, including a sexy woman in a bar.

Quayle still needs to win some people over: political satire found on the Internet.

alt.evil

Got a modest proposal for ending overpopulation and world hunger at the same time? Want to debate whether evil requires freedom, or just stupidity? Wrestling with a definition of evil? That's the kind of stuff that goes on here.

 alt.tasteless
This busy newsgroup is well named. Really well named. Take it from me, it's really, very well named. Some people avoid the sewers; others retreat into them, knowing they won't be followed. If you just want to (shudder) test the waters, there's actually a FAQ for this newsgroup. (It claims Jeffrey Dahmer as a former contributor, but you needn't believe everything you read.)

Internet Access Information: The alt.tasteless FAQ is posted regularly in the usual archives, just as if it originated from a pillar of online society. Try alt.answers and **rtfm.mit. edu**, and within the newsgroup itself. God's mercy on you.

 alt.tasteless.jokes
"Parachute, used once, never opened," is about as clean as it gets amid the lewd, rude, and crude material offered up here to an enthusiastic audience. The entire ethnic joke genre has retreated to this corner of the universe, leaving everyone else with only lawyers to chew on. Thus fueled, the denizens here are experimenting with a new joke genre that shows lots of potential: anti-Microsoft. Meanwhile, my theory is that this newsgroup is the source of the colo-rectal-rodentia stories you will eventually see being thrashed out anyplace online where standards have fallen. Formerly creditable people have even sworn in my presence to the existence of a newsgroup called alt.sex.gerbils.duct-tape (there is a semi-bogus one called alt.sex.ham-

CHAPTER 12

ster.duct-tape). Anyway, there's a discussion of this branch of human knowledge in the FAQ of the alt.folklore.urban newsgroup. The result of someone's extensive research: It's all a myth. However, they also note that gerbils are illegal in California [CA Reg. Title 14, Sec. 671 (c)(2)(J) 1].

alt.sex.fetish.diapers

Yes, they're serious. And if you feel the same compulsions they do (to wear diapers decades after you've outgrown them), you can come here for understanding and advice from the Diaper Pail Friends. There is, in fact, a lot of advice, especially on diaper brands: which are better, where to get them, how to modify them, and how to live a normal life. There's also a periodically posted FAQ file, with diaper vendor information, details on the group's private IRC chat channel, their ftp archives, and how to find the "adult baby" forum on CompuServe.

And Finally

alt.suicide.holiday

People actually post descriptions here of their unsuccessful suicide attempts, sometimes barely hours after the sleeping pills were snatched away. Others wrestle with depression, or try to help those who do, although anyone who comes across as a "shiny bright savior" tends to get flamed. Last I checked they were trying to write a FAQ file focusing on reasons to live. Pray you'll never need to read it. Or their other FAQ, the "methods file."

Saving Face:

You ask? Well, should you opt to become a bunnyhunter, remember—the war must go on! You'd spoil it for everyone if you actually won the thing. Likewise, when following a boarding party over the gunwales in alt.fan.dan-quayle, remember that overreliance on facts and logic will get you denounced as a war criminal. As for the other groups, if you need to read them, you'll know. If you have doubts, try taking two aspirin and going to bed.

COMMERCIAL SERVICES

Traditionally, the commercial services have been worlds unto themselves, with their own collections of programmed offerings, conferences, files, chat lines, and e-mail domains. You can think of them as miniature Internets, with one big difference:

You pay for them.

This may not seem like a big disadvantage when you realize that Internet access, too, has to be paid for, directly or indirectly. And commercial services have a central point of management, which has to consider the wrath of its users and the reality of competition from other services. The result is that you are more likely to get what you pay for. For instance, on the Internet it is not uncommon to encounter response time problems and mysterious outages that, from a commercial service, would bring groveling apologies and billing adjustments.

Meanwhile, with BBSs, you can indeed rig things so you data surf forever for free, but what you'll find out there will be strictly random.

Things you can expect from an online service include:

☞ Reference works (encyclopedias, the Bible, etc.)
☞ Airline guides and ticket sales
☞ News from various news wires, including business, weather, and sports
☞ brokerage services
☞ Stock market data
☞ Corporate data
☞ Travel services (hotel booking, tour booking, car rental, tourist information, etc.)
☞ E-mail, with gateways to other services
☞ Telex transmission
☞ Fax transmission
☞ Commercial database access
☞ Discussion conferences, with associated files and chat lines
☞ Chat lines (by themselves)
☞ Online games
☞ Attentive customer service

There are often several levels of pricing. The basic fee (which we'll list with each service) covers basic services, which normally include chatting, e-mail, most conferences, Internet access if any, and most games. Surcharges may be added for things like 9,600-bit-per-second access, brokerage services, business database searches, e-mail over a certain size, some conferences sponsored by third parties, fancier games, and certain specialized services.

Today, there's an additional trend of Internet access, and you see Usenet newsgroups with back-and-forth responses originating from users of multiple commercial services. Internet access has also eased the start-up dilemma that faces new services, which would otherwise have no ongoing conferences to attract the users whose input embodies the conferences. The result is that hardly a week goes by without the announcement of a new online service of some sort.

In this book we have restricted ourselves to established commercial services that provide a medium for the expression of the user's grassroots urges. Those geared toward digital entertainment (like Prodigy) or one-way database searching (like Dialog) or to mirror the contents of specific publications were omitted. (Such services, though, have their place in the scheme of things.)

AMERICA ONLINE (AOL)

Other commercial services offer some sort of optional graphics front end, but America Online is built around one. The Windows program (or similar windowed Macintosh or DOS interfaces) you get with your subscription handles all the interfacing chores, including dialing in. All you have to remember (after you get it set up initially with the correct phone number, etc.) is your password. Every time thereafter, you just click on a screen button and (after the usual handshaking rigmarole) you're online.

When you get online with AOL, you're presented with welcoming screens, and as you pick each option and get deeper into various menus, you are presented with more and more windows, laid atop each other. In the end you feel like you're going around pulling aside curtains to see what's behind them. If you feel frustrated at ever getting the big picture, there's a keyword command that will give you a list of the available keywords, and from that you can size up the entire domain.

The main drawback has been the connection speed. Although 9,600-bits-per-second access is becoming available in most major cities, the standard connection speed has been 2,400 bits per second. Accessing text-based offerings at 2,400 bits per second is slow but not unmanageable—they have rigged it so you can start reading text in a window before it has all arrived. If the system has to download a new icon before showing the next window, the system might seem to stop for half a minute. Downloading large files, meanwhile, can be painfully tedious—some can take hours. In the end you may feel as if you are running Windows off a slow but huge floppy disk, one you'll probably never manage to explore completely.

AOL has been aggressive in getting popular magazines to sign up with online editions, such as *Omni, Consumer Reports,* the *Smithsonian,* and *Scientific American. Time* magazine came out with its first daily edition on AOL.

All in all, I keep running across people remarking to the effect that AOL, with its undemanding software and proven, context-rich offerings, is "what Prodigy should have been." The proof is in the pudding—AOL's subscription list grew about 142 percent during 1993, to about 530,000, and at this writing is well over 800,000. (Most services are coy about giving out subscription totals, incidentally.)

The cost is $9.95 per month for up to five hours access anytime during the day, and $3.50 an hour thereafter. For information, call 800-827-6364.

To send mail to another service, in the "To:" field on the "Compose Mail" screen just input the Internet version of that person's mail address. Similarly you can get mail from other services via the Internet bridge using the form "your-name@aol.com" where "yourname" is your AOL user name (what AOL calls your "screen name").

BIX

The Byte Information Exchange was originally started by *Byte* magazine as an auxiliary service to the magazine, and many of the conference moderators were associated with *Byte,* either as editors or contributors. Its subsequent sale to the same firm that runs Delphi has not changed things much—BIX is still 98 percent conferences. Files and games, and its chat area (called CBIX), are only incidentals.

BIX, like Delphi, offers full Internet access—just type "gopher" or "ftp" or "telnet" or "nn" (for reading Usenet newsgroups) from the command prompt. BIX's Internet conference is said to be its most popular discussion area. The professional programming conferences are also popular, and there is a large concentration of Amiga users and developers.

For current events and general talk, the tojerry conference is popular. It's hosted by science fiction author and *Byte* columnist Jerry Pournelle.

The basic subscription is $13 a month, plus $3 an hour during the weekends and evenings, and $9 per hour during business hours (called primetime in the online world.) The price includes that of the packet-switching services you'll be traversing. If you are in a position to call them locally (in Cambridge, Massachusetts) or access them via Internet telnet, you can save money, since those routes only cost $1 an hour at any time. For information, call 800-695-4775.

To send Internet mail, just use an Internet address in the "to" line when sending mail. You can receive Internet mail, or mail form other services using the Internet as a bridge, with the address "yourname@bix.com" where "yourname" is your BIX user name.

COMPUSERVE

The CompuServe service is owned by H&R Block (the national tax accounting firm) and is one of the oldest services around. The former fact probably explains CompuServe's emphasis on investor services. The latter probably explains CompuServe's emphasis on hardware and software-specific conferences and forums, since it was personal computer users seeking information and software that got the commercial services off the ground. Many of CompuServe's computer forums are brand-specific and are moderated by the manufacturer itself. For some software firms (including divisions of Microsoft) "customer support" has come to mean posting patches in the CompuServe forum that bears its name.

The conferences usually have their own libraries and chat areas as well as the conference postings. All in all, CompuServe's list of services is broad and well developed—the total is said to be about two thousand.

For $8.95 a month you get unlimited access to CompuServe's basic services. Surcharged services (and that includes most conferences) costs eight cents a minute. Access of 9,600 or 14,400 bits per second is another sixteen cents per minute. Certain stock market and database services carry additional charges. And keep in mind that if you are traversing a packet switching service, its charges are an additional surcharge, and will vary with time of day. For information, call 800-848-8199.

To send mail to an Internet address, or to someone on another service via the Internet: when CompuServe Mail asks you for the address of the recipient, say "Internet: address" where "address" is the Internet address. Note that there is no space after the colon.

People can send mail via the Internet to you on CompuServe by using your CompuServe address with the comma changed to a period, followed by "@compuserve.com". If your CompuServe address is 123456,987, your Internet address is 123456.987@compuserve.com.

DELPHI

You can gauge the trend at Delphi when you realize its corporate name used to be General Videotex Corporation, but in 1993 (after being bought by Rupert Murdoch's empire) it changed to Delphi Internet Services Corporation. And the Internet remains the big draw that Delphi uses. It has its own set of conference forums (called SIGs—Special Interest Groups), but its ads tout Internet access—five hours free for joining up. Which is great, except that most Delphi connections are still at 2,400 bits per second (that is changing) and five hours at 2,400 bits per second is not enough to scratch the surface of the Internet. Within the speed restriction, you can carry out all the common Internet functions: ftp, Usenet, telnet, IRC, gopher, archie, e-mail, the World Wide Web, etc.

Delphi has additionally taken the concept of conferences one step forward with the use of custom forums that are created and run by members—a sort of in-house alt. hierarchy. There are about 150 of them, ranging from animal rights to divorce support. Some are open to all comers, and some are private clubs you have to ask for admittance to.

Delphi offers two basic plans, called 10-4 and 20-20. The 10-4 plans offers four hours a month for $10 and $4 an hour thereafter. The 20-20 plan is $20 for 20 hours and $1.80 an hour thereafter. There is also a $9 surcharge prime-time use if you're accessing GEnie through a packet switching network. (Direct-dial and telnet access carry no surcharge at any time.) Internet access costs an additional $3 a month flat fee.

You can join online by calling 800-365-4636. At the Username prompt, reply with JOINDELPHI. At the password prompt, reply NWS94. Or you can talk to someone (or at least listen to a recording) at 800-544-4005.

To send mail out to someone on another service, use the Internet version of their mail address. Go to either the mail prompt under the main menu or the mail prompt under the Internet Services menu and say Send. When it asks "To:" input:

```
Internet"name@internet.address"
```

Note that there is no space after Internet.

You can receive mail from the Internet, or from another service using the Internet as a bridge, with the address "yourname@delphi.com" where "yourname" is your Delphi online user name.

GENIE

GE Information Services offers GEnie. Like CompuServe, services are divided into interest areas, each with its own file library, conferences, and chat areas. In GEnie's, these areas are called roundtables.

Superficially, GEnie touts itself as a service for the business and professional user, with access to the Charles Schwab brokerage, plus Dow Jones News/Retrieval, TRW business credit profiles, Dunn and Bradstreet corporate profiles, investment analysis services, portfolio management services, and other business research tools and an investors roundtable.

Scratch the surface, though, and you immediately see that it's really a consumer service. One of its busiest conference areas (especially during the summer) is the Disney Roundtable, offering travel information concerning Disney's theme parks. There are also quite a few role-playing and adventure games online, and more than 150,000 files.

The monthly subscription is $8.95, which gets you four hours of evening time. Evening time is $3 an hour thereafter. Primetime is $9.50 an hour. For information, call 800-638-9636.

You can send mail to people on other services and the Internet by using their Internet address. After GEniemail asks for their address, give their Internet version of their address followed by @inet#. Note that there is no space before the @.

Meanwhile, you can receive mail through the Internet (or from other services using the Internet as a bridge) at "your-name@genie.geis.com" where "yourname" is your GEnie user name.

BBSs AND ECHO NETWORKS

BBSs can be thought of as one-person commercial networks. When online with a BBS, you may or may not be able to tell the difference between being online with CompuServe—you're still getting files and participating in conferences—and perhaps running a game. Except that, in all but a few cases, the online resources of a BBS are only a tiny fraction of the resources of a commercial service. The BBS is, after all, basically just somebody's PC that you're using remotely. (However, the use of echo networks, explained in this chapter, greatly expands the available conferencing resources.)

So what's the big deal? Well, BBSs have one enormous advantage over commercial services or the Internet:

They're free.

Most are set up as hobbies, and hobbies they remain. Many of the larger ones will charge you a yearly subscription so the owner won't feel so guilty about what he's spending on his toy, and a few have thousands of subscribers and a paid staff. But even in those cases you can call in as a "guest" for free. Your access will simply remain limited until you pay up—maybe you can only stay online for half an hour, maybe you'll be limited to the amount of downloading you can do, maybe certain files and conferences will be denied you, or all three may apply. Otherwise, you can count on data surfing for only the cost of the phone call. And if you can line up a list of BBSs within your local toll-free calling area (and most cities have scores of BBSs these days) you can count on data surfing cost-free. And if you find a local board that's part of one of the larger echo networks (explained later) you can converse with like-minded people worldwide on a sort of low-budget version of the Internet. On some nights it may work as well as the Internet.

Businesses, meanwhile, have embraced the idea of BBSs, using them for posting software patches, electronic mail, field automation, and customer support. Some, additionally, even belong to echo networks.

Some jargon:

QWK—File extension used by many mail reader software packages for conference material to be uploaded or downloaded for a specific user.

Door—A program, such as a game, order-taking facility, or database search tool, designed to be invoked by the BBS program. The BBS program loads the door and then drops out. The door runs, using the serial connection set up by the BBS program. When through, it drops out and reinvokes the BBS program. For doors to work on a multiline BBS, each line normally has to run on a separate PC (linked via a LAN) or in a memory partition.

Integrated—BBS software intended to handle multiple lines from one machine (using special multiport serial boards) performing its own multitasking. Doors are not possible, but the software will include its own programming language and/or offers a programming interface for adding custom features. Examples: TBBS and The Major BBS.

Mail Reader—User software (which usually invokes a door on the BBS) that lets you download new conference postings, read them offline, write comments, and upload the comments. Thus you can have full participation in your favorite conferences for a fraction of the long-distance phone charges it would otherwise take. The appearance of mail readers is what caused BBSs to take off in the 1980s, since the users no longer felt the "clock ticking."

Multinode—BBS software intended to run on a LAN, one line per node, to facilitate running doors. (Small systems can use a memory manager instead of a LAN.) Examples: PCBoard and Wildcat.

PCBoard—Brand of BBS software from Clark Development Company.

RBBS—Freeware BBS software.

RIP—Remote Imaging Protocol, system used to create graphics-based BBSs.

Sysop—System operator, usually meaning the guy who owns the BBS.

TBBS—The Breadboard System, a brand of BBS software from eSoft, Inc.

The Major BBS—Brand of BBS software, from Galacticomm, Inc.

Wildcat—A brand of BBS software from Mustang Software.

SOME GREAT BBSs

Online, you can regularly encounter user-collected lists of hundreds of different BBSs—getting two thousand BBSs appears to be a chore, not a challenge. Despite the size of the lists, there may not be much overlap—some people estimate there are as many as fifty thousand public BBSs out there. The number of private ones, used for a business's e-mail or an organization's member support, could easily be double that.

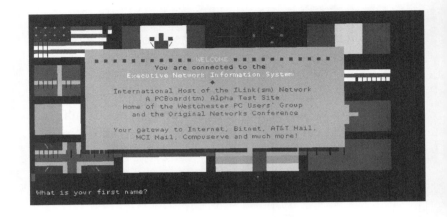

The problem with such lists is that BBSs are ephemeral. Any surplus 8088 and modem will serve to host a single-line BBS, and shareware or freeware BBS software is widely available online for the asking. (Many commercial telecommunications software packages include all the facilities you need to set up a simple BBS with no echoes or conferences.) Therefore, many people and organizations find they can set one up for no more than the cost of the phone line. And then they can take it down with the flip of a switch.

So it's no mystery why my own luck using such lists has ranged from poor to grim, mostly getting me an education in what "line no longer in service" messages sound like in various parts of the country.

The following, however, have been around for a while and appear to have firm foundations. Hopefully they will still be around when this book comes out. If all else fails, you can start with them, look for lists, and work backward to your own neighborhood.

- ☞ Aquila   708-820-8344, large Chicago BBS
- ☞ EXEC PC   414-789-4210, located in Wisconsin, it has nearly 300 dial-in lines and is said to be the largest BBS in the world
- ☞ Channel 1   617-354-8873, large Boston-area BBS

Check This Out:

Lists of BBSs also appear in certain magazines, including *Boardwatch, Computer Shopper, BBS* magazine, and *On-Line Access.*

Welcoming screen of Rusty-n-Edie's BBS, using PC ANSI graphics.

☞ Boardwatch 303-973-4222, located in Colorado, this BBS is run by *Boardwatch* magazine
☞ Rusty & Edie's 216-726-0737, this large board is located in Ohio
☞ The Well 415-332-6106, this San Francisco Bay Area Unix system offers Internet access, and is a hotbed of Bay Area-ness

Echo Networks

We mentioned echo networks. The idea is simple: In the same way the individual users download new conference messages and upload new comments, individual BBSs will upload and download new conference traffic to each other. (Sometimes e-mail and files are also carried.) Usually the traffic goes through a central BBS serving as the hub. Larger networks may have multitiered systems with local, regional, continental, and global hubs.

The result is that you have a slow version of the Internet. Assuming all the nodes are echoing during the night (when it's cheaper) to their hubs, BBSs across the world can be carrying the same conference traffic current to within two days. More and more of them echo several times a day, making it increasingly likely the traffic you'll see will be nearly real-time.

And Check This Out:

Increasing numbers of larger BBSs are boasting Internet access. Sometimes this means they have an Internet mail address, sometimes it means they carry Usenet newsgroups, and sometimes it means they have full ftp and telnet facilities. You have to ask.

BBSs AND ECHO NETWORKS

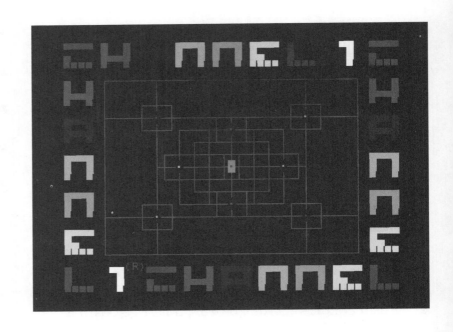

**Check
This Out, Too:**

More and more of the larger BBSs are accessible through packet-switching services, which should be cheaper than long-distance phone access. If your favorite BBS is on such a network, it can supply you with the access details.

The problem with echo networks is that they are only slightly less ephemeral than BBSs. You can set one up at the drop of a hat. The common procedure is to rely on FidoNet protocols, contact some sysops with similar interests, set up some conferences, give the collection a name, iron out the echo procedures, fire up the modem, and you're an echo network.

The best single point of information on echo networks that I found is the IBMBBS Forum on CompuServe. In the libraries section of that forum, item ten is labeled "BBS Networks." It contains information files and sysop membership applications for start-up networks. (There is similar material in the GEnie BBS RoundTable—enter the library and use the Set Software Libraries, and use setting 57, "BBS Lists and Ads.") The "othernets" conference on FidoNet is also cited as a good source of information.

As for what shows up—name it, it's there. I've seen sysops trying to raise interest in echo networks whose topics included:

- ☞ Pilots
- ☞ Earthbound flight simulator users
- ☞ Psychologists
- ☞ Canadian gays
- ☞ Jews
- ☞ Christians
- ☞ Pre-Rapture Christians
- ☞ Masons
- ☞ Yankees
- ☞ Southerners
- ☞ Programmers
- ☞ "Truth seekers"
- ☞ Writers
- ☞ Artists
- ☞ Eco-activists
- ☞ Sex enthusiasts seeking "sensitive" themes
- ☞ Sex enthusiasts who are beyond such concerns
- ☞ Cross-dressers
- ☞ Real estate agents
- ☞ Outdoor sportsmen
- ☞ Residents of various corners of the globe setting up regional nets, from Oregon to Osaka

By and large, these are all start-up networks and may or may not be around when you set out to track them down. Paralleling the case with BBSs, getting a list of thirty is no problem, but may not overlap someone else's list.

The established main-line networks don't need to advertise—sysops come to them. Some of the established ones include the following:

- ☞ FidoNet   FidoNet is a faithful old dog, being the oldest of the hobbyists' echo networks and assuredly the largest. Lately it boasts over twenty-five thousand nodes worldwide. A major North American hub is at The FidoNet Eastern Star, at 717-657-2223.
- ☞ ILink   ILink has "only" a few hundred nodes, as it seeks to restrict membership to "quality" boards. The

Check This Out:

It's common to see BBSs belonging to more than one echo network. On the other hand, while some networks offer hundreds of conferences, few BBSs will carry all the conferences of a particular network. What's carried by a BBS is entirely decided by the sysop, based on his or her tastes and/or the capacity of the machine.

BBSs AND ECHO NETWORKS

hub is at the Executive Network Information System BBS at 914-667-4684.

☞ **RelayNet** A very inclusive network with more than a thousand nodes worldwide, its hub is at the Running Board BBS at 301-229-5623.

☞ **SmartNet** Looser than ILink but tighter than RelayNet, SmartNet's hub is at the Sound of Music BBS at 516-536-8723.

☞ **NANet** Also called NorthAmeriNet, this network is a sort of feeder network for Canada Remote Systems BBS, the large BBS that also serves as its hub, at 416-213-6003.

People Talking About BBSs

As you might imagine, the best way to learn about BBSs is online. Some online resources devoted to them include the following:

 alt.bbs.lists
This newsgroup is where lists of bulletin boards show up, often grouped by area code, geographic region, or software type. Plus, people post requests here for lists of BBSs in particular regions—requests that frequently get responses. Many sysops maintain lists of other BSSs in their neighborhoods, so all you have to do is trigger a response from the right person. The only problem with relying on this newsgroup for lists that you can use to get online with is that to get the lists you already have to be online—the old chicken-and-egg problem.

 alt.bbs
This busy newsgroup plays host to a lot of general software questions from sysops struggling with their systems. Plus there are people

looking for boards in particular areas, or boards that have a particular specialty—Confederate history, for instance.

comp.bbs.misc

This newsgroup differs from alt.bbs mainly in that there is more international traffic. If they are looking for boards in Toledo, they could just easily mean Spain as Ohio.

alt.bbs.internet

If you have any kind of question concerning BBSs that offer Internet access—setting up software, or where to find one—you'll be in good company here. From the postings here, yearning for Internet access is universal—people are looking for sites in Saipan, the West Bank, Kenya, Oman, and even Albany, New York.

BBS Corner (AOL)

This AOL department can be reached through keyword: BBS. There are regional lists of BBSs, *Boardwatch* magazine online, a forum sponsored by the National Association of Sysops, software support libraries from several BBS software vendors, and wide-ranging discussion forums.

BBS (BIX)

This BIX conference includes sysops-related discussions centering on the main BBS software systems, plus developments in the world of virus fighting, and FidoNet news. There is a topic titled "Recommended" where people post information on their favorite BBSs. Sometimes these are individual reviews, sometimes regional lists, sometimes sysops promoting their own boards. The moderator removes logons, access codes, blatant advertising, and other dubious things.

IBMBBS (CIS)

On CompuServe, if you GO IBMBBS you're delivered to the IBM Bulletin Board Systems forum, part of the IBM users forum. There are wide-ranging discussions concerning topics of interest to sysops using boards based on the IBM PC architecture, including files of utilities and doors. There is a strong FidoNet presence.

BBS SIG (Delphi)

This Delphi forum can be reached by selecting the Computing Group at the main menu, and then the BBS SIG. As well as a chat area and a discussion where sysops wrestle with software, there's a database area offering whole BBS shareware systems, plus, for example, doors, utilities, mail readers, graphics front ends, and mail readers.

THE INTERNET

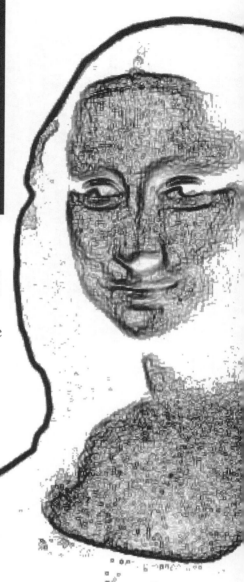

The Internet is what people are usually thinking of when they talk about the Information Superhighway (unless they are talking about electronic commerce via interactive cable TV, an idea that many consider bogus). The Internet is basically a huge echo network using high-performance hardware and telecommunications links. You should be able to sit at an Internet machine and interact in (almost) real-time with any other machine on the Internet. There are said to be thirty thousand large computers or networks connected to the Internet, with as many as twenty million users, with monthly growth figures said to be in the double digits. The range and volume of the information available on the Internet defies description, and all of it is just a few keystrokes away.

So you can see why people get excited about the subject. But everything has its down side, and with the Internet the downside is spelled c-h-a-o-s. No one entity owns or runs the Internet—each site participates on the basis of its own comfort level and/or budget. Basically, all any Internet node has in common with any other is that it can be reached, eventually, from any other site through data communications links and will respond to a short list of least-common-denominator Unix commands. The procedures you need to use are arcane, and what's available changes endlessly.

Meanwhile, to use the Internet you must be sitting at a terminal inside one of the Internet's nodes or must be hooked remotely from a desktop computer via modem to an Internet node. In the latter case your desktop is acting as a terminal on the Internet node, but you will (usually) have to add the extra step of downloading any files you get from your Internet node to your desktop machine.

HOW IT ALL BEGAN

In the beginning was the Cold War. And the U.S. military looked on their avowed enemies to the East and thought, "Look at them—like Frederick the Great with rural electrification. But if they ever manage to pop a nuke in our neighborhood, the resulting meltdown of random phone network components could negatively impact the flow of paperwork. How can we ensure that our telex messages always get through?"

And so they cooked up a protocol called TCP/IP, by which messages are herded through network nodes like tourists through airports, to be reassembled in a coherent fashion at their destination. They rigged up a network using it, connecting military research institutions with academic research sites and other interested parties. They called it Arpanet, for Advanced Research Projects Administration Net.

And it was discovered that a network that could continue to function in the face of random damage could also continue to function in the face of random growth. And grow it did, until the tail was wagging the dog, and the military decided to takes its marbles and go elsewhere. But the Internet—as they now called it—got along fine on its own. And although participation was a voluntary thing, the Internet soon became an indispensable tool for many.

Astronauts repairing a satellite in a photo retrieved from the Internet via ftp.

INTERNET BASICS

There are five basic things you can do on the Internet—ftp, telnet, archie, Usenet, and mail lists. Much of this book concerns them. Other, more exotic things will be covered later in the chapter.

FTP

FTP stands for File Transfer Protocol, and it allows someone at one Internet computer to get files from another. Files are sent from the remote site to the user's site. If the user then wants to download them to his or her PC, that involves an extra step, normally employing ordinary file transfer protocols.

Meanwhile, across the world, countless organizations with Internet nodes have set up certain files on their systems as being open to "anonymous ftp." The files are usually arranged in a hierarchy under a directory called /pub/. The files may have been placed there to promote the dissemination of knowledge, to enhance the organization's reputation, or in the spirit of a farmer who plants some vegetables outside the fence to distract the rabbits. It doesn't matter. All that matters is that anyone with an Internet connection can get at these files and copy them back to their own machine. Except for the basic connection costs involved in being online, there is no charge.

So, sitting at your Internet node, you have the world at your fingertips. At least, it can be after you understand the use of the following ftp commands:

ascii—Switch to ASCII mode. ASCII mode is the default mode and used for transferring text files.

binary—Switch to binary mode. For transferring binary files like .ZIP files or .Z files. You must use this mode for binary files or the files will be corrupted.

cd—Change the directory on the remote computer, as with an MS-DOS machine.

cdup—Move up (or backward, as you please) a directory level.

dir—List the files in the current directory on the remote computer, showing file sizes and other information.

get—Copy a file from the remote computer to yours.

hash—Puts a '#' on the screen for every 1,024 bytes transferred during a "get" or "mget" operation, so you'll know the computer is still working during long file transfers. (Otherwise, nothing may appear to happen for minutes on end.)

help—Gives help on the use of commands within the ftp program.

ls—List the files on the remote node, in the working directory, giving file names only.

mget—Copy multiple files from the remote computer to yours. You can use wildcards to get lists of files, such as "mget read*" to get readme and read.me.

pwd—Shows the present working directory (pwd) so you'll know where you are on the remote node.

put—Opposite of get (often disabled).

The procedure is that you call up your local node's ftp facility, and then, when prompted, supply the name of the Internet node you want to reach, such as "rtfm.mit.edu". Your node then goes out on the Net and establishes the connection. The next thing you'll see is the remote machine asking for your log-in name. Traditionally, you supply the word "anonymous." You are then asked for your password. Traditionally, you supply your e-mail address.

At that point you are logged on to the remote system and are free to use the commands just listed. Restrictions apply—as mentioned, anonymous users are allowed access only to certain directories.

Saving Face:

You must use the binary command if you are getting anything but an ASCII text file, or it will be corrupted at your end. Most such files are compressed, and the first sign of trouble is usually when the decompression program can't handle the file.

Saving Face:

On some nodes you have to move in one leap to a specific subdirectory: You have to say "cd /pub/pc/software/" rather than doing a separate cd for each directory level. That's because access to the intermediate subdirectories is restricted.

You can then use cd and cdup to navigate through the directory hierarchy, using ls or dir to examine the file names. When you see what you want, you can use the get or mget commands to copy it to your local node. FTP is not instantaneous—large files can take several minutes. To steady your nerves, you might want to use the hash command.

When you are through, you can break the connection with close or quit, or whatever your host machine uses.

All computers have a limit to the number of connections they can service, and Internet sites usually have an additional restriction to the number of simultaneous anonymous connections they will permit, lest the machine be taken over by remote callers, leaving the local users unable to get anything done. If the limit is fifty and you are caller fifty-one, you will get a (usually) polite message telling you that the connection is refused. If the site has this problem repeatedly, try using it only in the evening. And it's always best to use the nearest sites (when there's a choice) to cut down on network congestion.

It is possible to perform ftp via e-mail, by sending a message to the site to trigger the transmission of the file to your e-mail address. The practice, however, seems to be in disrepute due to the congestion it can cause (the files can be unexpectedly huge), and some sites don't allow it or pass on the traffic. Check with your site about whether it's allowed, and the procedure.

Telnet

Telnet is a facility by which you can login to a remote computer through the Internet. You use your name and password, and function as if you were sitting at one of the remote computer's terminals. This assumes, of course, that you have an account on that remote computer. Some hosts have telnet services that anyone can use with a generic password, such as "guest," or the abbreviation of the name of the service you wish to use. This is especially the case with library card catalogs and government database services, where telnet access can provide a "user friendly" interface.

Check This Out:

Most Internet nodes are Unix machines and therefore "case dependent" when it comes to handling files and navigating subdirectories. Saying "get read.me" will not work if the file is named Read.me or READ.ME. Likewise, using Anonymous will not always work as your login—always use anonymous (lowercase) for better results.

Archie

Archie is short for "archiver." Several sites monthly poll other sites to see what files they have posted, and then post that list. Using archie, you can search that list for a given file name (or, rather, a file name that contains the text string you give). There are archie servers you can telnet into, but most sites worth mentioning have an archie facility to handle the searching for you. Check your documentation.

Note again that what archie searches is the file names, not the contents of the files. You can't know if you've really found what you are looking for until you get the file into your machine and examine it. And the list could be a month out of date.

Usenet

Usenet is the set of conference forums (called "newsgroups") usually associated with the Internet. Actually, Usenet is carried by services other than the Internet, and there is no requirement that an Internet site carry Usenet. But the two are usually found hand in hand.

As conferencing systems go, Usenet is the mother of them all. There are, in worldwide circulation, more than forty-five hundred newsgroups, covering topics as wide apart as locksmithing and deviant sexual practices. It is estimated that two hundred thousand people participate in Usenet newsgroups, from sites all over the globe. Traffic at this writing amounts to 3.5 gigabytes per month. A question posed in Cleveland can trigger answers from night owls in South Africa, Singapore, and Italy—within minutes. (Actually, though, it can take a couple of days for a message to propagate to all Usenet sites, so responses can dribble in for a while.)

When approaching newsgroups, you have to understand that they are divided into "hierarchies." If you see one

```
open oak.oakland.edu
Connected to oak.oakland.edu.
220 oak.oakland.edu FTP server (Version wu-2.4(3) Thu Apr 14 15:45:26 EDT 1994) ready.
Name (oak.oakland.edu:lamont): anonymous
331 Guest login ok, send your complete e-mail address as password.
Password:
230-Please read the file README
230-  it was last modified on Tue Apr 26 11:56:15 1994 - 2 days ago
230 Guest login ok, access restrictions apply.
ftp> cd /pub/msdos/filedocs/
250 CWD command successful.
ftp> binary
200 Type set to I.
ftp> hash
Hash mark printing on (1024 bytes/hash mark).b
ftp> get mailserv.inf
200 PORT command successful.
150 Opening BINARY mode data connection for mailserv.inf (2615 bytes).
######
226 Transfer complete.
local: mailserv.inf remote: mailserv.inf
2615 bytes received in 1.4 seconds (1.8 Kbytes/s)
ftp> close
221 Goodbye.
ftp> quit
```

*A typical ftp session. I opened an ftp connection to oak.oakland.edu. The
remote system asked for my name. I responded "anonymous" and it
responded affirmatively and asked for a password, which it did not echo.
Thereafter, input from the remote system began with a three-digit number—
the code for that response. Input at my end was prompted with "ftp>". As you
can see, there was a welcoming message telling me to read the README file.
(Actually, there were several paragraphs of notices, but I edited them out.)
Then I did a "cd" to the directory I wanted. Then I gave the "binary" command to make sure binary files would get through uncorrupted. Then I gave
the "hash" command so I could watch the progress of the file transfer. Then I
gave the "get" command to trigger the file transfer. The file was short and
came over in only 1.4 seconds. I then ended the connection with the "close"
command. The "quit" command told the local machine to leave ftp mode.*

whose name starts with "aus." you can assume it concerns Australia. If you see one named "aus.computers," you can assume it's a general computer conference from Australia. If it's named "aus.computers.ibm-pc," you can bet the conference is about the use of PCs in Australia. Meanwhile, if the name ends with "-d" that means the conference is devoted to free discussions, usually of a software or moderated postings of material in another newsgroup of the same name, but without the -d at the end. The main hierarchies appear to be:

☞ biz.—Business newsgroups, usually specific to a corporation
☞ comp.—Computer-related subjects
☞ misc.—Miscellaneous material
☞ news.—News, usually about the Usenet and the Internet
☞ rec.—Recreation
☞ sci.—The sciences
☞ soc.—Sociology, culture, social concerns

And there are dozens of others, often of regional concern. Plus there's the alt. hierarchy, not considered one of the standard hierarchies. There, anything goes. Each site can decide what newsgroups or hierarchies it will carry. A common decision involves whether to carry the alt. hierarchy, and especially the alt.sex. hierarchy (see Chapter 11).

Some newsgroups are moderated, and postings should be sent as e-mail to the moderator, whose name you'll doubtless see when reading the conference messages. In some cases, postings or replies are automatically routed to the moderator.

Many (but not all) conferences have FAQ files, answering Frequently Asked Questions about the conference and the subject it covers. You should read the FAQ file before launching questions of your own, lest you discover they've already been covered a hundred times. The FAQ file is often posted at intervals in the conference, usually at least monthly, since most sites don't keep newsgroup postings online for more than a month. FAQ files are often archived at several central locations, including **rtfm.mit.edu** and **ftp.uu.net** in North America; **ftp.uni-paderborn.de**, **ftp.germany.eu.net**, **grasp1.univ-lyon1.fr**, and **ftp.win.tue.nl** in Europe; and **nctuccca.edu.tw** in Asia. The newsgroup postings themselves are rarely archived, but information such as data files and background material concerning the newsgroup's subject are often archived with the FAQ file. (FAQ files are usually written by the moderator or a volunteer, often with ongoing input from the users. With the rise in the Internet's visibility, some FAQ writers have become celebrities.)

If you are new to Usenet, you also should not run out and start posting until you are sure you have the hang of your software. There are newsgroups in most hierarchies with names that end in .test. Try posting to a test newsgroup, and then see how your contribution looks. Other than that, there are a couple of technical tricks specific to Usenet that you will need to know.

uuencoding—There has been no way of attaching binary files to newsgroup postings, frustrating those who wanted to post programs or artwork. To get around this, they use uuencoding, where binary data is encoded as ASCII text strings. Other users download the postings (usually it is in several "threaded" messages, most binary files being too long for one newsgroup message), string them together, and perform uudecoding. (Various freeware decoders for the PC are in circulation—I have had very mixed luck with them.) Your site may have a uudecoder and a mail reader that can submit a selected posting to the decoder and then present you with the resulting binary file. The latter is a much easier way of doing it. Check your documentation. Newer mail readers are supporting a protocol called MIME by which binary material is detected and automatically converted.

Beauty is in the

eye of the

beholder.

rot(13)—To avoid giving offense, off-color jokes and the like are often posted in a code called rot(13), where the position of the letters in the alphabet are rotated forward 13 positions. Performing rot(13) a second time restores them. Your Unix server may list rot(13) as one of its file conversion facilities. Otherwise, check the documentation of your mail reader utility.

Mail Lists

An Internet mail list is a sort of inverted conference. The basic idea is that instead of posting messages in a common text database where it can be read with all the other messages in that database—which is what a conference or newsgroup amounts to—you send your contribution to an e-mail address. Software at that site then resends the message to all members of the mailing lists.

In practice, most mail lists are moderated, and incoming material is not immediately retransmitted. The moderator gathers and culls incoming material and sends batches out periodically. In essence, the result is an electronic newsletter, one created by its own readership.

In this book, mail lists are listed along with conferences and newsgroups, with a different bullet:

newsgroup

This is the name of a newsgroup, conference, or forum, and can be reached through the carrier mentioned here in the description. If none is mentioned, it's a Usenet newsgroup. The number represents my subjective rating of the conference's noise-to-information ratio, with one indicating all noise, and five indicating all information. Flaming and pointless chatter count as noise, although, admittedly, that's the whole point of some conferences.

mail-list-name

This is an Internet mail list. Send your subscription request to **listaddress@host.site**. The number represents my estimate of the mail list's noise-to-information ratio, with one indicating all noise, and five indicating all information.

If the subscription address for a mail list starts with "listserv" or "majordomo" the standard protocol is that if you want to subscribe, you send a single-line "listserv command" to the contact address, thusly:

```
SUBSCRIBE MAIL-LIST-NAME yourfirstname yourlastname
```

Notice that you should list your real name, not your e-mail address, which the software can get from the header of the message. SUB can be used instead of SUBSCRIBE. Should

Check This Out:

Uuencoding and -decoding are standard Unix features. If you are on a Unix system, try typing "man uudecode" to see a help listing. If you are stuck on a PC with a uuencoded file, a DOS uudecoder that has been highly spoken of is uuexe525.zip in the Garbo file archive (see Chapter 8). You can get it from there via anonymous ftp **garbo.uwasa.fi** in the /pc/decode/ directory. You can also get it from the many Garbo mirrors, and doubtless from scads of other places.

THE INTERNET

you later change your mind, you can unsubscribe by sending the message again, adding UN in front of SUB or SUBSCRIBE. Do not put anything else in the message—a human being will not read it, and any extra verbiage may confuse the software.

If the address does not begin with "listserv" or "majordomo" you can assume that a live person will read your message, and accordingly write a polite message asking to be added to the list.

However, there are variations. Sometimes the listserv command should be in the header instead of the body of the message. Sometimes is should be on the second line of the body, with the first left blank. And sometimes you need to send your qualifications to the moderator. Most mail lists are associated with a conference, whose FAQ will give the details.

A list of publicly accessible mailing lists is available through the FAQ archive at **rtfm.mit.edu** in the /pub/ usenet/news.answers/mail/mailing-lists/ directory. It is probably at mirror sites as well. There are about eight hundred such mailing lists, and there is no estimate as to how many private ones might exist.

SOME INTERNET TRICKS

The good news about the Internet is that developments unfold faster, and in more directions, than you can keep track of. The bad news about the Internet is that developments unfold faster, and in more directions, than you can keep track of. But some developments that offer improvements over classic ftp access include gophers, WAIS, and WWW.

Gopher

Gopher is an attempt to wring order out of the primal chaos of the Internet. If your Internet site or access provider has a gopher service, you can call it up and see a menu of

Internet offerings, by category. You pick a category and go deeper and deeper into the menu until you get to an actual online service. Gopher then connects you to that service. If you are using gopher for file access, some gophers can download it to your desktop machine at the same time it is transferring it via ftp from the remote site. Some will even perform any necessary decompression on the fly. The range of offerings on the Net that are accessible through gopher is called "gopherspace."

Gopher is possible because many of the sites that offer gopher themselves put together a gopher menu of what they offer (if anything) and post it. These menus are gathered and compiled by a sort of super gopher at the University of Minnesota.

There are, at this writing, as many as six thousand participating gopher sites. Many of the Internet resources mentioned in this book can be found via gopher, but not all, and your results will vary from day to day and site to site.

"Veronica," meanwhile, is a facility for performing keyword searches on gopher menus.

WAIS

Wide Area Information Servers (WAIS) is similar to gopher, except that after you pick a likely information source from the menu, you can use keyword searches to find what you want, based on full-text searches of the available material. You can then display or retrieve any files that have been located. About five hundred databases are available over WAIS at this writing, covering bibliographies, technical documents, newsgroup archives, and even recipes and movies.

WWW

The World Wide Web offers hypermedia browsing—references in one document can call up another, possibly located around the globe. Hypertext can be thought of as fancy,

computerized footnotes—except that when you call up the footnote, it could be another whole document or other data resource. When reading a document in WWW, the text will be interspersed with numbers in square brackets. These are the hypertext markers. Typing one of those numbers will take you to the hypertext reference.

Artist's vision of a Mars landing, found on the Internet.

With online viewers, such as Mosaic for Windows and Macintosh, AMosaic for the Amiga, DOSLynx for MS-DOS, or Cello for Windows, you can read text that has been formatted specially for the screen in the HTML mark-up language, and even look at any referenced artwork online. All these viewers are available on the Internet as free downloads.

Such viewers have their own address protocols, called URL (Uniform Resource Locator.) When you see something that looks like an FTP address but is referenced as URL, you'll know it's material intended for use with a WWW viewer.

But such viewers, at this writing, require at least SLIP, PPP, or similar connections, where TCP/IP connectivity is extended directly to your desktop.

More and more online organizations, entities, or activists have been rushing to offer URLs with HTML "home pages," the whole thing coalescing into a legitimate trend. But from all accounts, a nifty home page with some graphics and hypertext links to Finland is not always superior to a collection of raw text files, especially as the users may have to spend five minutes for their modems to draw down the home page. As often happens, our technology outstrips our skill at using it.

The Future

Currently, the Internet is paid for by those who own the sites that run the hosts, and rent the necessary high-speed data links to hook to their neighbor. Each site has total control of the Internet at that site. There is no single point of control, but once a consensus on how to do something forms, few Interneters seem willing to buck it on most issues.

The situation, therefore, is similar to the state of road building in medieval cities. Each householder was responsible for paying for the paving of the street in front of his or her house, the king paid for the crossroads, and country roads were handled by corvées of feudal labor. The so-called Information Superhighway and National Information Infrastructure initiatives in the United States are, basically, attempts to replace data feudalism with something approaching the modern system, where the government builds and maintains roads with income derived from apportioned taxes—or at least encourages such activities with subsidies and tax breaks. Certain basic issues remain to be hashed out, though:

☞ Who pays?
☞ How much?
☞ Which locales get on-ramps?
☞ Which ones get relegated to the backwaters?

Meanwhile, it is likely that in the foreseeable future there will be an internet, rather than an Internet, as the Internet, commercial services, echo networks, and other online entities mesh closer and closer. (You can, for instance, already login to some commercial services through the Internet, although you still need an account there. And more and more Usenet traffic originates from outside the Internet.) Methods are being experimented with that will do away with modems and open phone lines to direct, high-speed data transmissions, so that data speeds and bandwidths will no longer be an issue. Meanwhile, your microwave oven, garage door opener, and burglar alarm may all get Internet addresses so you can control them from anywhere. You may feel that you're living inside one huge computer.

And, at some point, you will be. But don't let that worry you—as can be seen by this book, it will still be a human place.

GLOSSARY

ALPHANUMERIC.

Refers to characters of data that are represented by keys on the keyboard. Alphanumeric characters are transmitted as a character code, such as ASCII.

ANALOG.

Where information in one medium is converted into analogous information in another medium—as in the phone system, where sound is turned into electrical vibrations.

ARCHIVE.

A compressed file, created by using compression software like PKZIP. Several files can be compressed and stored together in one file that must then be decompressed before being used. Compression is important on the Net because the smaller the file, the less time it takes you to get it. An archive can also be an online storage area used by a particular conference, forum, or newsgroup.

ARITHMETIC COPROCESSOR.

A chip that extends the command set of the microprocessor to include calculator functions, such as arithmetic, higher math, and trigonometry, performing those calculations many times faster than they could be performed by software. The use of such a chip can greatly speed up calculation-intensive software, such as computer-aided drafting.

ASCII.

American Standard Code for Information Interchange—the computer character code in common use except in IBM mainframes. Similar versions exist for various European languages. Text files saved in ASCII format can be read by virtually anyone on any machine.

ASSEMBLER.
Highly complicated programming language that directly controls the inner workings of a computer. Used mostly by professionals on projects where high-speed execution is essential.

ASYNC.
Asynchronous, the start-stop style of data communications used in the PC world.

ASYNCHRONOUS.
In data communications, signals that are not synchronized to any timing signal. Asynchronous data are sent in discrete bytes of information with random space between them.

AT COMMAND SET.
The set of standard modem control commands pioneered by Hayes Microcomputer Products, Inc. Each command starts with the letters AT.

BAUD.
This is a widely misunderstood term. A modem's baud rate indicates how many times it can change its frequency per second, thus sending discrete electronic signals down a phone line. Different modems can send different amounts of bits (or characters) with each signal, so baud rate is not the same as the bits-per-second speed. A modem's bps (bits per second) rating ultimately determines how quickly you can transfer files. For example, what's usually referred to as a 9,600-baud modem is really a 2,400-baud modem that can attach 4 bits of information to each signal, resulting in 9,600 bps (2,400 baud * 4 bits = 9,600 bps). See also BITS PER SECOND.

BBS.
Stands for bulletin board system. BBSs are run on personal computers (such as IBM, Mac, or Amiga) and usually have e-mail, discussion conferences, games, and file libraries. Most BBSs are run as a hobby and don't cost anything to join. Some larger BBSs and most business BBSs do charge annual fees.

BINARY.
A base-2 system number system, using only the integers 1 and 0. This is the ultimate lingo that every computer understands.

BIT.

A single binary integer—a single 1 or a single 0.

BITNET.

Because It's Time Network. A worldwide network connecting more than five hundred universities, colleges, and research organizations. Today it can be thought of as part of the Internet.

BITS PER SECOND.

The speed rating of a data communications connection, referring to the number of bits—including data and framing bits—that can be moved in a second. It is not the same as the baud rate, which is the rate signals that are introduced into the line. See also BAUD.

BOGUS.

When it is used to describe a Usenet newsgroup, it means that the newsgroup is not accepted by all sites, usually due to a flaw in the newsgroup creation procedure or because it has questionable (or no) content.

BTW.

By The Way. "BTW, your margins are off."

BUFFER.

Special computer memory used to hold data that are in transit from one place to another.

BYTE.

Eight binary integers (bits) which gives 256 possible code permutations (two raised to the power of eight). All character codes in the PC world represent alphanumeric characters (that is, any character you can generate by pressing a key on the keyboard) with bytes.

C.

Popular programming language commonly used by professionals and hobbyists.

CALL WAITING.

Every sixteen-year-old's dream—a special telephone service option whereby someone talking on the phone can answer a second incoming call and switch between the two conversations. If you're online and you get another call, the Call Waiting tone will knock your modem offline. To avoid this, disable call waiting *every time you dial by entering the modem command: ATD*70, phone number.*

CAT.
A Unix command for listing a text file on-screen, without interruption, so you can catch it on your local machine. Cat lets you avoid downloading. Downloading text files from Unix to MS-DOS machines is often problematic since the two environments have different ways of ending lines and paragraphs.

CATS, GENDER DISTINCTION VIA SPY SATELLITE.
Tomcats have larger, squared-off heads.

CHAT.
A special place on many online services (including the Internet) where you can go and "chat" with other people in that same "location" by typing back and forth with each other in real time.

COMPATIBILITY.
Refers to the ability of hardware and software to work together, regardless of their origins.

COMPRESSION.
Methods of making files consume fewer bytes for easier storage or faster transmission. Fifty percent compression is usually possible, but actual results depend on the peculiarities of the individual file and vary enormously. On Unix systems, compressed usually end with a .Z, and need to be decompressed (and perhaps recompressed using PKZIP) before downloading to a PC.

CONFERENCE.
A message base devoted to discussion of a specific topic. Also called a forum, roundtable, or special interest group (SIG). The word is also sometimes used to refer to a chat session.

CP/M.
Control Program for Microprocessors. A disk operating system for eight-bit computers, which preceded DOS.

CRASH.
The complete, utter failure of a computer system, usually by locking and ignoring everything you do (even the three-finger salute). It's time to flip the big switch.

CURSOR.

The flashing spot on the screen where any impending screen activity will take place. Its hypnotic effect has caused many midnight programmers to fall into a light coma.

CYBERPUNK CANON.

Science fiction novels that define the cyberpunk scene—dark, brooding settings in which the Little Man seeks to escape being steamrollered by runaway, authoritarian-controlled technology. There is usually some VR angle. Read: Orson Scott Card's Ender's Game, *William Gibson's* Neuromancer *and* Virtual Light, *Karie Jacobson's (as editor)* Simulations: 15 Tales of Virtual Reality, *Neal Stephenson's* Snow Crash, *and Vernor Vinge's* True Names . . . and Other Dangers.

CYBERSPACE.

The Net, and everything that happens online.

DIGITAL.

Communication method where data is encoded in binary form.

DITTOHEADS.

People who quote excessively from conference messages they are replying to.

DOS.

Disk Operating System, usually of a PC. DOS is the basic system software that actually controls the machine. Application programs that use specific machine functions (such as writing or reading disk files, writing to the screen, or handling keyboard input) generally do so through DOS functions. Application software, therefore, is generally not written to run on a particular machine, but rather on a particular operating system. For the PC, the commonest are MS-DOS from Microsoft, PC-DOS from IBM, and DR DOS from Digital Research. Application software intended for DOS should run on either.

DUPLEX.

Refers to the ability of a telecommunications connection to carry data in both directions. Full duplex means data are traveling in both directions at once, half duplex means data can go in either direction, but only in one direction at a time. (Simplex means data can only go in one direction, period.) However, duplex is often used to describe whether data is echoed locally or remotely, regardless of the actual nature of the connection. Full duplex means a remote echo, and half duplex means a local echo.

EASTER EGG.
A hidden surprise when a rare set of conditions are met. These are commonly found on Macintosh and Windows programs. Many Windows applications from Microsoft will display running lists of the developers' names after receiving an arcane series of commands.

EBCDIC.
Extended Binary Coded Decimal Interchange Code. A character code used by IBM mainframes.

ECHO CONFERENCE.
A "message base" that is echoed—regionally, nationally, or even globally—among multiple BBSs, who are members of an organized echo network.

ECHO FLAG.
A flag on a conference message that means it will be echoed to other members of the echo network.

ECHO NETWORK.
An organized network of BBSs that exchange (echo) the contents of selected conferences. Some are run entirely by hobbyists, but have hundreds of participating BBSs, located all over the globe.

EDI.
Electronic Data Interchange, automated electronic mail between business systems, using formats set by industrial organizations, for tasks like automatic invoicing, ordering, and shipping notification.

ELDER NODES.
Members of the secret guiding body behind the computer revolution. Includes you, after you read this book.

EMOTICONS.
Alphanumeric creations that substitute for the writer's facial expressions in otherwise sterile text files. Heavy reliance, on the other hand, generally produces an off-putting saccharine syrup. Vast collections have been assembled. Some examples:

-> Tongue firmly in cheek
(o.-) Wink
(O.O) Wide-eyed amazement or interest
(@.@) Total shock
:-) Smile face (sideways)
:-(Frown face (sideways)
B-) Smile face with glasses (sideways)
B-(Frown face with glasses (sideways)
;-) Winking and smiling (sideways)
!@#$%&* Generic expletive (Qwerty keyboard)

EMULATION.

(1) The use of software to make a PC act as if it were a particular kind or brand of terminal. (2) The ability, through software, of one computing platform to run the software of another, incompatible platform. With native code, the speed degradation is usually a factor of about six. Windows emulation can be much faster, since the software that services the Windows function calls is usually translated to native mode.

ENCRYPTION.

The process of encoding information so that only the person who has a decoder can view the information. Encrypted text appears to be random gibberish to anyone who does not have the decryption key. There are many "grades" of encryption algorithms that give different levels of security. Some are classified by the government, others are banned from export from the United States.

ESCAPE.

The Esc (Escape) ASCII code is used to signal a device that the data that follow should be interpreted as commands rather than as text.

FAQ.

Frequently Asked Questions. An informational file concerning a specific Usenet newsgroup explaining the group's purpose and answering questions frequently posed by newcomers. Reading the FAQ and about two weeks of traffic is considered a wise move before doing any posting. FAQ files are found in separate archives (try rtfm.mit.edu or one of its mirrors on the Internet) and may also be posted at intervals in the newsgroup itself.

FILE TRANSFER PROTOCOLS.
Specific ways of accomplishing file transfers. See Kermit, YMO-DEM, and ZMODEM for the chief examples.

FILE TRANSFERS.
Using computers to send and receive files via modems. For more information on file transfer protocols, see XMODEM, YMODEM, ZMODEM, and Kermit.

FLAMERS.
Online users engaged in producing flames. Self-conscious flamers often begin and end their flames with <flame on> and <flame off>, but most are blind to their own sins.

FLAMES.
Online messages, usually in discussion conferences, that constitute a heated exchange, quarrel, or feud between two or more users.

FORUM.
Another name for a conference.

FRAMING BITS.
Bits used in async connections to separate bytes from each other.

FUBAR.
F***ed Up Beyond All Redemption. Test or demo files are often named foo.bar. Makes you wonder, doesn't it?

FUD.
Fear, Uncertainty, and Doubt—the ruling emotions in many niches of the computer market.

FUDD.
(1) Elmer Fudd, cartoon character, shotgun-wielding nemesis of Bugs Bunny. (2) Firesign Theater law-giver.

FWIW.
For What It's Worth. "He's just flaming, FWIW."

GATEWAY.
Connection between an e-mail service and some other service or mode of transmission, such as to the Internet, a fax number, the telex network, or even surface mail via hardcopy printouts.

HACKER.
(1) Dedicated programmer who uses intuitive, seat-of-the pants methods to solve complex programming problems—hacking at a

problem until it's solved. (2) Online intruder who gains unauthorized entry into a computer system or voice mail systems.

HEXADECIMAL.
A base-16 number system that programmers use to represent binary numbers. The hexadecimal numbers run 1 through F (15). Hexadecimal numbers are often marked with an "h" to distingusih them from decimal numbers: 10h is equivalent to 16 in our decimal system.

HTML.
Hypertext Markup Language. Used to format text intended for use in a URL on the WWW, or some other TLA.

IC.
Integrated circuit—a "chip."

IMHO.
In My Humble (or Honest) Opinion. "IMHO, you're mistaken."

INTERNET.
A network of networks, all sharing the same addressing scheme and transmission protocol, comprising more than thirty thousand subnetworks, mostly at academic, research, government, and corporate institutions. There may be more than two million nodes and as many as twenty million users.

IOW.
In Other Words. "IOW, you don't agree¿"

ISDN.
Integrated Services Digital Networks. A scheme for converting the phone system to digital technology.

K (KILOBYTES).
In discussions of salaries, K refers to 1,000, but in computer science it actually stands for two to the tenth power—1,024. Hence, 640K is actually 655,360 bytes.

KERMIT.
File transfer protocol, inherited from the minicomputer world. Slow, but reliable.

KILL FILE.
A list kept by your news reader software, so that a particular posting will not be downloaded if it was written by someone you don't

like, or its subject line includes a particular keyword you're not interested in.

LAN.
Local Area Network. A group of computers that are usually hard-wired together (but may be connected through infrared or microwave beams) so that they can share information and hardware resources.

LOGOFF.
To issue the necessary commands to end a connection with a remote host in a controlled fashion, as opposed to simply hanging up.

LOGON.
To complete the necessary steps to connect with and use a remote computer.

M.
In computer science, M means million, not thousand.

MACRO.
A simple program that (usually) plays back a series of keystrokes and thus automates a chore or task, such as setting up a word processing document or drawing emoticons. Many application programs include some sort of "macro language" for this purpose, varying from simple keystroke playback utilities to elaborate programming facilities.

MAIL LIST.
Also rendered mail.list or mail-list. A sort of inverted conference. Postings mailed to the list's e-mail address are automatically forwarded to everyone on its subscriber list. Some lists are moderated, which means that someone gathers the postings, culls and edits them, and sends them out in one batch, basically as a newsletter.

MEGABYTE.
1,048,576 bytes.

MEGAFLOP.
One million floating point operations per second. A measure of computer performance similar in intent to the MIP (see entry), except that the FLOP is easier to define. Floating point operations are handled very differently from integer operations: the former would be $2.0 \times 2.0 = 4.0$ and the latter would be $2 \times 2 = 4$. Integer operations are much easier for the computer to handle.

MEGAHERTZ.

One million cycles per second. In references to radio it refers to transmission frequency, but in computer science it refers to the speed of the computer's internal clock—the original PC ran slightly under five million cycles per second, and the latest Pentium machines run at about one hundred million. In the first microcomputers it took multiple cycles to accomplish any meaningful operation, but the latest machines are down to one-half cycle or so per operation.

MESSAGE BASE.

All the messages posted in a particular conference.

MIPS.

Millions of Instructions Per Second. Since there is no clear agreement on the definition of "instruction," MIPS is more of a marketing term than an engineering term, but one still sees it used to rate computers. A sixteen-megahertz 80386 PC is generally equated to three MIPS, and a sixty-six-megahertz 486DX2 PC at about forty MIPS.

MODEM.

Short for modulator/demodulator. The hardware interface device between a computer and the phone line that is responsible for transmitting and receiving data.

MODERATOR.

Someone who monitors the traffic in a particular conference or newsgroup, settling quarrels and keeping discussion on track.

MS-DOS.

Microsoft Disk Operating System. The basic system software of the PC that defines the interactions of the disk drives, serial port, keyboard, and other system components. Compatible variants include PC-DOS from IBM and DR DOS from Digital Research. MS-DOS programs will run under OS/2 and Microsoft Windows as well.

MUD.

MUDs, MOOs, MUCKs, MUSHs, and others are multi-user gaming environments that can be experienced on the Internet. People from all over the world can play the same game simultaneously and interact with each other. Most participants use English, though German and Japanese are popular as well.

MULTITASKING.

The ability to run multiple programs at the same time, as opposed to loading multiple programs but running only one.

MULTI-USER.

The ability of a computer to support more than one user at a time. Multi-user games (like MUDs) allow many people from all over the world to play the same game simultaneously and communicate with each other.

NCSA.

The National Center for Supercomputing Applications is associated with the University of Illinois in Urbana. Among other things, this group created the first version of Mosaic for Unix, Windows, and the Macintosh. Most commercial versions of Mosiac so far are based on the NCSA's code.

NEWS READER.

Software that lets you download unread messages in conferences or newsgroups you belong to, read them offline, write comments, offline, and then upload the comments.

NODE.

A computer that is a participating member of an established network. Elder Nodes are members of the secret guiding body behind the computer revolution.

NSA.

National Security Agency. U.S. governmental agency involved in cryptography. True believers "know" that the NSA is omnipresent and monitors every phone call and e-mail message in the country, and so put keywords they think the NSA computers look for—"food for the NSA line-eater"—in their e-mail signatures, to thus perhaps overload the NSA and strike a blow for freedom everywhere.

ONLINE.

The act of firing up your modem and visiting cyberspace.

OS/2.

Operating System/2, the operating system introduced in 1987 for the IBM PS/2, more lately championed by IBM as a faster, multi-user, and multitasking answer to Microsoft Windows. Most commonly used on network file servers.

OTOH.

On The Other Hand. "OTOH, we may both be wrong."

PACKET SWITCHING NETWORK.

Any of several commercial services offering nationwide (or regional) data communications services through shared use of high-speed data lines leased from the phone companies. Each line is shared through "packet switching"—"packets" of data from each user are interspersed on the line at one end and sorted out at the other. In metropolitan areas the services can be reached through local phone calls.

PARITY.

Error-checking bit optionally added to each async byte.

PARALLEL.

Data connection where each bit in a byte has its own line. Used for printers and similar peripherals.

PC.

A microcomputer based on the Intel chip set that can run software written for the MS-DOS operating system. The "architecture" of the PC was defined by the original IBM PC that came out in 1981, but it is now cloned by hundreds of vendors—which is legal, as long as they don't copy the IBM PC ROM BIOS. The main chips that have been used in the PC to date are as follows:

- ☞ 8088—Original version
- ☞ 8086—Original with sixteen-bit bus
- ☞ 80186—Faster version of 8086
- ☞ 80286—Heart of the PC/AT, three times more powerful than an 8088
- ☞ 80386—Thirty-two-bit chip, four times more powerful than an 80286
- ☞ 80486—Enhanced 80386 with internal arithmetic coprocessor, about twice as powerful as the 386
- ☞ 486SX—Cheaper 80486 without the arithmetic coprocessor
- ☞ 486DX2—Runs twice the clock speed as the bus, allowing for cheaper components
- ☞ Pentium—Twice as powerful as the 486
- ☞ P6—Unreleased at this writing, presumably twice as fast as the Pentium (final name: Hexium? Sextium?)

Since clock speeds have also increased along with power (the 8088 ran just under five megahertz, while the 486 and Pentium can go up to about a hundred) a Pentium can run the same software several hundred times faster than an 8088, assuming there are no disk access or screen display bottlenecks. But while software for earlier chips will run on later ones, the reverse is not always true. For instance, Microsoft Windows 3.1 requires at least a 286, and full functionality requires a 386 or better.

Several RISC processors, especially the PowerPC, the DEC Alpha, the MIPS, and the Intergraph chips, can function as PCs by virtue of running a version of Windows NT.

PHONE PHREAK.

A phone system hacker who takes control of phone company switching equipment in order to make free long-distance phone calls or prevent his or her calls from being traced while computer hacking.

PIN.

Personal Identification Number, the form of password protection used primarily by automatic teller machines, security "tokens," and smartcards.

PLATFORM.

The combination of hardware and operating system that defines a particular, standardized computing environment.

PPP.

Point to Point Protocol. Extends TCP/IP connectivity over high-speed modems directly to a desktop computer, giving it full Internet participation. Similar to SLIP, but is slower because it offers more error detection and correction features.

PSTN.

Public Switched Telephone Network. If you can pick up a phone and dial another phone that is outside your organization, then your phone is attached to the PSTN.

PS/2.

Personal System/2, a variant of the PC produced by IBM in a futile effort to recapture the PC market from the clone makers. It is software-compatible with the PC, but not always hardware compatible.

QWERTY.

The standard-style American keyboard, so named because of the arrangement of the left-side keys in the second row. The layout was intended to make certain letter combinations difficult and thus prevent jamming, and to put an anagram of the word typewriter *in the top row to facilitate sales demos. The main variant is the Dvorak keyboard, named after its inventor.*

RAM.

Random Access Memory. The memory embodied in the memory chips inside the computer, as opposed to the data stored on the hard disk or the diskettes. The name refers to the fact that you can address one byte without scanning through all the others first, as you would have to do with magnetic tape. Data stored in RAM are "volatile," meaning it goes away when the power is turned off.

REBOOT.

To boot when the machine is already turned on, usually after a software glitch has locked up the system or sent it into an infinite loop. This can be done on a PC by pressing the Ctrl, Alt, and Del keys at the same time. Many PCs also include a red reboot button, in case the computer is ignoring the keyboard. Rebooting wipes the slate clean—you might as well have turned the system off and back on.

ROTFL.

Rolling On The Floor, Laughing. "Comment re: your posting: ROTFL."

ROUNDTABLE.

Another name for a conference.

RS232.

Designation for the serial ports used by PCs.

RTFM.

*Read The F***ing Manual. Used to get rid of people who ask stupid questions about software. Also as a common name for anonymous ftp site file directories.*

RYFM.

*Read Your F***ing Manual. Variant of RTFM.*

SCRIPT FILE.
A record of the commands necessary to (usually) logon to a remote system, used with a modem software package to automate the procedure.

SELF-PROGRAMMING.
Those who have been using the C programming language too long will slip command lines into their conference messages, such as, "#dripping_sarcasm_mode(ON)."

SERIAL.
Data connection in which all the bits of every byte are sent sequentially and serially down the same line. Used for modem connections and for certain peripherals.

SERIAL PORT.
Input/output connection on a computer designed to be used with a modem or modemlike device (such as certain printers or scanners).

SESSION.
The time between logon and logoff that a user spends on a system.

SIG.
Special Interest Group. Another name for a conference.

SIG.
Abbreviation of signature.

SIGNATURE.
Personalized billboardlike presentation of ASCII characters at the end of a message or posting, to add personality and authenticity to an otherwise sterile medium. Signatures are often created using macro utilities, or are stored in special files in the user's machine. The custom of limiting them to four lines is often observed in the breach. (Handwritten signatures can, of course, be scanned and transmitted for inclusion in hardcopy mail.)

SLIP.
Serial Line Internet Protocol. Extends TCP/IP connectivity over high-speed modems directly to a desktop computer, giving it full Internet participation. Similar to PPP, but faster while less reliable.

STORE AND FORWARD.
The mode that most e-mail uses, whereby messages are stored until forwarded to the receiver, usually when the receiver eventually logs

in, or immediately to a fax machine or to a hardcopy printer for surface mail.

SYNC.
Synchronous communications, in which two devices are locked in a
continuous communications link with each other, and the meaning of
each bit is determined by its placed in the data stream.

SYSOP.
System operator, generally the person who runs a BBS, but can also
be someone who moderates a forum or conference.

TELEX.
Electromechanical teleprinters formerly relied on for data communications, generally using the five-bit Baudot code, or uppercase
ASCII. A telex number that can be reached directly instead of
through a store and forward arrangement is called "conversational
telex." "Telex" should not be confused with the computer hardware
and hearing aid maker of the same name, or with Telix, a brand of
modem software.

THREAD.
Messages within a conference that address the same theme—usually they are comments on the same original posting. Some software
allows you to read a particular thread in a conference to the exclu-
sion of other messages.

TINAR.
This Is Not A Review/Recommendation. "I liked version 3.2, but
TINAR."

TLA.
Three-Letter Acronym. There's no end to them online. Some people
render IMHO as IMO, apparently just to make it a TLA.

UPLOADING.
To transmit a file of any description using a file transfer protocol, as
opposed to "autotyping" a text file.

VAPORWARE.
Any software product that has been announced and perhaps even
reviewed in the press, but has yet to appear on the shelves. There
have been products that existed in no other form. Very popular
among marketing types at many software companies.

VENDOR CONFERENCE.

A BBS echo conference devoted to technical support for a particular product, usually with participation by the vendor's technical or customer support department.

VR.

Virtual Reality. The creation of a computer-generated 3D graphic world that the user can walk around in and manipulate.

UNIX.

Also rendered as UNIX. An operating system, originated by AT&T, designed for multi-user systems, with built-in telecommunications functions. It is popular mostly in the academic and scientific communities. There are versions that will run on the PC, but it is rarely used for that purpose. The name is a play on Multics, a prior operating system. MS-DOS users face five hard lessons when dealing with Unix:

☞ Unix is case sensitive. Whereas MS-DOS translates everything to uppercase, saying "get Read.me" on a Unix system will not work if the file is named "read.me" or "Read.Me," etc.

☞ Unix uses long, rambling file names. The file eat.flaming.death would have to be renamed to death.eat before you download it to a PC.

☞ When typing subdirectory extensions, you use the / (divisor slash) instead of the \ (gray slash.)

☞ Unix uses different end-of-lines than does MS-DOS, so that ASCII files downloaded from Unix to DOS machines may not format correctly. Capturing them as they scroll on the screen, however, normally works.

☞ You usually do not have to include a carriage return after inputting single-letter menu commands.

URL.

Uniform Resource Locator. Addressing protocol for items intended to be used with WWW graphical file browsers over TCP/IP connections.

USENET.

A semiformal echo network associated with the Internet, although also carried by other networks. Individual conferences are called newsgroups. There are in worldwide distribution, at last count, about forty-five hundred.

VIRTUAL.

Something that exists in computer terms, but will not be found in the real world. Virtual memory, for instance, is RAM that the computer thinks exists, but is really part of the hard disk.

VIRUS.

In the computer world, a self-replicating program that attaches itself to a legitimate program (such as an operating system utility) and seeks to attach copies of itself to other programs. Most viruses are created as pranks or to cause serious damage to your computer.

WORM.

(1) A self-replicating program that attempts to take over the computer it is resident in and also propagate copies of itself through whatever network it is attached to. (2) Someone who tries to make unauthorized use of a system. The term is preferred over "hacker" by many insiders.

XMODEM.

Original file transfer protocol for microcomputers. Considered too slow today, especially when used over packet switching networks, but usually available when nothing else is.

X-WINDOWS.

Graphics user interface for Unix, reminiscent of (but not compatible with) Microsoft Windows.

YMODEM.

File transfer protocol. Basically, an improvement of XMODEM, but not as good as ZMODEM.

ZIP.

Most popular method of file compression in the PC world (there are others, however) using shareware programs PKZIP and PKUNZIP. They are widely available, but be sure you get version 2 (officially 2.04g), since files zipped with version 2 cannot be unzipped with version 1. Be warned: There are bogus versions of PKZIP floating around with version numbers like 1.20, 2.0, 2.02, or 3.05. They are probably hacks of a intermediate version of PKZIP, and may contain viruses. However, IBM's version 2.06 is equivalent to 2.04g.

ZMODEM.
Popular file transfer protocol, the fastest in common use.

APPENDIX A:
ASYNC COMMUNICATIONS

Assuming you're accessing the Net from a microcomputer, getting online involves something called "async communications." (*Async* is short for "asynchronous," meaning not synchronized.) Succeeding requires several things:

- ☞ Background knowledge
- ☞ A computer with a modem
- ☞ A phone line without too many splices in it
- ☞ Communications software.
- ☞ Usually—but not always—a subscription with some kind of online service provider.

All these aspects have to work together for things to run smoothly. Sadly, the least little thing can knock you offline, or prevent you from getting on. If you're new to this, don't worry. It's nearly impossible to do physical damage to your computer (or yourself), so hang in there and read on.

Computers store and send data in binary format, meaning everything is broken down into ones and zeroes. Each individual one or zero is called a bit. Bits are commonly clumped into groups of eight, called bytes. A byte can have 256 possible meanings (two raised to the eighth power), which is enough to cover all the characters on the keyboard, upper- and lowercase both; some special characters, accents, and umlauts thrown in to keep some foreigners happy; plus screen graphics characters to make it possible to prettify the screen without going to graphics mode. The standard way of representing bytes is called ASCII (American Standard Code of Information Interchange, pronounced *asky*). It is possible to use only the first seven bits of the code (128 meanings, still enough for the keyboard but cutting out the graphics characters). Five-bit and six-bit codes also exist.

The byte, as it turns out, is the basic unit of telecommunications for desktop computers. The standard transmission method of sending bytes is, as we noted, async. (The opposing method, called sync, is used mostly by mainframe terminals, or desktop computers pretending to be mainframe terminals.) Most of what you need to know about telecommunications concerns the nature of async, which we'll now cover.

ASYNC COMMUNICATIONS

Desktop telecommunications methods are derived from those used by the original electromechanical telex machines to transmit manual keyboard input. The timing of each keystroke was (in machine terms) random. Therefore, the data representing a keystroke—a byte—had to be transmitted as a separate, stand-alone entity. This was accomplished by adding "framing bits." The data byte is framed by a preceding start bit, and followed by an optional parity bit, and then a stop bit.

The start bit was originally a signal of a special length that would cause the clutch of the telex machine's printing mechanism to engage. Today's is a disposable bit to warn the system that a data byte is following.

After the data byte is an optional parity bit, which can assure the system that the bits in the data byte are all correct. With "even parity," there must be an even number of ones, and the parity bit is set according. For instance, if there were three ones in the data byte, the parity bit is set to one to make four. With "odd parity" the result must be an odd number. Note that this method only works if one bit is corrupted—two bits being wrong could cancel each other out. And the error is only detected—there is no provision for correcting it. The system can only pass along the obvious garble, replace it with a question mark or something else, or just freeze up.

The stop bit follows the parity bit. Its original purpose was to make sure the telex mechanism had time to reset itself before the next character arrived, and two bits were used. With computers, one is used, as a separator.

The result of all this is that you will see BBSs and online services listed with annotations that look like this: 8-N-1, or 7-E-1. The first means eight data bits, no parity, and one stop bit. The second means seven data bits, even parity, and one stop bit. To use these services successfully, the telecommunications settings in your modem software will have to match.

Check This Out:

Most services and BBSs today use 8-N-1. The Internet uses seven data bits, which is why uuencoding (see Chapter 15) is needed.

YOUR COMPUTER

The computer needs to have a serial port, often called an RS232 port. Alternately, the computer can have an empty expansion slot that could accommodate an internal modem, as described earlier. It must be installed with modem software, and it must have enough RAM to run it.

And that's about it. At all but the highest speeds, telecommunications is not a demanding task for a computer.

Saving Face:

Knowing the jargon of computer connections may save you some headaches:

Gender—In RS232, male has the pins, female has the sockets. If you have to connect like genders, you can get intermediate "gender-menders" to fix the situation.

Saving Face:

Assuming eight bits and no parity, or seven bits and parity, each byte ends up being ten bits. Therefore, you can figure your transmission speed in characters per second by dividing the modem speed in bits per second (as explained later) by ten.

Null Modem—With a modem or serial cable intended for connection to a terminal or printer, the in and out data pins might be reversed. You can get a null modem to re-reverse them. It will also let you connect computers directly together through their serial ports.

Parallel—The connection used for most printers, using eight parallel data lines. The other lines are for "handshaking."

RJ-11—The standard phone cord plug in North America—a block with a little spring level, with four connector leads.

RS232—Standard connector port on a computer, with either twenty-five or nine pines. There are adapters to connect the two varieties.

Serial—The connection used for modems, plus some mice and some printers. There is one inbound and one outbound data line. The rest of the lines are for "handshaking" or optional use.

THE PHONE LINE

If you can pick up the receiver, get a dial tone, and dial a number without having to negotiate with a live operator, that means you are on the PSTN (Public Switched Telephone Network) and your phone line is suitable for getting online. There are, however, several complicating details.

Call Waiting

American phone companies have been successful at selling the public on an option called Call Waiting, whereby the phone gives you a signal tone when another call is coming in while you are already talking. The signal tone can addle the modem and knock you offline. It is usually possible to disable Call Waiting when dialing your modem, by using the following command: **ATD *7** followed by the number you want to dial.

PBXs

If you are dialing from inside an office phone system, you usually have to add a prefix to the phone number—commonly, the number 9—to get an outside line. Most modem software will let you do this—check the documentation.

Hint: Assuming your modem uses the so-called AT command set (most do) you might find the following commands useful when dialing through a PBX:

, (comma) —Pause for two seconds

/ —Pause one-eighth second

@ —Wait for an answer

W —Wait for the second (outside) dial tone

! —Flash-hook (hang up, then reconnect)

When dialing through a PBX, you might precede the phone number with ",,9W". The commas cause the modem to wait four seconds for the PBX dial tone, 9 gets you an outside number, and the W causes the modem to wait for the second dial tone.

Hotels

Calling from a hotel, you will not only be going through a PBX, but you'll be using phones that are often not intended to be unplugged by the guests. Some will have a modem port—an unconnected RJ-11 connector—in the body of the phone. If nothing else works, and you feel brave and technically equipped, you can dismantle the phone or wall junction box and get at the phone wire, splicing it to your modem cable. Remember, connect the red to the red, and the green to the green, and ignore the other wires.

Cellular Phones

It is possible to get online through a cellular connection, but it takes special adapters and modems, throughput is likely to be slow, and driving and typing don't mix.

Packet Switching Networks

To reach an online service in another city, you are sometimes directed to use a packet switching service. You dial into a local number, get online, and then step through a few simple commands to get connected to the online service. Once there, you login as if you had called directly, and the packet switching network becomes invisible. Your online service should provide documentation on the details of the procedure, and the number to call.

Such a network consists of leased high-speed digital phone lines, reached through special modems that divide the data from the various callers (who are using lower speeds) into packets that can share the high-speed line. At the destination, the packets from each caller are picked out and turned into separate data streams again.

Using a packet switching network incurs extra expense (which will be billed to you by your online service) but is generally cheaper than calling directly.

MODEMS

You cannot go online without a modem, which connects your computer to the phone line. The word stands for "modulator demodulator." A modem takes the digital on-off signals generated by the computer and modulates them into noises on the phone line. (You can listen to the noise, but don't bother—it's usually a very unpleasant shrieking.) At the other end it demodulates the noise back into digital signals.

You need a modem because what Alexander Graham Bell invented was, and is, an instrument for the transmission of the human voice. It is very good at that. But to keep matters simple, the phone only transmits a "bandwidth" of about 4,000 cycles per second. This band covers most of the resonance of the human voice, although it is only about a fourth of the bandwidth you can hear (barring attendance at a lot of rock concerts). This is why music will sound "tinny" over the phone, and why people with a certain range of hearing loss can converse face-to-face but not over the phone.

This limitation explains why modem connections are slower than direct connections—that 4,000-cycle bandwidth forms a rather narrow pipe into which to pour high-speed data. Nevertheless, the modem makers have been coming up with more and more tricks to play with that 4,000 cycles, and today modems that can achieve 28,800 bps have become affordable.

Modem technology amounts to a pretty much endless subject, with variations and permutations all over the landscape. But for the average user who wants to get online, there are three things you need to understand: speeds and protocols, compatibility issues, and connection methods.

Speed/Protocol

Protocol refers to details of how the modems "talk" to each other, and is the main thing you need to consider. Speed is part of a protocol's specification.

There are more protocols than you'll ever want to hear about. But the ones in use on public networks in North America are pretty much as follows:

☞ Bell 103 (300 bps)
☞ Bell 212A (1200 bps)
☞ V.22 (1,200 bps)
☞ V.22 bis (2,400 bps)
☞ V.32 (9,600 bps)
☞ V.32bis (14,400 bps)
☞ V.34 (28,800 bps); V.34 was not standardized at this writing

Modems are (usually) backward compatible, meaning that, for instance, a V.32bis modem should be able to connect to a

Saving Face:

The cognoscenti quibble about the definition of "baud" and "bits per second" (bps.) The baud rate is the number of times per second that signals are introduced into the line, while bps is the communication speed. At 300 bps, baud and bps are the same. As you get faster, they're not—the baud rarely gets higher than 2,400, as the modem squeezes multiple meanings out of each sound wave.

Bell 103 modem. In fact, they often use the slower protocols as "fallback" speeds on noisy lines. At this writing, it is not possible to go faster than 9,600 bps over most links of most packet switching networks, and many commercial services are still geared to 2,400 bps.

Compatibility

The computer's software has to be able to control the modem, to give it the commands to pick up, dial, hang up, etc. Fortunately, most modems today adhere to the AT command set pioneered by Hayes Microcomputer Products, setting standard commands for controlling modems.

Unfortunately, most vendors have not been able to suppress the urge to embellish or "improve" the AT command set, so compatibility is not assured. Most modem software packages come with lists of modems they support, just as word processors list compatible printers. Just be sure, before buying one or the other, that your software can support your modem.

Connection Method

A modem is either internal or external. If internal, you install it as a board in your computer, taking up an expansion slot. On a PC, it usually only needs an eight-bit slot. If there is a half-length slot behind the disk drive, it might fit there. You then plug the phone line into the board's RJ-11 port (explained later), facing the outside through the end tab. There may also be a second port on the board where you can connect a phone or answering machine, with the line passed through to the first port. That line will be functional as long as the modem is off. (Beware: Sometimes the line remains functional when the modem is on.) Upon installation, the board becomes one of the computer's COM ports. You can usually select which COM port the modem is using through switches on the board. Just make sure that no other device is using the same COM number, and make a note of what the number is, since you'll have to tell the modem software when the time comes to configure it.

If the modem is external, it will be housed in its own enclosure, which you will need to plug into a power supply. It will connect to the computer through an RS232 serial connector, either twenty-five-pin or nine-pin. The modem will also connect to the phone line through an RJ-11 connector. Your computer, of course, has to have a serial port, but most PCs come with two. Establish what the COM number of the port is before plugging in the modem, since you'll have to tell the modem software when the time comes to configure it.

Some external modems are "acoustic," meaning they connect to a phone through little rubber hoods that go over the handset. You should need an acoustic modem only if you are planning a lot of international travel—some countries have phone systems with incompatible electrical standards, possibly ruling out the direct-connect modem you brought from home.

Final Word

Get the fastest modem you can afford—you'll thank yourself every time a download takes thirty minutes instead of an hour. However, you may not always want to use it at the highest speed, especially on services that charge a premium for speed. If you are just browsing, there is no need to go faster than 2,400 bps—you can't read any faster than that.

COMMUNICATIONS SOFTWARE

The computer does not know that there is a modem connected to it. Before anything can happen, there has to be software running that tells the computer to move data to and from the keyboard, the modem, the screen, and the disk drive. These are not exotic requirements, and there are perfectly good modem (or telecommunications—either term is used) software packages that are modestly priced, or given

 **Saving Face:**

Fax modems also use digital transmissions methods, but they are not compatible with data modems—fax and data are two different worlds. However, many vendors offer fax/data modem combinations. Whether the device is acting as a fax or data modem depends on the software controlling it. It cannot be both at the same time. However, we will probably soon see fax machines with data storage used for e-mail.

away free as premiums with modems, or downloadable from bulletin boards.

Still, make sure the software:

☞ Supports your "platform" (computer brand, operating system, RAM size, display, etc.)
☞ Supports your modem (brand and protocol)
☞ Includes any file transfer protocols you think you'll need (protocols are explained in Chapter 1)

Certain secondary features might also interest you—or leave you cold.

Emulation

The remote computer may want your computer to emulate (pretend to be) a specific brand of terminal. The standard TTY (Teletype) terminal mode turns your computer into an electronic telex machine ("glass TTY"), capable only of printing characters, line spaces, and carriage returns. Other terminal emulations usually add some level of cursor control, and possibly color control. As with modem compatibility, you need to make sure the one you want is supported.

Chat Mode

Some e-mail and online services offer chat mode for real-time exchanges between two or more users. Chat mode in your software will let you compose and edit a reply while watching incoming text.

Mini BBS

This is an answer mode that will let the caller use the facilities of your computer, within parameters that you establish.

Learn Mode

Logging on to a remote system usually involves repetitive steps. With Learn Mode the software can "watch" these steps and repeat them later, automating the process.

Script Languages

If you want to automate something more complicated than logging on (say, doing overnight unattended file transfers), you'll want a package with its own programming language. These languages are usually called "script languages" since they are less arcane, more specialized—but more limited—than conventional programming languages.

Text Editors

A simple, built-in text editor is useful for writing messages for immediate transmission. Alternately, some packages let you "shell out" to the word processing program of your choice.

Mouse-Click Response

Clicking a word on-screen will cause that word to be sent to the remote computer, optionally followed by a carriage return. This feature lets you select from menu options without typing.

INDEX

Uppercase, use online, 20
URL, defined, 310, 330
Usenet
    definition, 330, 331
    FAQ files, 302–3
    hierarchy, 302
    Oracle, 93
    using, 302–4
Users, IRC, example, 206
Uuencoding, 12, 303–4, 305
Uuencoding, of erotic pictures, 228
Uuexe525.exe, 305

V

V-Rave, chat line, 148
Vaasa, University of, 159
Vacuum, effects, 88–89
Validation, in AI, 27
Vampire, mail list, 186
Vaporware, definition, 329
Vectrex, game system, 184
Vending machines, online, 122
Venus, image of "Gumby," 243
Verification, in AI, 27
Veronica, Internet facility, 307
VGA-Planets, game, 186
Vidvue, 46–47
VIRTU-L, mail list, 60
Virtual Worlds, BIX forum, 61
Virtual Reality, defined, 51–52
Virtual citizens, rights of, 177
Viruses
    discussed, 24
    satirical, examples, 100–101
VR386, 54, 56–58
VRAP-L, mail list, 60
VT52/VT100, Delphi forum, 194

W

WAIS, Internet facility, 307
Waiting for the Electrician or Someone
    Like Him, 114
Wall Street Journal, 109
Wargames, CIS forum, 192
Warp Speeds, 70
Warren Commission, 261
Wayne's World, 107
Weak AI, defined, 27
Wetleather, mail list, 236
Whining, 262–65
White Wolf, game system, 186
WNY-Raves, mail list, 148
Wodehouse, P.G., 121
World Wide Web, *see* WWW
WWW, Internet facility, 307–9

X

X Files, TV show, 254
XDZebra, artwork, 129
XMODEM, 12
Xpilot, game, 186

Y

YMODEM, 12

Z

Za.humour, newsgroup, 99
ZIP, definition, 331–32
Zippy, dog, 118
Zips, 115
ZMODEM, 12